Revelations

Revelations

Alpha and Omega

David Allen Rigsby

Writer's Showcase
San Jose New York Lincoln Shanghai

Revelations
Alpha and Omega

All Rights Reserved © 2002 by David Allen Rigsby

No part of this book may be reproduced or transmitted in any form or by any means, graphic, electronic, or mechanical, including photocopying, recording, taping, or by any information storage retrieval system, without the permission in writing from the publisher.

Writer's Showcase
an imprint of iUniverse, Inc.

For information address:
iUniverse, Inc.
5220 S. 16th St., Suite 200
Lincoln, NE 68512
www.iuniverse.com

This is a work of fiction. Although inspired by actual events, the names, persons, places, and characters are inventions of the author. Any resemblance to people living or deceased is purely coincidental.

ISBN: 0-595-21293-X

Printed in the United States of America

Dedication

To my wife and *Earth angel*, Angela Rebekah…you are truly the virtuous woman of Proverbs 31.
To my one and only child, Katrina Danielle…may you follow your own path too.
To my mother Elizabeth Anne and stepmother Carrie Ann.
To Laurie Ann Rigsby.
And to anyone who still believes in the one true God and His only begotten Son.

Epigraph

"Give ear, O my people, to my law: Incline your ears to the words of my mouth. I will open my mouth in a parable: I will utter dark sayings of old: which we have heard and known, and our fathers have told us. We will not hide them from their children, showing to the generation to come, the praises of the Lord, and His strength, and His wonderful works that He hath done. For He established a testimony in Jacob, and appointed a law in Israel, which He commanded our fathers, that they should make them known to their children: That the generation to come might know them, even the children which should be born; who should arise and declare them to their children: That they might set their hope in God, and not forget the works of God, but keep His commandments: And might not be as their fathers, a stubborn and rebellious generation; a generation that set not their heart aright, and whose spirit was not steadfast with God."

Psalm 78:1-8

Contents

Dedication v

Epigraph vii

Foreword xi

List of Abbreviations xiii

Introduction xv

Revelations Alpha 1

Revelations II Omega 231

Conclusions 459

Foreword

"Again the word of the Lord came unto me saying, Son of man, speak to the children of thy people, and say unto them, when I bring the sword upon a land, if the people of the land take a man of their coasts, and set him for their watchman: If when he seeth the sword come upon the land, he blow the trumpet, and warn the people; Then whosoever heareth the sound of the trumpet, and taketh not warning; if the sword come, and take him away, his blood shall be upon his own head. He heard the sound of the trumpet, and took not warning; his blood shall be upon him. But he that taketh warning shall deliver his soul.

But if the watchman see the sword come, and blow not the trumpet, and the people be not warned; if the sword come, and take any person from among them, he is taken away in his iniquity; but his blood will I require at the watchman's hand. So thou, O son of man, I have set thee a watchman unto the house of Israel; therefore thou shalt hear the word at my mouth, and warn them from me."

Ezekiel 33: 1-7

List of Abbreviations

INT. interior
EXT. exterior
M.O.S. without sound
POV point of view
AD LIB dialogue not scripted
b.g. background
f.g. foreground
O.S. off screen
V.O. voice over

Introduction

Like most Americans, I remember exactly where I was on the morning of Tuesday, September 11, 2001. I was glued to the TV screen as I watched, in shock, the events unfolding in New York City. I watched both World Trade Towers as they fell from the terrorist attacks that day. This prompted my memory of the first and last time I stood at the base of both towers. The first was as an eighteen year-old just arriving in New York City for the first time in the fall of 1979. Ironically, the last time I stood between the towers was just one day before the first terrorist attempt to topple them on February 26, 1993.

Maybe it was that close encounter that inspired me to include a terrorist attack on the towers in my story *Revelations, Alpha and Omega*. In the original version of this story, I chose New Year's Eve on Y2K. It seemed a very likely scenario, as did other things I included in the story happening on that night. As a storyteller, I used dramatic license by putting all the events on one night. It made for a more dramatic effect. After Y2K passed uneventfully, I simply changed the year to 2004 as that appeared to be the absolute latest when the event could happen and still have the impact my story had given it. But I remained convinced it had to happen before the signing of the seven-year peace treaty between Arabs and Jews, authored by the Antichrist. I knew our troops would then go overseas and security here would be increased to a point just shy of Martial Law. Even our rights guaranteed by the Constitution would be convincingly whittled away out of fear. We'd gladly give up some of our rights for peace and safety. I also knew that every time

xvi   Revelations

something horrible happened in the world, it would have a uniting effect. Patriotism would escalate. Recently, one man was featured on the front page of our local paper sporting a new tattoo of our flag and the letters "USA" on his forehead. It fit exactly the future my story had outlined. The reason for this natural progression of events will unfold before your very eyes as you read *Revelations, Alpha and Omega.*

Something else my story had predicted after the collapse of the World Trade Towers came to pass shortly afterwards…our economy's demise. This happened for a reason. The *why* is something you'll also discover as you read the entire story. I don't want to give anything away here because I know you'll only get the whole picture by reading the story. That's the reason why I wrote it…so you'll understand everything. That's also why my story goes back to the beginning. The very beginning. You have to have that foundation of knowledge and understanding or my story's true purpose will elude you.

I've embedded a lifetime of research in this story. It has taken over five years to finish the version you're about to read. The original version was registered with the Writer's Guild of America (WGA) on November 27, 1999 as a screenplay trilogy. Professional editing pared it down to its current two-part version. No one else before me has ever put so much historical, scientific and Biblical knowledge relating to each other into a single story. It was a real challenge to keep the story moving and entertaining as a result. I think I've managed to do the impossible. Now it's up to you to do me one better…actually take the time to read it and understand your own history from a viewpoint never before taken. As you do this, try and place yourself back in time when everyone thought the Earth was flat and the sun revolved around us. This is something you and I can laugh about now but back when Galileo promoted Copernicus' theory of a round Earth revolving around the sun, he was condemned to spend the rest of his life in exile for heresy. *Think about that.* What if the theory my story presents is true? The reason I wrote it as a story instead of a textbook was so that you could grasp these far-fetched concepts more easily. I'm asking a lot from you but I can promise you this…you'll never look at the world around you in quite the same way again. The difference between my theory and others, most notably Darwin's theory, is that I used the Bible as the unshakable truth to which science and history have to conform. Refusing to let go of God's word as the foundation made all the difference. It literally opened new doors. Even church theology, if it didn't fit the actual words found in the Bible, was tossed aside. Before you call that heresy, remember the lesson learned from Galileo.

The events I've outlined after the demise of our World Trade Towers *will* come to pass. Forget the dates I've assigned them as I only used them for the purpose of telling a story. But I can promise you future things outlined in *Omega* will happen. I just want the world to know and understand why these things are really happening. It's like looking in the mirror and being honest with yourself concerning your appearance. Do you really need to lose some weight or have you managed to put on rose-tinted glasses and convince yourself otherwise? I hope to remove those rosy glasses and show the world around you the way it really is. You may not like the truth but that doesn't change the reality of it. That extra weight you're carrying around your midsection or thighs is still there no matter how much you pretend it is not. But you can do something about your weight. Even if you can't do anything about the world's future, you can at least prepare for it. If you knew something horrible was about to happen to the plane you were about to board, would you still get on? Of course not. If you knew the right course of action, I'm sure you'd take it. That's *why* I wrote this story…to give you a fighting chance so you can control that part of your future.

To quote Douglas James Mahr in his prophetic foreword for his own book, *Voyage to the New World*: "Every once in a while a book comes along that has great impact on the world, its societies, its belief systems, its people…" The impact of *Revelations, Alpha and Omega* will be measured in these terms…Good luck. And may God bless you. Did you know that just studying the book of *Revelation* carries its own blessing? "Blessed is he that readeth, and they that hear the words of this prophecy, and keep those things which are written therein: for the time *is* at hand." *Revelation* 1:3

David Allen Rigsby

Revelations Alpha

◆

"Have you ever wished you could go into the future and see what it holds? Or go back in time and see what *really* happened? Hold on to your seat 'cause I'm going to take you on a ride you'll never forget. Stories, myths and legends. I'll show you where they all began. And more importantly, how they'll end." *Laurianna*

The Beginning and the First

FADE IN:

Subtitle: revelation n. 1. The act of revealing; a disclosure, esp. by supernatural means. 2. A striking accession of information.

Subtitle: "It is a fortunate thing for governments that men don't think."…*Adolph Hitler.*

Subtitle: "Those who forget the mistakes of the past are condemned to repeat them."

Subtitle: This is based on a true story.

Subtitle: "c.850 BC, Israel."

EXT. ISRAEL—NIGHT

Two men are walking through the desert. It's very windy. A storm is approaching. We can SEE LIGHTNING and HEAR THUNDER in the b.g.

They come to a river. The older man throws his mantle in the water, causing the waters to magically separate.

The two men walk across the dry bed with water on both sides. The old man walks past his mantle, picking it up.

The river returns to normal as they reach the other side.

The STORM gets worse. The bald-headed younger man, ELISHA, yells to his master as the WIND separates them more.

Suddenly something very bright and LOUD, like the noise of great waters, comes from the sky between them.

BRIGHT OBJECT'S POV—THE TWO MEN BELOW

We're not sure what we are in but we know we're inside the flying object headed towards them.

BACK TO SCENE

The older man is missing now as the object climbs into the sky. Elisha is left behind holding his master's mantle.

ELISHA
(yelling)

Elijah! Master! E-l-i-j-a-h!

He tears his clothes as he falls to his knees onto the desert sand.

ELISHA'S POV—SKY

Where the bright object disappeared.

NARRATOR (V.O.)

I guess this is where I come in. Have you ever wished you could go into the future and see what it holds? Or go back in time and see what *really* happened? Hold on to your seat 'cause I'm going to take you on a ride you'll never forget. Stories, myths and legends. I'll show you where they all began. And more importantly, how they end.

We SEE an ELECTRONIC GLITCH like the changing of a television channel or frequency.

EXT. SKIES OVER GERMANY—NIGHT

We HEAR an old WW II airplane as it comes from behind us. It flies right through us, PULLING US

INT. AIRPLANE'S COCKPIT

Alongside the pilot.

Subtitle: "World War II, March 1945. Somewhere over Germany."

The SOUNDS of RADIO CHATTER mix with SWING MUSIC as we HEAR a pilot's AD LIBS to his wingman.

We're in a P-51 Mustang with an American, JOHNNY ROCKWELL, twenty.

JOHNNY

> Have you guys heard about David's biggest fantasy?

EXT. JOHNNY'S PLANE

Reveals "Shooting Star" written across the nose, under a picture of a comet's tail.

EXT. WIDER VIEW

Various B-17 bombers flying in formation, being escorted by the P-51 Mustangs. Various pilots AD LIB their remarks to Johnny's question.

Flying beside Johnny in a P-51 Mustang is DAVID SMITH, twenty.

INSERT—NOSE OF DAVID'S PLANE

Showing a pinup girl with angel wings painted above the words "Guardian Angel."

INT. DAVID'S PLANE

> DAVID
>
> You're just jealous because my fantasies are better than yours.

> JOHNNY (V.O.)
>
> Oh, I'm sorry...making it with my guardian angel...doesn't excite me.

The other guys LAUGH and tease him with AD LIBS.

> DAVID
>
> Not a REAL angel...I said a girl that LOOKS like an angel.

> JOHNNY (V.O.)
>
> Give me a girl with horns over one with wings any day.

David LOOKS at a photo of an almost nude girl taped inside his cockpit. The girl is wearing a halo and dressed like an angel.

> DAVID
>
> You can have your farm animals freaky-boy; I

personally like things that fly between my legs.

EXT. DAVID'S PLANE

David breaks off from the pack in a barrel roll as our VIEW WIDENS. Johnny, David's wingman, follows him with the same maneuver.

EXT. WIDER VIEW

Also flying in a Mustang with the Americans is one British fighter of the Royal Air Force and twelve B-17's, or Flying Fortresses.

A PILOT'S VOICE (O.S.)

How much further to Berlin?

INT. B-17

A BOMBARDIER looks through his bombsight, lining up their target.

BOMBARDIER

Just a little bit closer.

INT. JOHNNY'S PLANE

JOHNNY

How long have we been in the air?

INT. DAVID'S PLANE

> DAVID
> (looking at
> his watch)

Too long. That's what I hate about new watches, they rarely lie. Best Christmas gift I got last year.

> JOHNNY (O.S.)

As your only friend, I believe that's the only present you got.

> DAVID

Did you know this watch even tells you what day it is?

> JOHNNY (O.S.)

Really? What day is it? Even I've lost track.

> DAVID

It's Wednesday…or Wodensday, or however you Scandinavians say it in your Norse mythology.

INT. B-17 BOMBER

A Mexican-American machine gunner, PEDRO, loads a bullet into his gun, which says "HITLER" on it. He joins in via two-way radio.

PEDRO

They call him Odin. We call him Wodan. Same guy though. They say he's the father of gods, we say he's the grandson of old man Noah. Wodan built a tower to reach heaven, but work stopped when the Great Spirit Teotl gave each family a different language.

As our VIEW WIDENS, we find all the bombs also say, "HITLER," on them.

PEDRO
(continuing)

He's supposedly the founder of our race so we named the middle day after him. We called it Wodansday but now everyone calls it Wednesday too.

INT. DIFFERENT B-17

A British pilot, NORM, with obvious Scandinavian features is piloting one of the other B-17's and adds his input.

NORM

Okay…I'll bet you didn't know all the OTHER days of the week come from OUR Teutonic myths. Tuesday and Thursday…from Tyr, the god of war and Thor, the god of thunder…both sons of Odin—the father of OUR gods. Friday, from Freyja or Frigg, the goddess of love…or wife of Odin.

INT. PEDRO'S B-17

> PEDRO
> (interrupting)

Let me guess…Sunday, in honor of the Sun god and Monday, the Moon goddess and…

> JOHNNY (O.S.)
> (joining in)

…and Saturday, the Roman god…Saturn?

Suddenly a LOUD ALARM goes off in the forward cockpit where the radar man, nicknamed RADAR, observes some blips on his monitor.

> RADAR

We've got company!

EXT. REAR B-17

Gets hit as the first German plane comes into firing range.

EXT. WIDER VIEW

They all come under attack from anti-aircraft fire on the ground and a whole squadron of German planes.

> DAVID (O.S.)
> (shouting)

Johnny, I've got one on my tail…I can't shake him!

JOHNNY (O.S.)

I'm on him!

Just as a German plane's machine gun fire is about to line up with David's plane, Johnny takes out the enemy and he EXPLODES!

Johnny's plane pulls up sharply, beginning a vertical roll.

Other German fighters in formation take out some of the B-17's.

Norm and Pedro's B-17's return fire and several of the German fighters are taken out by a frenzy of machine gun fire.

INT. PEDRO'S B-17—MACHINE GUN TURRET

The shells with Hitler's name on them are SEEN automatically loading.

INT. BOMBARDIER'S COMPARTMENT

The BOMBARDIER lines up the image below him through his bombsight.

BOMBARDIER

There it is! Bombs away! I repeat...bombs away!

EXT. WIDE VIEW—ALL B-17 BOMBERS

Open their bomb bay doors and begin dropping bombs.

EXT. NORM'S B-17—CLOSE ON—OIL

Leaking from the bullet-ridden British bomber.

INT. BRITISH B-17—COCKPIT

The pilot, Norm, notices the oil gauge losing pressure, shakes his head and signals his copilot as they pull off and head home.

> NORM
>
> Sorry boys, we're losing oil!

EXT. DAVID'S PLANE

Has come under attack from two more German fighters now on his tail.

EXT. WIDER VIEW

Johnny's P-51 Mustang has finished climbing and comes at the enemy straight on, taking out one of the German Messerschmitt BF 109's.

The German plane crashes into another German plane, taking him out too.

> DAVID (O.S.)
>
> Thanks!

> JOHNNY (O.S.)
>
> Just making the skies a safe place for angels to fly.

Two Germans come after Johnny now. David's plane goes into a steep nosedive, reversing Johnny's maneuver to come full front.

INT. PEDRO'S B-17—RADAR ROOM

Radar observes a new group of fast-moving, green blips on his screen.

RADAR

Be on alert guys...I'm picking up some fast-moving blips...they might be those super advanced Messerschmitt Me 262 jet airplanes we've been hearing about...and they're joining us!

EXT. DAVID'S PLANE

As he levels out, he fires at a German plane coming towards him. Someone suddenly FIRES, hitting David from behind!

One of the more advanced German planes, responsible for the direct hit, comes into VIEW. David comes down in a tailspin.

INT. DAVID'S PLANE

He tries to eject but the lever is jammed.

Song "SOMEONE TO WATCH OVER ME" by Gershwin begins.

As he is going down, his LIFE FLASHES before his eyes.

FLASHBACK—DAVID'S LIFE

We SEE him going backwards in his life, getting younger as these flashes get shorter and INTERCUT with his face as he passes out.

The final flash is from an elementary school Christmas play, where a young David is dressed as Joseph. A LITTLE GIRL dressed like an angel is looking down at him from the makeshift manger.

LITTLE GIRL

Angels are God's messengers. They'll watch over you and protect you...

END FLASHBACK

DAVID'S POV—THE GROUND

Her words ECHO as her little face INTERCUTS with the approaching ground before he BLACKS OUT from the g-force.

ELECTRONIC GLITCH

Like the changing of a television channel or frequency.

Chorus of "SOMEONE TO WATCH OVER ME" begins.

FADE TO: BLACK

FROM BLACK, we SEE a light getting closer. It APPEARS that David has died and is flying to this place, which now materializes.

The NARRATOR'S female voice offers our only explanation.

NARRATOR (V.O.)

What happens after you die? Where does the spirit go? To know where one is going, it helps to know where one has been.

The SOUND of MUSIC and SINGING can be heard from a distance. We are flying and HEAR the sound of RUSHING WIND. Our VIEW is like the one that we got when something picked up Elijah.

NARRATOR (V.O.)

This is where it all started…about ten billion miles from your sun. Where one day is as a thousand years and a thousand years is as one day.

EXT. PARADISE—HIGH ANGLE

Its topography is like none ever seen before. Mountains made of brass, gold, and silver.

NARRATOR (V.O.)

The elusive "Planet X," a.k.a. Paradise…orbiting your sun like an electron orbiting the nucleus of an atom. It could be said Heaven has no mass…a spiritual place. Can you see an electron? But you don't doubt its existence, do you? Now, can you visualize Heaven?

EXT. GOD'S CITY—HEAVEN—DAY

A city of gold APPEARS. We enter through a gate made of solid pearl. The street is pure gold. The SINGING and MUSIC builds.

INT. GOD'S THRONE ROOM—CLOSE ON—LITTLE GIRL ANGEL

As she presents a bouquet of flowers at God's feet.

LITTLE GIRL

Good morning, God.

Our VIEW WIDENS as all ANGELS finish a SONG of praise to God.

Five gold, mechanical creatures, each with six helicopter-type wings, surround the throne itself.

Each is generating one of the five VISIBLE colors of a rainbow: violet, green, blue, yellow, and red. They encircle God's throne.

> NARRATOR (V.O.)
>
> Now, you're wondering...I thought angels had feathered wings? Only Ezekiel ever DESCRIBES an angel's wing in detail. Only one division of angels has them. Isaiah called them Seraphim. John called them zoa, or living creatures. Yet Ezekiel described them as they are *called*...the cherubim.

INT. CLOSE ON—EACH CHERUB

One resembles a lion, one a man, one a calf, one a flying eagle, and one a serpent with legs and arms.

They all SING a different NOTE as they sing, "Holy, Holy, Holy."

> NARRATOR (V.O.)
>
> These are the five original cherubim...representing the highest order of all created flesh and blood. They surround God's throne and never rest from praising Him. When they unite, they function as the vehicle, which carries God's throne whenever He leaves Heaven.

INT. THRONE ROOM—VARIOUS ANGLES

On other angels, which we discover are all naked. They look very human but almost glow from their brightness.

Some look like identical male and female twins.

All have identifying marks, like a birthmark. Twins have complimentary marks.

LILILEA and RABEELALIA, female twins, have an "S" on the back of their hands. The "S" shape makes sharp, right-angled turns.

The SONG ENDS. We can SEE a glimpse of God through the light.

The angels hurriedly finish putting away their instruments and AD LIB about attending "the first wedding."

INT. FEMALE ANGEL'S ROOM

The female angels are all gabbing and excited. A beautiful, dark-haired angel, LAURIANNA, sits at her dresser looking in an oval-shaped mirror.

She opens a gold box sitting on her dresser and removes one of two gold bracelets. She admires it.

MICHAEL, early twenties with dark wavy hair and blue eyes, enters.

>   MICHAEL

>   The rings?

We SEE they are in the golden box.

>   LAURIANNA

>   Don't worry. My brother is the ring bearer.

Before closing the box, she puts the one bracelet on her wrist. The distinctive mark on her hand matches the one on the bracelet. She tucks the box into her hair piled up in a bun atop her head.

EXT. OUTER SPACE

As we leave Heaven, we head into DARKNESS.

>   NARRATOR (V.O.)

>   In the beginning, there was darkness until God

became light.

We approach our solar system, and the sun becomes brighter.

NARRATOR (V.O.)

Your sun...comprised mostly of hydrogen. Through fusion of these hydrogen atoms, the sun produces its heat and light.

We see an OVERHEAD VIEW of all the planets in our solar system.

NARRATOR (V.O.)

This is the way your solar system used to look.

We DROP DOWN from above the planets, heading towards the sun. We first FLY BY the two outermost twin planets, Uranus and Neptune. The planet Pluto doesn't exist...yet.

Then, we PASS Saturn and discover it has no ring.

We CONTINUE on towards the sun and now PASS Jupiter without its famous giant red spot at 19.5 degrees S. latitude.

Continuing, we CLOSE IN on a large and very bright planet. This is where our current asteroid belt is located.

NARRATOR (V.O.)

This is the fifth planet, known as Tiamait. It was the middle planet of your solar system...four before it and four after it. Whether entering or leaving the solar system, it was always the fifth planet. From this stone of fire, angels were created.

Orbiting Tiamait is a moon with water and a living atmosphere. It contains many beautiful landscapes and angelic cities, resembling Paradise with its topography of precious metals.

NARRATOR (V.O.)

This moon, the companion of Tiamait, was the inhabitable place where angels could dwell.

We FLY towards another planet, Mars, with an atmosphere and water. We now head towards our planet.

NARRATOR (V.O.)

Your home…the THIRD planet.

EXT. EARTH'S ORBIT—OUTER SPACE

A layer of clear material covers Earth. We pass through this outer-protective layer to discover it is made of water.

NARRATOR (V.O.)

God divided the waters from the waters and placed this water canopy above the firmament, which He called Heaven. Water is the only substance on Earth occurring naturally in three forms: liquid, solid, and gas. Every living thing needs water to live. Two-thirds of man and Earth's surface is water.

EXT. INSIDE EARTH'S ATMOSPHERE—OVERHEAD VIEW

We SEE one large ocean and one huge continent divided by rivers.

There appears to be a globally warm climate.

In the center of the landmass is a huge garden, which is located near modern-day Gulf of Mexico and southwest of the Florida coast.

> NARRATOR (V.O.)
>
> The Garden of Eden, at precisely 19.5 degrees north latitude...the foundation stone of the north.

Eden looks like an island with one huge river flowing from and around it.

This crystal blue river then splits into four smaller rivers as they cut through various parts of the huge, single landmass. These river paths seem to outline some of our present-day continents.

> NARRATOR (V.O.)
>
> The River of Eden divided into four other rivers: Pison, Gihon, Hiddekel, and the Euphrates.

Passing through the "Strait of Gibraltar," we SEE three of the rivers separating from the main one.

> NARRATOR (V.O.)
>
> These three are the Gihon, Pison, and Hiddekel.

The Hiddekel River continues northeast through Asia.

> NARRATOR (V.O.)
>
> This would cut through and separate modern-day Russia from Mongolia and China, a mountainous region in your time.

Modern-day South America and Africa are separated here by one of these three rivers, the Gihon, which completely surrounds Africa.

Antarctica is connected to South America at the bottom, then wraps around the bottom of Africa, with the bulk of Antarctica just east of Africa. The Gihon River surrounding Africa separates them.

Northeast of Antarctica's northern-most tip sits India and Australia, both separated from Asia and each other by the Pison.

Australia is just east of India, separated from Asia AND India by a portion or tributary of the Pison River.

The fourth division of the one river from Eden flows north.

> NARRATOR (V.O.)
>
> The original Euphrates River used to separate North America and Europe and ran northward.

WE CONTINUE OUR DESCENT DOWN TO

EXT. GARDEN OF EDEN

We SEE various forms of now extinct vegetation and many different TYPES of monkeys and other prehistoric animals. The various dinosaur types are about the size of the average pet dog today.

Finally, there appear two intelligent serpents, exact duplicates of the serpent cherub we saw in Heaven earlier. Resembling a modern-day Grey alien with legs and arms, each has only three fingers and toes and walks upright.

They watch a huge egg beginning to hatch.

> NARRATOR (V.O.)
>
> So which did come first…

INSERT—CLOSE ON—EGGSHELL

As a baby serpent breaks out.

BACK TO SCENE

The parent serpents are proud of their newest member.

> SERPENT
>
> Should we name him, or let the man name him?

EXT. NEAR RIVER BANK—DAY

Subtitle: "Garden of Eden."

A naked man, ADAM, walks by. We notice he has no belly button.

He picks up a stick and swings at some pebbles next to the river of Eden. The pebbles land in the water, upsetting a school of eels.

He notes how far they sail, landing in the middle of the river.

On the horizon, the early morning sun is rising. The constellation Gemini is above the horizon and is fading.

GOD, who looks like Adam's identical twin, joins Adam.

He picks up a slightly larger stick and begins to hit pebbles too.

> GOD
>
> Are you nervous?

SMACK! The SOUND of the stone hitting the stick is like the crack of a homerun hit. They watch the stone soar high into the air.

ADAM

Why should I be? You made her for me. She's perfect.

GOD

Both of you are perfect in my eyes. Your love for the woman is perfect...in a perfect world.

God's stone finally lands on the other side of the huge river, three times that of Adam's best distance.

ADAM

Why did you make her for me?

GOD

Because you were lonely and needed companionship with someone just like you, but different.

ADAM
(looking at God)

Why did you make me?

GOD
(pause)

For the same reason.

Adam's eyes again find the spot where God's stone landed.

ADAM

I challenge you to a stone hitting contest.

GOD

Okay…but let the one who is without sin go
first.

Adam shrugs his shoulders as they both go at the same time.

Adam's stone falls short into the river where the eels dive after it. God's
lands on the other side again.

ADAM
(curiously)

What's sin?

We SEE a large fruit tree behind them as our VIEW WIDENS.

NARRATOR (V.O.)

The Tree of Knowledge…of Good…and Evil.

While looking at the fruit on the tree and listening to God try to explain
to Adam the definition of sin, we

CUT TO:

EXT. GARDEN OF EDEN—FLOWER BED—CLOSE ON—LAURI-
ANNA'S BOX

Still tucked in her hair. Laurianna, Angelea, and the twins Rabeelalia
and Lililea are busy helping fix Eve's long hair.

EVE, mid-teens, also has no belly button. She is stunningly beautiful.

Eve studies her hair in a reflection in an oval-shaped hand mirror.

EVE

Something is missing.

Eve notices the little gold box in Laurianna's hair.

EVE

I love how it looks in your hair.

LAURIANNA

It's my phylactery.

She takes it from her hair, takes the rings and bracelet out of the box, and puts the second bracelet on her wrist and the rings on her finger.

She adorns Eve's hair with the box.

LAURIANNA

There…something…borrowed.

She LAUGHS nervously, showing her sentimental attachment to the box.

EXT. GARDEN OF EDEN—CENTRAL AREA

Subtitle: "The first wedding."

Beautiful voices are SINGING as we see a naked Eve adorned with flowers in her long hair, which covers her butt and breasts.

Adam watches her walk towards him. He's standing in front of a tree with twelve different fruits.

NARRATOR (V.O.)

The Tree of Life.

EXT. EDEN—SURROUNDING AREAS

Gathered around the huge outdoor ceremony are representatives of every beast of the field and air. We SEE a lion beside a lamb. The lion is eating grass while the lamb is licking the lion's ear.

EXT. PATH TO ALTAR

A little boy angel and a little girl angel walk in front of Eve, scattering flower petals for her to walk on.

As Eve walks down the path in the garden, WE FOLLOW her. We come to seven male angels participating in the wedding.

> NARRATOR (V.O.)
>
> These are Adam's groomsmen and the original seven archangels: Michael, Gabriel, Yekun, Kesabel, Gadrel, Raphael, and Uriel.

We CONTINUE along the path where three more angels bow, showing their respect for the bride.

> NARRATOR (V.O.)
>
> These three are Raguel, Seraqael, and Haniel. They will be promoted to archangels…soon.

We PASS BY two more high-ranking angel chiefs.

> NARRATOR (V.O.)
>
> Samyaza and Azazyel.

As Eve takes her final steps toward the altar where Adam is standing, we SEE four male angels.

> NARRATOR (V.O.)
>
> Four more Princes…Amazarak, Penemue, and the twins, Turyal and Tarel.

Seven female angels surround Eve as her bridesmaids. The only ones we recognize are Angelea and the twins, Lililea and Rabeelalia.

EXT. THE ALTAR

God stands under the Tree of Life, ready to perform the marriage ceremony. He faces Adam, who watches Eve walk down the aisle.

As WE LOOK into Adam's eyes, Adam has a

FLASHBACK—EVE'S FIRST DAY

Adam is awakened from a deep sleep by someone he's never seen before. This new person, Eve, has been placing flowers in his hair.

As he awakes, she runs off LAUGHING. Adam tries to get up suddenly to give chase but notices his side hurts and sits back down.

END FLASHBACK

ADAM'S POV—THE WEDDING

God begins the ORAL part of the ceremony. As God directs His words and attention to Eve, Adam looks into her beautiful blue eyes.

EVE'S POV—OF ADAM

While looking at Adam, she remembers

FLASHBACK—BESIDE THE RIVER

HUMMING to herself while taking a bath in the river.

Adam has crept up behind a tree to watch her.

She notices him and comes out of the water unashamed by her

nakedness to greet him.

Adam has made a wreath from the flowers Eve placed in his hair. As he places it on her head, they smile at each other.

END FLASHBACK

BACK TO SCENE

We are back at the wedding where both Adam and Eve exchange smiles.

We notice Eve is wearing the same wreath of flowers in her hair, now adorned by Laurianna's gold box.

We LOOK into God's eyes.

GOD'S POV—OF EVE

He looks into her eyes and remembers creating her.

FLASHBACK—EVE AND ADAM'S CREATION

Adam is asleep on the ground. God is holding a rib in his hand. He begins morphing it into a woman.

Using the same molding motions of His hands, we now

DISSOLVE TO:

God sculpts something out of clay. His hands are muddy. The completed clay statue of a lifeless Adam stands before Him.

As He gives mouth-to-mouth to Adam, we see the clay become flesh.

NARRATOR (V.O.)

The breath of life...creating the living body, soul and spirit.

>   GOD
>   (to Adam)
>
> Happy birthday.

END FLASHBACK

BACK TO WEDDING

God looks at the angels, archangels and cherubim assembled for the wedding. We HEAR His thoughts O.S. as He remembers their creation.

FLASHBACK—ANGEL CREATION

>   GOD (O.S.)
>
> And from the rock I cut off a great fire, and from the fire I created the incorporeal ten angel troops. Their weapons are fiery and their raiment a burning flame.

God is hammering on a bright rock with a golden hammer. The sparks created from the hammer striking the rock are the substance He uses to mold and create the angels.

>   GOD (O.S.)
>
> But firstborn of the angels was you, Lucifer. The brightest, wisest and made from the finest gold. The workmanship of your pipes and sockets was prepared in you the day I created you.

We SEE LUCIFER'S golden serpent head, six helicopter-style wings and hundreds of lamps or electric-type bulbs that cover his perfection giving him a very bright appearance. With these lamps, he generates the color red in the rainbow over God's throne.

GOD (O.S.)

The Red Dragon, in whose image the serpent was made.

He's also covered with precious gemstones and in the center of his body near his chest is an oval-shaped looking monitor.

GOD (O.S.)

Truly, you are the Prince of the Air. Of the five cherubim created to carry my throne, I placed you at the top.

All five cherubim attach to each other around God's throne.

They complete a five-pointed star with a circle or rim surrounding them, which connects to them at each of the five points. Lucifer is at the top of the five-pointed star.

Each of the five cherubim now has five faces, showing how when they UNITE, they each SHARE each other's characteristics.

A large blue firmament is above them, containing air for God.

The pentagon-shaped base created in the center is the floor that God's Throne sits upon and where the cherubim attach.

The six wings of each cherub MORPH down to four wings as they UNITE. These wings are just underneath their five-faced heads.

As the cherubim land, their wings stop turning. Two of their blades point toward the two blades of the nearest cherub. The other two blades drop down beside each cherub, motionless.

OVERHEAD, their outstretched wings perfectly outline a five-pointed star.

As the landing process ends, we SEE a wheel within a wheel unfold from each cherub and set down upon the ground.

God's Throne faces Lucifer as He looks at him.

> GOD

Happy birthday!

END FLASHBACK

BACK TO WEDDING

LUCIFER stands by playing music and is one of the five VOICES SINGING a song, along with the other cherubim also surrounding the Eden altar.

Underneath their wings, which have dropped down and cover their bodies, a mechanical-looking hand is being used to PLAY a harp.

The body of each cherub acts like a large pipe organ PLAYING various NOTES. Each cherub plays one TONE each to complete a five-toned sonatina, sometimes resembling the Intel and "CLOSE ENCOUN-TERS" tones. Lucifer's golden body always vibrates the lower note.

> LUCIFER
> (thinking to
> himself)

I am made from fire and covered with gold and precious stones. This man and woman are made from the dirt and clay that I walk upon underneath my feet.

Standing beside Lucifer is the earthly serpent performing a BEAT to the wedding music. He's PLAYING a type of DRUMS made of hollowed-out trees. He holds the drumsticks with his three-fingered hands.

EXT. FRONT OF ALTAR

The little boy angel, APOLLYON, and little GIRL ANGEL are standing behind Adam and Eve now.

GIRL ANGEL
(telepathically)

Do you still have the rings?

He answers by showing them on his thumbs, giving a "thumbs up" sign.

Apollyon starts talking nonstop AD LIBS to the little girl angel telepathically until God interrupts him by SHUSHING him mentally.

GOD

Apollyon, give Adam the rings.

Apollyon is having a hard time getting them off his thumbs so Michael, the archangel who appears to be the best man, lends a hand.

Michael hands Adam both rings. Adam places one on his own finger.

While Adam places the ring on Eve's finger, the little girl angel takes a bracelet off her wrist and places it on Apollyon's wrist.

GIRL ANGEL
(telepathically)

I made it for you.

She shows off her matching bracelet with the same crest or mark they both share on the back of their right hands.

> GOD

I pronounce you…man and wife.

Adam kisses Eve on the cheek.

> NARRATOR (V.O.)

This was the very first kiss.

Apollyon and the little girl angel are both embarrassed and blush.

> APOLLYON

Thanks for the bracelet, sis.

He then turns towards her and imitates Adam's kiss by kissing her on the cheek. She blushes again while pushing him away.

> NARRATOR (V.O.)

That was the very first…angel kiss.

> GOD

What I've joined together, let no one separate.

As He says this, an apple-like fruit FALLS from the Tree of Life.

> GOD

Stop!

It does so, in mid-air, just above Adam's head.

The little girl angel backs away, still blushing from her brother's kiss. She then MORPHS back into an adult angel, where we discover it's Laurianna, as she runs off into the thick garden.

Adam looks up at the apple above his head.

ADAM

Come to me.

It obeys. He takes a bite and offers it to Eve.

Eve takes a bite as the surrounding hosts of angels APPLAUD.

God thoughtfully looks around at all of His creations.

GOD
(to Himself)

I can't believe I'm finished. I created all this.
Seems like only yesterday, I was alone.

FLASHBACK—GOD'S FIRST DAY

We are in total DARKNESS. Suddenly, a bright LIGHT APPEARS. It then separates into THREE LIGHTS or stars in the center of the blackness.

The three stars line up like the belt of Orion. Then, the star Sirius appears. Then, one by one, the other stars of Orion appear.

The lower belt star BECOMES God while the five stars: Betelgeuse, Bellatrix, Rigel, Saiph and Sirius BECOME the five cherubim.

God sits in the center of the cherubim and looks at all five of their monitors. He holds some kind of light pointer that affects images onscreen as He touches them.

GOD

Now, what would it look like if I added a bill?

He touches the screen in front of Him with the pointer.

GOD

That's interesting…now what if I add a tail?

Our VIEW WIDENS revealing that God is actually creating the image of a duck-billed platypus.

> GOD
>
> It looks funny, but maybe the man will like it.

> NARRATOR (V.O.)
>
> God experimented with all His ideas this way before He actually created them. He had five computers to animate with. After all, He had never done this before. God was a Spirit only until he realized He could separate from Himself and become three-dimensional.

END FLASHBACK

BACK TO SCENE

Adam and Eve kiss again. God gives a nod to the five cherubim, signaling them to begin playing again.

> GOD
>
> All angels come now and show respect to my final creation as all instruments begin playing again.

The cherubim begin playing as the angels kneel, bow or curtsey.

> LUCIFER
> (to himself)
>
> I'll never glorify this thing made from the clay

of the Earth I once ruled. How dare God give them dominion over the planet He first gave to me?

EXT. EDEN—GOD'S THRONE—LATER

Lucifer joins the other cherubim as a flying machine.
Our VIEW WIDENS to include Michael, the last angel to bow.

EXT. GARDEN OF EDEN—OVERHEAD VIEW

The five cherubim lift-off to carry God's Throne from Earth.

INT. CHERUBIM THRONE—GOD

Addresses everyone below.

> GOD (V.O.)
>
> This is the beginning of my day of rest from creating all things. The Earth will revolve around its sun 1,000 times when this day is to be complete.

As the cherubim reach Earth's outer atmosphere, their wings fold up just over the wheels and a fiery propulsion system kicks in.

EXT. TIAMAIT'S MOON

God arrives as the cherubim land in the throne room. He addresses the angels.

> GOD (V.O.)
>
> Let this seventh day begin a day of feasting and

celebration.

He toasts all the angels gathered here as they begin feasting.

> NARRATOR (V.O.)
>
> All angels split into three groups. One third remained here. One third went to God's Throne. The other third went all around the universe. After every 333 revolutions of the Earth around the sun, the angels would rotate.

INT. TUNNEL OF LIGHT

Rising above the Earth and heading off in different directions. Wormholes transport the angels individually.

> NARRATOR (V.O.)
>
> Angels move at the speed of thought through these 540 gateways or ladders...known as Jacob's Ladder.

Subtitle: "666 years later."

EXT. OUTER SPACE—ABOVE TIAMAIT'S MOON

It's the final rotation as we SEE two identical twin male angels split up. PHANUEL to God's throne and KESABEL to Tiamait's moon.

Identical female twin angels, Rabeelalia and Lililea, go to Tiamait.

Two identical male twin angels, TURYAL and TAREL, go to Tiamait.

The fraternal twins split up the same way; the female, Laurianna, to God's throne and the male, Apollyon, to Tiamait.

Apollyon still looks like a ten year-old boy. Laurianna prepares to head off to Heaven in the tube of light.

LAURIANNA

Don't stay in that form too long, you might get stuck that way. And don't eat too much dessert.

APOLLYON
(laughing)

Yes, mother.

Laurianna gives him a stern look, and then cracks a smile as she joins the other angels going through the shaft of light.

Other angels are heading out to perform duties around the universe via these wormhole-like shafts.

Michael is leading these angel troops around the universe.

Gabriel is leading several troops to God's Throne.

Lucifer is hovering above Tiamait's moon and watches everyone leave.

NARRATOR (V.O.)

Lucifer is now in charge of all the angels on Tiamait's moon, planet Earth, and all the other stones of fire or planets in the solar system.

EXT. GARDEN OF EDEN—DAY

Eve walks through the garden and comes to the Tree of Knowledge. She SEES the two sticks used by Adam and God. She looks at the tree.

EVE

The forbidden tree. Didn't want any of your old fruit anyway.

As she walks away from the tree, our VIEW WIDENS to include the nearby river where we can SEE Lucifer through the bushes and ferns.

EXT. THE RIVER OF LIFE

Lucifer is filling his golden canteen with the life-giving waters as he looks up and notices Eve walk away from the forbidden tree.

Lucifer walks up to the tree.

> LUCIFER
>
> If God warned the man not to eat of the tree, there must be something He's hiding from them. Maybe I would be as all knowing as God if I ate from this tree myself. This new knowledge might enable me to overthrow God and become the supreme ruler.

He plucks one of the fruit from the tree. It looks like a cross between an apple, orange, and pomegranate.

> LUCIFER
>
> This fruit is like no other I've ever seen or smelled before.

He takes a bite. He immediately notices he's naked and tries to cover up with his wings and hands.

EXT. HEAVEN

Michael is leaving Heaven as Laurianna arrives.

> MICHAEL
>
> I'll look after your brother when I get to

Tiamait. I'm dying to try some gourmet dessert myself.

EXT. GARDEN OF EDEN

Lucifer is walking around enjoying his new view of things.

LUCIFER

I must take advantage of God's absence. I'll need support from the other angels to battle God for His throne. How can I make them understand my newly discovered point-of-view?

He LOOKS into his built-in monitor. He SEES God resting in Heaven. Then the image clouds up like a smoking mirror or crystal ball. It clears. He SEES Apollyon feasting on Tiamait's moon.

Lucifer's eyes light up along with all the lamps covering his body as a plan begins to form.

INT./EXT. TIAMAIT'S MOON—OUTSIDE KITCHEN

Lucifer has arrived on the angelic planet and is carrying bushels of the forbidden fruit from the tree in Eden. He's painted them almost like our modern Easter eggs to disguise them.

INT. KITCHEN

He brings them to the chef in the kitchen.

LUCIFER

Make as many dessert dishes from these as you

can and serve it to all the honorable angels.

Lucifer heads towards the banquet hall, passing the throne room. It's empty. He eyes the throne with a mischievous look.

INT. BANQUET HALL

The master chef enters with the desserts he's made for Lucifer.

The angels eat the pie, AD LIBBING comments on its "wonderful smell and taste."

Suddenly, they one by one realize they are naked and start looking for ways to cover up.

Lucifer enters the hall and SEES that his plan has worked. He doesn't even stay to see the rest. He becomes flight ready.

> LUCIFER
>
> Now, to take care of the man…and his companion.

EXT. OUTER COURT—BANQUET HALL

Michael arrives at Tiamait's moon just as the angels are discovering their nakedness. The first angel he encounters is embarrassed and tries to cover up. This puzzles him but he continues forward.

INT. BANQUET HALL

As he arrives inside the banquet hall, he OBSERVES angels eating dessert, and notices they immediately start covering their nakedness.

He SEES Yekun about to eat the dessert and heads towards him.

> MICHAEL
>
> Maybe I'll get a better understanding from one

of my fellow archangels.

He now witnesses Yekun's own conversion as he tries to cover up too.

MICHAEL

I sense some form of trickery is at play here.

EXT. TIAMAIT'S ORBIT

Michael stands at the base of the light shaft as Gabriel descends. Michael grabs him and together they climb back up onto the ramp.

MICHAEL

We better take the express route back to Heaven. There's trouble brewing here and we've got to warn the others.

EXT. GARDEN OF EDEN

Lucifer is in the garden now, watching Eve.

LUCIFER

The man will never willingly betray his creator. But, if I can trick the woman by mixing the truth with a lie, she will unknowingly betray God. And then the man will hearken to the voice of his beloved companion.

The serpent cherub becomes invisible and approaches the natural serpent.

LUCIFER
(telepathically)

Go to the woman. Talk to her.

NARRATOR (V.O.)

This is the first time dark forces manipulated someone's mind, as Lucifer used angelic telepathy, a form of communication not bound by the laws of sound waves.

SERPENT
(to himself)

I think I'll go talk to the woman.

EXT. FORBIDDEN TREE AREA

The serpent and Eve can be SEEN talking to one another.
Eve is still wearing Laurianna's golden box in her hair.

SERPENT

Yes, it is a perfect world. Except for one thing...that tree which looks and smells so good...but we can't be eating from it.

EVE

Oh, that tree. Sure, it looks nice but if God says we'll die when we eat from it, or even touch it—then that's enough reason for me to leave it alone.

Now Satan uses the same temptations on her that he himself suffered earlier.

> SERPENT/LUCIFER
> (together)

Ah…surely you won't…die! He wouldn't kill a pretty little thing like you. Why, you'll be just as smart as God…that's all He's afraid of. And He's afraid that too much knowledge will make you all independent and god-like yourself and you won't be needing Him anymore.

The serpent follows the urgings of Lucifer physically now, like a puppet as he picks up a forbidden fruit lying on the ground.

> SERPENT/LUCIFER
> (together)

Look…I'm touching it and I'm not falling over dead, now am I? Besides, look how pretty the fruit is and it smells absolutely delicious. How can you not wonder what it tastes like?

Eve is definitely considering all the serpent has said. She carefully takes the fruit from his hand, breathing a deep SIGH of relief because she's still alive.

She finally takes a bite of the fruit. While chewing, Eve realizes she's naked and covers herself. While doing this, the gold box falls out of her hair. As it hits the ground, the lid slips off.

INT. BANQUET HALL—TIAMAIT'S MOON—CLOSE ANGLE—APOLLYON'S BRACELET

He is STILL in the form of a boy and has become the self-appointed leader of the group on Tiamait's moon.

The archangel Yekun is in the front, nodding while Apollyon speaks.

APOLLYON

My fellow angels...our eyes have been opened.
We are as God.

We see other familiar angels becoming part of the rebellion: Samyaza, Azazyel, Amazarak, Penemue, Turyal and Tarel.

Two archangels, Kesabel and Gadrel, join Yekun as they are motivated by Apollyon's speech.

EXT. HEAVEN

Michael and Gabriel have made it to Heaven's gates by now and are busy informing the others. They're organizing and stationing their troops all around Heaven's perimeter.

We SEE the rest of the two-thirds that haven't been tricked by Lucifer now arriving as reinforcements in the b.g. God is still asleep.

EXT. GARDEN OF EDEN

Adam is calling to Eve, who is still crouching from embarrassment.

EVE

I'm over here.

As Adam approaches, she seems to be hiding.

ADAM

Why are you acting so strange?

EVE

Adam...I just ate of the forbidden tree...and I'm still alive. Look, you can touch it and still live.

Adam is obviously very grieved. He is looking at the fruit that she is holding in her hand.

EVE

My mind is open now and I'm still alive. The serpent was right! God lied to us about this tree. Nothing bad will happen to you...only good things!

Adam is visibly torn between obeying God and his love for her.

ADAM

You're sure we won't die?

Since he sees no immediate penalty, he finally takes a bite.

EXT. EDEN—NEAR RIVER

Lucifer is watching Adam. He LAUGHS a long, evil, sinister laugh.

Over his LAUGHTER, we see Adam squatting down to cover himself as he realizes his nakedness, like Eve did when she dropped the box.

NARRATOR (V.O.)

Adam's eyes were opened to the natural world...

Squatting now, he notices he's beside the golden box that Eve has worn since their wedding day. He SEES the lid beside it. He puts the lid back on the box, holding it as he weeps.

SATAN
(while laughing)

It's too late to put a lid on it now.

NARRATOR (V.O.)
(continuing)

...but his eyes would close to the spirit world.

INT. BANQUET HALL—TIAMAIT'S MOON—LUCIFER

Has traveled here at the speed of light and comes in at the end of Apollyon's speech.

LUCIFER

Apollyon is right. Together, we've opened your eyes, something only the true creator can do. Tell, me...do any of you remember who was here first, God or me? You've always taken His word that He created you. But look at me...I am the highest of all living creatures...even higher than the man who is in God's image. I tell you, I was first and it was I who created you from the fiery depths of Tiamait below.

Since they only remember Lucifer, Apollyon and God being around when they were created, they listen more intently.

LUCIFER

God is an impostor! He's just a potter who makes things from clay! You are made from fire

and light—only the brightest of stars can truly
illuminate you!

All of the angels start shouting, "Hail Lucifer, the brightest of all the
morning stars!"

APOLLYON

Then come with us, my brothers. We'll attack
God's throne and rule the universe together!

All of the fallen third make their way up the light shaft towards Heaven.
One third of all STARS in space become BRIGHTER like a supernova.

EXT./INT. THRONE ROOM—HEAVEN

As they arrive just outside the throne room, they fall into a trap set by
the remaining good angels. The fierce battle begins.

Here we see angels who were once close friends, some even related, having to fight each other. It saddens the good ones but doesn't seem to
phase the evil ones.

The angels use swords of revolving fire.

NARRATOR (V.O.)

Since angels are made of fire...they must fight
fire with fire.

Phanuel and Kesabel fight each other.

Michael fights Lucifer. This battle ends with Michael knocking the
flaming sword out of Lucifer's left hand with his golden slingshot.

Lucifer's left hand is badly damaged as he loses his sword.

Lucifer is cast from Heaven along with the other evil angels.

Gabriel towers over the smaller angel Apollyon as they fight.

Laurianna witnesses her brother being defeated as Gabriel gets the upper hand. Apollyon drops his bracelet as he's cast from Heaven.

Laurianna picks up the bracelet she made for her brother and WEEPS.

> NARRATOR (V.O.)
>
> The day I lost my brother became the darkest
> day I'd ever known.

We realize here that Laurianna is our Narrator.

FROM HEAVEN, we can SEE all stars in space. One-third suddenly stops shining, symbolic of the angelic third that just fell.

EXT. GARDEN OF EDEN—OVERHEAD VIEW

God arrives back on Earth. Only four cherubim carry him now, our first glimpse of how things are different. The united cherubim have only four faces—the man, lion, eagle and calf.

Gabriel and Michael have restrained Lucifer and bring him to the Garden of Eden. Lucifer's badly damaged mechanical left hand is covered with a black glove.

EXT. GARDEN OF EDEN—ORCHARD OF TREES

Adam, Eve, and the serpent are standing before God with their heads bowed. Adam and Eve wear aprons of fig leaves.

> GOD
>
> Why are you wearing these leaves?

> EVE
>
> Because we are naked.

50   Revelations

GOD

Who told you that you are naked? Have you
eaten of the Tree of Knowledge of Good and
Evil?

Adam and Eve both nod their heads.

GOD

Why?

Adam GULPS and points to the woman.

Eve GULPS and points to the serpent.

The serpent GULPS and points to Lucifer.

Lucifer just stands there and rolls his eyes.

God hands Adam and Eve clothing made from the skins of sheep.

GOD

Clothe yourselves with these, the white outer
garments of righteousness. From this day forward, all heavenly creatures will also wear garments of white so their nakedness cannot be
seen by men.

After the man and woman have dressed themselves, God looks at them
with a long face. He looks at Lucifer, then the serpent.

GOD
(to serpent)

You were the highest of creatures but because
of what you did, you are cursed above all cattle
and beasts. Since you deceived the man made

from dust and caused him to eat that which was forbidden, upon your belly will you now go and dust shall you eat all the days of your life.

God looks at the serpent and Lucifer now.

GOD

I will put an enmity between you and the woman, and between your seed and her seed. Their Redeemer shall come from her seed. He will ultimately crush you and restore man back to me. A place of fiery torment shall be prepared for you and all angels that followed you. After the same amount of time that it took me to create everything has passed, you will be cast there…forever.

God then looks at Eve.

GOD

I will greatly multiply your sorrows. In sorrow shall you bring forth sons and daughters. Your desires shall be subject to your husband. He shall rule over you. Man is now the head of the woman.

And finally, God looks at Adam. Since they look like identical twins, God is noticeably saddened.

Adam hangs his head in shame, avoiding God's gaze.

GOD

Because you listened to the voice of the woman

and disobeyed my own voice, the ground will be cursed to you. In sorrow will you eat of it all the days of your life. Thorns and poisonous weeds shall come from the ground with the herb that you shall eat, and by the sweat from your face shall you eat bread until you return to the ground from which you came.

NARRATOR (V.O.)

It was after this that Adam actually named the woman Eve, the mother of all living. Lucifer's name would be changed to Satan or the Devil. And because God feared that man, who now had knowledge of good and evil, would now eat of the Tree of Life and become immortal in this sinful state, man had to be driven out of the garden.

EXT. EDGE OF EDEN—DAY—LATER

As Adam and Eve leave the COLORFUL Garden of Eden, we SEE Laurianna's gold box still among their possessions.

The serpent family is also leaving Eden.

As they travel east, COLOR FADES from the world, which is now in BLACK and WHITE.

We SEE the four cherubim protecting the entrance to the Garden with a flaming sword. They stand protecting the path leading to the Tree of Life, the same path that Eve walked down on her wedding day.

NARRATOR (V.O.)

Man was never allowed back.

EXT. GARDEN OF EDEN/FORBIDDEN TREE—(COLOR)

God stands beside the Tree of Knowledge in the very same spot where He and Adam talked on his wedding day.

He can SEE Adam and Eve from far off, just past the entrance being guarded by the cherubim.

God has a tear in His eye.

> NARRATOR (V.O.)
>
> The separation of man and God began.

EXT. EAST OF EDEN (BLACK AND WHITE)

We SEE Adam and Eve eating wild roots, insects and honey.

As Adam constructs a shelter, he begins to till the ground for the first time. We see him planting seeds.

EXT. EAST OF EDEN—THE SERPENTS

Watch their eggs hatch for the first time since the fall. We SEE that their babies have no legs or arms. Their young have lost the ability to speak…they are mute.

The father serpent now speaks AD LIBS to his newborn with a forked tongue, which adds a lisp.

> SERPENT
>
> This poison stuff tastes awful.

> NARRATOR (V.O.)
>
> God not only divided the serpent's tongue,
> symbolic of speaking a lie with the truth with

one tongue, but He placed poison under the serpents tongue as well to forever show the real nature of a lie.

EXT. EAST OF EDEN—ADAM'S GARDEN—DAY

Adam is taking a break from his work in the field. He's sweating profusely. Eve gives him some water to drink as she wipes the sweat from his brow.

As she does, she notices something in Adam's hair. She pulls it out and holds it up to the light to inspect it closer…Adam's first gray hair.

NARRATOR (V.O.)

Man began to age.

EXT. HILL—OVERLOOKING ADAM

A dark, sinister-looking angel sitting upon a pale horse.

NARRATOR (V.O.)

DEATH became part of man's existence. As his body returns to dust, the water evaporates into the air, as does his spirit.

FADE TO: BLACK

FROM BLACK, we SEE shades of David's last FLASHBACK of the little girl's face, dressed as an angel in a school play.

VIDEO GLITCH happens again.

COLOR returns.

Subtitle: "Back to 1945."

EXT. BERLIN—DAY

We SEE a snake slithering from behind a building where KATY WEISS, a beautiful, sixteen year-old Jewish girl, is picking wild flowers and apparently praying.

> KATY
>
> Okay…God…As you know, I just turned sixteen…and…well, I've never…been on a date yet.

She looks around to make sure no one is listening while sticking some of the flowers in her long, dark-colored hair.

> KATY
>
> So naturally, I've never been kissed yet…by a guy…other than my father, that is. And that doesn't count…it's always on the cheek. What I was wondering was…do you think you could send me…someone?

As if to answer her, she HEARS something fall from above in some trees nearby. She runs to get a better VIEW of something hanging from a tree.

EXT. TREES NEARBY

Katy SEES that it's an Allied pilot, whose parachute is tangled in the tree. Feeling like he's an angel from Heaven above or at least the answer to her prayers, she rescues him by cutting him down.

DAVID'S POV—THE GROUND

As he falls towards it.

When his VISION FOCUSES, he HEARS ECHOES of the little girl he SAW as his LIFE FLASHED before him saying, "Angels will watch over you and protect you…"

We hear a REPRISE of "SOMEONE TO WATCH OVER ME."

His VISION CLEARS as he SEES Katy's face. The sun highlights her long hair, which is accented by the flowers. He mistakes her for an angel, thinking he has died.

KATY'S POV—DAVID

She SEES that he's kind of cute as he smiles at her.

BACK TO SCENE

KATY

Are you all right?

DAVID

I am now.

INT. KATY'S FAMILY HIDEOUT—LATER THAT NIGHT

Katy, her MOTHER and eight year-old little BROTHER are doctoring David, applying fresh bandages.

MOTHER

What will your father say?

KATY

It's just 'til he gets better.

MOTHER

Katy, you know how I feel about Americans.

Katy's mom quickly leaves the room, forcing Katy to explain her mother's remarks.

KATY

It was 1939. We were onboard the "ST. LOUIS" with 930 other Jews. We had sailed from Germany to Cuba. It was May twenty-seventh when we arrived. Only twenty-two were allowed off the ship. The United States wouldn't take ANY of us. We had to return to Europe. We've been on the run and hiding ever since.

There's a KNOCKING SOUND at the door. David falls out of his chair.

KATY

It's okay. It's my father…that's his secret knock.

INT. WEISS FAMILY HIDEOUT—LATER THAT NIGHT

The Weiss family is joined by Katy's FATHER as they sit around a makeshift kitchen table where David is the invited guest to a dinner of German rations.

FATHER

At night, I sometimes retrieve supplies dropped behind enemy lines. We're all losing weight from the occasional rationing.

MOTHER

I can almost get into my wedding gown again.

KATY

But you won't because you promised it to me.

MOTHER

Perhaps now that you are sixteen, I'll give it to you next Hanukkah.

FATHER

We had to spend last Hanukkah in this hiding place.

DAVID

I had to spend last Christmas on a bombing mission. "Peace on Earth and goodwill toward men…" while I defend bombers dropping exploding packages. I did get a nice gift though.

He shows off his watch that he got for Christmas.

DAVID

My wingman, Johnny, gave it to me. According to him, I'm always late for everything.

BROTHER
(to David)

I believe in Santa Claus!

Everyone LAUGHS.

FATHER

But none of us believe in your Jesus. That's why
we don't celebrate your Christmas.

DAVID
(to Katy's brother)

I can draw Santa Claus.

David takes a piece of paper and some crayons from the table and
begins drawing a picture of Santa Claus.

He hands the picture to Katy's brother. The little boy adds one of Santa's
helpers by drawing in an elf.

BROTHER

Santa's helper.

INT. WEISS HIDEOUT—LATER THAT NIGHT

David is reading a story out loud to Katy's brother.

DAVID

And Balder, the favorite son of Odin, was killed
because of Loki's trickery. All the gods and goddesses and animals wept for him. For his trickery,
Loki was chained to a rock with a great chain.

Katy and her mother are watching how good David is with her little brother.

MOTHER

Okay, we all need our sleep.

INT. SLEEPING AREA—LATER

David tries to sleep, but he's still in pain and feverish. Loss of blood contributes to short fainting spells. During one of these, he slips back into the same area of BLACK as when he almost died.

DREAM SEQUENCE

David SEES the little girl dressed as an angel in a Christmas play.

LITTLE GIRL

...bring tidings of good joy. For He is the promised one...the Redeemer through the seed of the woman...He will save you from the seed of the serpent, which bruises your heel but He will bruise the serpent's head.

She MORPHS into the adult female angel painted on David's plane. This sexy image causes him to WAKE UP SCREAMING!

END DREAM

His outburst gets Katy's attention, much to David's embarrassment.

KATY

Is anything wrong?

DAVID

No. Everything is…okay.

He rolls over, hiding the fact he just had a wet dream.

INT. NAZI CONCENTRATION CAMP—NIGHT

We WITNESS horrible experiments being performed on Jewish prisoners.

INT. THE VATICAN, ROME—NIGHT

We SEE a German, LICIO GELLI, in a secret meeting with bishops, cardinals, and several men in dark suits. One of these men wears a ring displaying Masonic symbolism.

LICIO

On behalf of the Third Reich, we thank the P-2 Masons and the Church of Rome for fighting on our side. We are close to figuring out how to resurrect the ancient flying serpent you so generously made available to us. It's just a miracle that your nuns have protected this mysterious flame all these centuries. Our top scientists and physicists are working night and day to understand its secrets. If Thor's hammer was meant to be wielded again, then it will be under the twisted cross.

EXT. USA DESERT/SECRET BASE—EARLY MORNING

American scientists are trying to develop the atomic bomb. Men in dark suits closely observe one of these experiments. Good and bad angels

INVISIBLY observe these tests also.

EXT./INT. AIR FORCE BASE (ENGLAND)—DAYBREAK

Johnny salutes an officer passing by on his way to his barracks.

Johnny takes off his hat and hangs it in his locker. He NOTICES David's hat still hanging in the locker they shared.

Johnny bows his head and a tear falls to the floor.

EXT. GERMANY—SECRET BASE

Nazi scientists are testing rockets.

> SCIENTIST
>
> We must get these things to fly with more accuracy so our boys won't have to risk their lives delivering bombs.

We SEE a failed rocket test under Wernher Von Braun.

INT. INDIA—DESERT TENT

Hitler's TRANSLATORS are busy poring over ancient Indian manuscripts. At the top of one page, we SEE the title "RIGVEDA."

> TRANSLATOR (O.S.)
>
> This one is supposedly a flight manual…showing how they used the iron flying machines.

EXT. PLATEAU OF TIBET—DAWN

Nazis are all over this archeological site, which is located northeast of India, near the Gobi Desert.

INT. UNDERGROUND TUNNEL

A Mongolian worker chipping away on a wall suddenly falls into a hole as the wall gives way.

                    NAZI OFFICIAL

          We've found the ancient tunnel!

EXT. GERMANY—SS WEWELSBERG CASTLE—NIGHT

We FOLLOW a little white dog returning from the nearby woods. He runs to his master and begins nipping at his heels.

The man picks up the dog as we SEE his face…it's ADOLPH HITLER!

INT. SS CASTLE

The SS or Secret Society, the secret police of the Nazis are in the middle of a secret meeting. They are conducting a secret Masonic ritual with lots of AD LIBBED references to Satanism and Saturn.

                    NAZI

          The Thule Society has given birth to the Nazi
          Party…and the Third Reich.

INT. HITLER'S PRIVATE BUNKER

Hitler is in his bunker talking to a spear tip he has encased there.

                    HITLER

          As long as I hold you in my possession, I will
          rule the world. I remember the first time I held
          you, October 13, 1938. I felt as though I had

held you in my hands once before, in some earlier century of history, and that I had once
claimed you as my talisman of power, holding
the destiny of the world in my hands. What sort
of madness invaded my mind, creating such
turmoil in my breast?

NARRATOR (V.O.)

Legends say many great world leaders have all
possessed this Sword of Destiny…Constantine,
Justinian, Emperor Charlemagne, Otto the
Great, Kaiser Wilhelm, the Hapsburg
Emperors…and now Hitler. Legends also stat-
ed…if they lost the sword, they would lose
their power.

INT. WEISS FAMILY HIDEOUT—NEXT MORNING

Katy's family sleepily lingers over a breakfast of military rations. Katy
stares at David, prompting an evil look from her mother.

MOTHER

After David's wounds heal, he'll have to move
to the abandoned warehouse across the street.

Katy starts to protest but retreats as her mother stares her down.

LATER THAT DAY

We HEAR a love SONG playing on an old RADIO. It's Trisha
Yearwood's "PERFECT LOVE." David is holding some thread while
Katy weaves and braids. She wears many braided wraps in her long hair.

They are beginning to fall in love.

We INTERCUT with FLASHBACKS of Adam and Eve's awkward beginnings at the same time we SEE David and Katy falling in love.

MONTAGE

A)   Adam SEES Eve bathing in a stream. He carries a wreath woven from the flowers Eve put in his hair while he was sleeping.

B)   Katy is taking a bath. She has the flowers in her hair that she picked when they met.

C)   Upon hearing Adam's approach, Eve doesn't know she's naked and gets out of the water unashamed to greet Adam.

D)   David accidentally walks in on Katy. She realizes she's totally naked and tries to cover up, as David quickly exits.

E)   Several days have passed and David's strength has noticeably returned while playing with Katy's little brother.

F)   Katy's mother sees how Katy and David are eyeing each other.

SONG AND FLASHBACKS END

INT. WEISS HIDEOUT—SEVERAL DAYS LATER

                    MOTHER

     I think David is strong enough to live on his
     own now.

INT. WAREHOUSE/ACROSS STREET—THAT NIGHT

David is setting up his hiding place complete with a bed.

INT. WEISS HIDEOUT

Katy places two embroidered rings she's made into a little leather box, a phylactery, and puts it in her coat.

Katy sneaks out her bedroom window.

EXT. WAREHOUSE

She tiptoes across the deserted road and enters the warehouse. She's unaware that the phylactery in her coat pocket has fallen out as she brushes past the small entrance.

As the lid comes off the box, the embroidered rings fall out.

INT. DAVID'S HIDEOUT—LATER

David and Katy are sitting on his bed talking M.O.S. They're holding hands. You can tell they have feelings for each other and neither one cares about the world outside.

> DAVID
>
> I've never cared about anyone before…not like this. I knew you were the one for me from the first time I saw you…it's like God Himself was telling me you were the one. It felt so right.

> KATY
>
> I know what you mean. It's like God answered the prayer I had just said, right as you fell into those trees. It's like our love is so perfect…

> DAVID
>
> Yes…a perfect love…in an imperfect world.

KATY

I know we talked about the fact that we'll probably never see a rabbi again...in fact, we may never see the outside world again. Tonight...may be all we have left.

DAVID

Do you want to...do it...tonight?

Katy breaks down in tears as she nods. She hugs David tightly, then searches her pockets for her phylactery but with no luck.

KATY

I had my phylactery right here...I had braided us two rings...just in case...we did decide...to do it tonight.

DAVID

I've got an idea.

He reaches for a braided hair-wrap in Katy's hair. He takes it and breaks it off.

KATY

Ouch!

DAVID

Sorry.

He then wraps it around both of their wrists and they begin exchanging wedding vows.

DAVID

Do you, Katy Ann Weiss, take me, David Adam Smith, to be your lawful wedded husband?

KATY

I do. Now...do you take me for your lawful wedded wife?

DAVID
(pretending to
think twice)

I do! And I've got an idea...

David takes off his 1945 military standard-issue watch and places it on her wrist.

Katy follows his lead and takes the braided hair-wrap and ties it around David's wrist.

KATY

Wait. We have to break something. It's traditional. It symbolizes the destruction of our temple...our sadness in this time of joy.

They both look around for something. David spots a piece of junk nearby and tosses it out a WINDOW, causing it to BREAK.

DAVID

There...that ought to cover that.

EXT. DAVID'S HIDEOUT

Two German soldiers are passing through just a couple of blocks away. They respond to HEARING the SOUND of the BREAKING GLASS by running in the direction of David's hideout.

INT. DAVID'S HIDEOUT

David is leaning towards Katy. Then, their first kiss. At first, he kisses her on the cheek.

FLASHBACK—GARDEN OF EDEN—FIRST WEDDING

We SEE Adam kiss Eve on the cheek.
While blushing, Apollyon kisses Laurianna on the cheek.

END FLASHBACK

BACK TO SCENE

David starts to kiss Katy on the cheek again but she turns towards him and this time their lips meet.
INTERCUT with FLASHBACKS of Adam and Eve kissing for the first time *after* the fall.

BACK TO SCENE

WE FOLLOW a trail of clothes to David's bed where he and Katy are making love.

FLASHBACK—EAST OF EDEN—ADAM'S HOME

WE FOLLOW a trail of sheepskins to Adam's bed where he and Eve are making love.

ADAM

Here's to perfect love…in an imperfect world.

FLASHBACK ENDS

EXT. DAVID'S HIDEOUT

A German soldier discovers the little leather box Katy dropped.

SOLDIER

A Jew! Probably hiding nearby.

He alerts other soldiers via radio to "search the entire area."
A Nazi soldier walking by the warehouse HEARS a SQUEAKING SOUND inside the building where David and Katy are making love.

INT. DAVID'S HIDEOUT—MOMENTS LATER

David and Katy are now lying in each other's arms.

DAVID

I'll love you for the rest of…your life.

KATY

I'll love you for the rest of…my life too.

There's a CRASHING SOUND as the Germans storm David's hideout.

EXT. DAVID'S HIDEOUT

As David and Katy are being led away in handcuffs, our VIEW SHIFTS to a window across the street. Katy's family tearfully watches their daughter being taken captive.

EXT. TRAIN STATION—NIGHT

Subtitle: "March 11, 1945. Bergen-Belsen, Germany."
A TRAIN WHISTLE can be HEARD as a train comes into VIEW.
Katy is herded from a cattle car as she arrives at the Bergen-Belsen Nazi death camp.

EXT. BERGEN-BELSEN CAMP—NIGHT

Katy walks past hundreds of Jews who are very emaciated and obviously starving to death.

INT. BERGEN-BELSEN CAMP

A soldier takes Katy to a room where she's ordered to strip.
A soldier confiscates all of her possessions, including David's watch. Another guard is shaving her head.
Her long hair falls to the floor.

INT. BUNK AREA—LATER THAT NIGHT

Katy climbs into the bunk where she'll sleep that night. She's bald now. The EYES of a young, frightened girl meet her gaze.
After the guard leaves, Katy tries to befriend the girl.

                              KATY

What's your name?

The feverish girl's face is LIT UP by LIGHTNING.

                              GIRL
                            (coughing)

        Anne…Anne Frank.

The SOUND of THUNDER punctuates her words.

EXT. GERMAN DIRT ROAD—NIGHT—RAINING

David is being transported to a POW camp. Suddenly, the driver runs into a washed-out place in the road causing the jeep to overturn.

David is thrown from the wreck. He gets up slowly. Realizing this is his chance to escape, he runs for it.

One of the Nazi soldiers is snapping out of his confusion and SEES David running.

He levels his GUN at the fleeing American…and FIRES!

                              CUT TO:

EXT. BERGEN-BELSEN CAMP—NIGHT

We SEE and HEAR GUNFIRE as a Bergen-Belsen guard is helping other guards execute prisoners at point-blank range.

INT. BERGEN-BELSEN—GIRL'S BUNK AREA

Anne Frank is in great pain. Katy is trying to comfort her.

EXT. WASHED-OUT ROAD—RAINY NIGHT

David is lying on the ground. His bloody hand stops moving. He's still wearing the braided hair-wrap bracelet on his wrist.

He dies face down in a puddle.

INT. BERGEN-BELSEN—GIRL'S BUNK AREA—CLOSE ON—ANNE FRANK

She closes her eyes and dies.

WE MOVE to another room nearby where WE SEE piles of jewelry.

Katy's watch, given to her by David, is lying atop a huge pile.

EXT. BERGEN-BELSEN CAMP—STORMY NIGHT

We SEE the ovens burning bodies of slain Jews. The smoke from the ovens rises. Over this, we HEAR the VOICE OVER of a CHILD.

> CHILD (V.O.)
>
> I was once a little child who longed for other worlds. But I am no more a child for I have known fear and I have learned to hate...

INT. WEISS FAMILY HIDEOUT—NIGHT

Katy's family is dead. They have all been shot to death. Her little brother is lying face down in a pool of blood. His body lies next to the picture he and David drew of Santa Claus and his elf.

> CHILD (V.O.)
> (continuing)
>
> ...How tragic, then, is youth that lives with

enemies, with gallows ropes. Yet, I still believe I
only sleep today, that I'll wake up. I'll be a child
again, and start to laugh and play.

EXT. BERGEN-BELSEN CAMP—NIGHT

We FOLLOW the smoke from the ovens as it RISES all the way up to

EXT./INT. HEAVEN/GOD'S THRONE ROOM

Where the smoke reaches God's nostrils. Sadness fills God's face.

FADE TO: BLACK

Video GLITCH again.

FROM BLACK:

We FOLLOW smoke DOWN to its origin.

EXT. CAIN'S CITY—CENTER COURTYARD—DAY (BLACK AND WHITE)

We discover the smoke is coming from a young child being burned on a sacrificial altar.

Subtitle: "City of Enoch or Cain's city."

As several people from the city surround the burning child, we HEAR AD LIBS complaining about the bad crops last year.

MAN ONE

We're supposed to sacrifice a young male child
to lift this curse from us. Isn't that what Cain
said the redeemer would do?

MAN TWO

Yes…a male child through the seed of the woman would be a sacrifice to lift the curse.

MAN ONE

I wish we could sacrifice one of those behemoths. They break down our fences and eat all our crops.

MAN TWO

I had one as a pet several hundred years ago but those reptiles never stop growing.

MAN ONE

And they live as long as we do…hundreds of years.

EXT. FOREST OUTSIDE CITY

We SEE these large lizards as the man finishes speaking…they are dinosaurs!

INT. CAIN'S HOUSE—NEXT MORNING

Subtitle: "Earth, August 13, 3113 BC."

Cain is getting out of bed and admiring the view of the city. We SEE he has an "X" on his forehead, surrounded by a circle.

NARRATOR (V.O.)

Cain, the mayor of his own city, wears God's

mark to protect him from other men.

A girl gets out of bed and joins Cain at the window. He kisses her.

NARRATOR (V.O.)

Cain married his sister, a daughter of Eve and Adam. This was before Moses' Law. The gene pool was not yet weakened. Adam and Eve had numerous daughters before finally giving birth to Cain and Abel, but only the male was ever mentioned in His word.

FLASHBACK—EAST OF EDEN—ADAM'S FARM

Eve is suffering labor pains. Adam HEARS her SCREAMS and abandons his hoeing to join her under the tree where she's giving birth.

ADAM

Does it hurt that badly?

As if to answer him, she grabs the hoe from his hand and smites the ground just behind Adam.

He turns to discover she has decapitated a snake that was coiled up only inches from them both, which was about to strike his heel.

EVE

Yes, it hurts...but the snake was why I was screaming.

ADAM

Kind of ironic...they got us into this.

We HEAR a baby CRYING as Eve is now holding a baby boy.

NARRATOR (V.O.)

This was the birth of Seth. The new beginning
for the righteous seed after Abel's death.

We SEE the umbilical cord still connected to Seth.

END FLASHBACK

EXT. HOLY MOUNTAIN—CLOSE ON—SETH

He stands on the mount's edge, looking over the City of Cain.

NARRATOR (V.O.)

Seth, now 757 years old, dwells on this Holy
Mountain with the rest of the Righteous. Here,
they live separated from the children of Cain.

These righteous sons and daughters are busy constructing houses from
stone. Among them are LAMECH and his father, METHUSELAH.

We SEE them moving the stones just by verbally commanding the rocks
to cut themselves and move.

NARRATOR (V.O.)

They had the faith of their forefathers since
most of them still lived.

Some of the stones move to the SOUND of a TRUMPET or FLUTE
while being played by one of the Sethites.

EXT. CAIN'S HOUSE—MID-MORNING

Cain and his family are constructing a large house overlooking the city. They obviously don't have faith as many different mechanical rigs are being used to hoist their construction materials.

As Cain hammers and chisels on a large rock slab, we SEE a

FLASHBACK

Of Cain killing Abel with the same hammering strokes. He kills his brother with a rock.

> NARRATOR (V.O.)
>
> Cain killed Abel over jealousy of Abel's sacrifice to God.

We see, in the distance beyond Abel's body, a lamb burning on Abel's altar while fruit and corn burn on Cain's altar.

> NARRATOR (V.O.)
>
> It was on the eve of Abel's wedding that he was killed.

Eve's beautiful daughter is visibly grieved by Abel's absence.

END FLASHBACK

BACK TO SCENE

We HEAR the music of a wedding in Cain's City.

EXT. CAIN'S CITY/TOWN SQUARE—DAY

A young couple is exchanging their first kiss as their wedding ceremony concludes.

Our VIEW EXPANDS, showing men and women dancing very sensually. There are hundreds of girls but only a few dozen men in attendance.

As we PULL BACK to include the entire city, we NOTICE boundaries between neighbors.

Weights and measures are being used in a marketplace.

REACHING the outskirts of town, we RISE ABOVE fortified walls surrounding the city.

As WE CONTINUE past the high walls, we SEE why they're so tall…for protection from dinosaurs and other wild beasts.

DISSOLVE TO:

INT. TIAMAIT'S MOON—THRONE ROOM

INSERT—SATAN'S OVAL MONITOR

The IMAGES from Cain's city appear onscreen.

BACK TO SCENE

Satan and Apollyon are watching the events on Earth. They are sharing the images with fallen angel chiefs gathered in a meeting.

SATAN

> There you have it. That's what we have to work with. Now, unless all of you want God's words to come true and be ultimately defeated by

His...Redeemer, then I urge you to help me destroy the man and his seed. If we don't, then He will come through the seed of the woman...right on schedule.

APOLLYON

You, that have been chosen by lot to accompany Samyaza and Azazyel with your mission...go now...and spread the light...our light...to all the world.

EXT. MT. HERMON—EARLY EVENING

Two hundred of the fallen angels, a.k.a. the Watchers, are gathered here. They aren't well dressed and many of them are unshaven.

SAMYAZA

Lucifer has entrusted us with a great mission. Anyone thinking of backing out?

All of the other angels look around, shaking their heads.

SAMYAZA

Then it's agreed. We must satisfy our lust and take wives from the daughters of Cain.

AZAZYEL

But what will happen to us for committing such a crime? Won't God punish us greatly for this most forbidden union?

There is much unrest now among the other angels.

SAMYAZA

We are already condemned to eternal punishment. This is our only chance to change that verdict. Do you want to go back and explain your cowardice?

AZAZYEL

If I'm going to burn, I might as well burn brightly!

All of them hold hands and swear an oath to continue with the plan.

NARRATOR (V.O.)

A female angel, Lililea, also joined them.

INT. CAIN'S CITY—DRINK HOUSE—LATER THAT NIGHT

All the wedding guests and townspeople are now inside a huge tavern. Everyone is drinking a strong drink made out of corn. The man serving up the brew and in charge of the music is GENUN.

GENUN

Drink up everybody! It's time!

The crowd is getting very drunk and rowdy. Many of the guests are becoming increasingly lustful and lewd.

The band of trumpets and horns, string instruments, cymbals, lyres, harps, and flutes keep the place hopping.

EXT. THE DRINK HOUSE

We HEAR the MUSIC drifting out of the building, traveling in the air and heading up a nearby mountain.

EXT. HOLY MOUNTAIN—NIGHT

These righteous sons and daughters are assembled and HEAR the MUSIC down below. They are listening very intently.

DISSOLVE TO:

EXT. HOLY MOUNTAIN—NEXT MORNING

The MUSIC starts back up again and drifts up the hill from Cain's city below. Some are up and busy constructing houses from stone.

MUSIC from below gets LOUDER than music being played to move rocks, causing some rocks to slip and fall. This causes concern for their leader, JARED.

> JARED
>
> Children, oh my good and innocent and holy children. Know that once you go down from this holy mountain, God will not allow you to return to it.

EXT. CAIN'S CITY—DAY

LOUD MUSIC spills into the streets. Genun notices some of the Sethites are still gathered at the edge of the hill, obviously curious.

He turns to some girls who've been drinking and dancing all night and motions to them. They stagger over to him in a very sensual dance-like walk. He tears off one of the girl's tops.

GENUN
(pointing up)

Dance where they can see you.

EXT. CAIN'S HOUSE

Cain is setting up an elaborate system to raise a rock slab for the roof of his house.

EXT. BOTTOM OF HOLY MOUNT—DAY

The 200 Watchers, now standing at the bottom of the hill by the river, SEE the beautiful girls of Cain's city, dancing.

The twenty WATCHER Chiefs are looking through telescopes. ONE of them doesn't have a looking glass and walks up to one that does.

WATCHER ONE

Hey, let me have a peep.

The Watcher begrudgingly hands the eyepiece to him.

WATCHER ONE

Thanks Tom. I'll let you have it back in a moment.

EXT. CAIN'S CITY STREETS—DAY

Everyone is watching the sexy, topless girls dancing now. The girls remove more layers revealing more skin as they dance. They are very sexy indeed, tossing their well-adorned long hair seductively.

These girls can SEE the children of Seth atop the mountain.

EXT. HOLY MOUNTAIN—DAY

Some of the men NOTICE the girl's almost-naked bodies through eyepieces of their telescopes. They are obviously enjoying this.

EXT. NEARBY MOUNTAIN—DAY

Satan observes the Sethites, the Cainites, and the Watchers.

> SATAN
>
> Time to desegregate the world.

EXT. BOTTOM OF HOLY MOUNT—DAY

Genun leads the almost-naked dancing girls, other band members, and townspeople to the same place where the Watchers were just standing.

Genun's face reveals that Satan is now talking through him like he did when he talked through the serpent in Eden. He LOOKS UP to the curious Sethites.

> GENUN/SATAN
> (yelling)
>
> Come on down!

EXT. HOLY MOUNT—DAY

The Sethites look around, seeing no way to come down the mountain. ENOCH, firstborn son of Jared, SEES his brethren are being tempted.

> ENOCH
>
> Hear me, oh sons of Seth, small and great. I
> adjure you, by the death of our father Adam,

and by the blood of Abel, of Seth, of Enos, of Cainan, and of Mahalaleel, to hearken to me. Do not go down from this holy mountain; for the moment you leave it, you shall no longer be called children of God, but children of the devil.

The majority of the pack ignore him and yell back AD LIBS to Genun below that they "don't know how to come down."

EXT. BOTTOM OF HILL

SATAN/GENUN

Come to the western side of the mountain. There you will find a stream of water that comes down to the foot of the mountain. Come to us that way.

EXT. BACK OF MOUNTAIN

The children of Seth are making their way down the mountain.
They load rafts into the stream, riding it down the hill.

EXT. CAIN'S CITY—ALONG THE RIVER

The fallen chiefs MATERIALIZE in physical, 3-D bodies. They are dressed in COLORFUL clothes. They approach the girls in the city, who are still dressed—barely, in BLACK and WHITE.

The Watchers "ask the girls for a dance" and exchange a bow and curtsey. As Genun's MUSIC gets LOUDER, the dancing between the angels and women gets seedier.

As the Sethites arrive along the bank of the river, they OGLE the women scantily draped in COLORFUL linen.

Satan, invisible to the humans, smiles at the Sethites as they approach. He also smiles at the fallen chiefs, now in human form, sitting along the stream, watching over their new brides with lust.

As the children of Seth get out of their crudely built rafts, they "command them to rise" out of the water. The boats obey their voice, to the amazement of the Cainites.

The girls with the fallen angel chiefs look at them, bewildered.

> GIRL
> (to angels)
>
> Can you do that?

The angels exchange looks and nod their heads in unison.

> CAIN
> (to the Sethites)
>
> Greetings! I'm Cain, Mayor of this city. Please
> come to my house as an invited guest.

The first Sethite off the raft shakes Cain's hand and follows him.

The other Sethites give in to their newfound lust as the women throw themselves at them.

Satan LAUGHS a long, sinister laugh and then vanishes.

While several women lustfully attack one Sethite, he NOTICES an oar from one of their rafts slowly drifting downstream.

He reaches out, "commanding the oar to return," but it keeps drifting away. This puzzles him and concern covers his face.

He stops the girls and pulls away. He LOOKS UP at the other Sethites watching from above.

HIS POV

They are slowly turning away with sadness.

He SEES several rafts coming down the river with more Sethites.

EXT. THE BOAT—COMING DOWNSTREAM

The boat approaches the shore, where the now frightened Sethite from the first boat tries to warn the others to turn back.

They never notice him, as the women YELLING at the new arrivals drown his voice out.

EXT. RIVER BANK

Lililea goes over to the Sethite who is trying to warn the others.

> LILILEA
>
> I want you for my husband. Your seed is about to be enlarged. We'll make babies of…titanic proportion.

EXT. CAIN'S HOUSE—LATER

The Sethite invited to Cain's house raises the roof slab VERBALLY.

The workers rigging a crane intended to do the job are dumbfounded.

Cain's oldest daughter grabs the young man and takes him into their newly roofed house with a lustful look in her eyes.

EXT. BESIDE THE RIVER

An orgy is now in full swing alongside the river.

There are plenty of women to go around. Each of the two hundred fallen angels have a woman or two while the Sethites each have one as well. Samyaza has taken several women.

NARRATOR (V.O.)

> The fallen angels began teaching various skills and secrets of the universe to mankind. The reason...to cause mankind to fulfill fleshly desires with no regard to God and to learn new ways to destroy themselves.

EXT. CAIN'S CITY—DAY

Subtitle: "Nine months later."

The CRYING SOUND of babies being born fills the air, and is mixed with the SCREAMS of pain from their mothers.

INT. CAIN'S HOUSE

Women give birth while their angelic husbands look on with pride.

Lililea gives birth to a redheaded, green-eyed baby girl while her Sethite husband admires his newborn daughter.

LILILEA

> We'll name her...Lilith.

EXT. HOLY MOUNTAIN—DAY

Subtitle: "3013 BC, one hundred years later."

From the sky, we SEE something bright descending.

Enoch is quietly tending this vineyard and looks up to see whatever is coming down from the sky. As it gets closer, we SEE it's similar to what picked up Elijah in the opening scene.

The vineyard is empty now as we FOLLOW the flaming chariot all the way UP until it disappears.

> NARRATOR (V.O.)

> And Enoch walked with God: and he was not for God took him.

EXT. CAIN'S CITY

The giant children are now full-grown adults. They are playing alongside reptiles that have grown into full-sized dinosaurs.

Lilith is fully-grown too. She stands about eighteen feet tall and is very well proportioned.

EXT. CAIN'S CITY—DAY—OUTSIDE THE WALLS

The giants are hunting and killing the dinosaurs for sport since they are big enough to be a challenge for them.

Fire-breathing leviathans use their flames in self-defense.

INT. HOLY MOUNTAIN—NIGHT—LAMECH'S HOUSE

Subtitle: "2944 BC, 69 years later."

Lamech's wife is giving birth to their firstborn son.

> LAMECH

> We'll name him…Noah.

EXT. JUST OUTSIDE CAIN'S CITY—DAY

The giants are fighting each other in a tournament. Some of their mothers are in attendance. The giants tower over them.

EXT. INSIDE FIGHTING RING

The fighting between the giants gets rougher. Several giants in the b.g. are chasing after a fire-breathing leviathan.

EXT. OUTSIDE THE RING

The violence spreads to the crowd watching the fight as TWO GIANTS start hitting each other.

> GIANT ONE
>
> You insulted my mother! Now take it back!

> GIANT TWO
>
> Not in another hundred years!

The intense fight ends with GIANT TWO being killed.

Our VIEW WIDENS as the fire-breathing dragon being chased in the b.g. comes upon the freshly killed giant. His fiery breath chars the dead giant's remains before it runs off and dives into a river.

The surviving giant looks at the dead, burnt giant he just killed. He bites into the flesh of the dead giant, tasting his blood and flesh. He likes it and continues his blood feast.

Our supernatural eyes are opened as we SEE the soul of the dead giant leaving his body.

NARRATOR (V.O.)

God determined that the souls of the giants
would not be redeemed and their bodies would
never be resurrected, therefore their souls
would wander to and fro looking for a place of
rest…or a body to inhabit.

The dead giant's spirit approaches a normal-sized male spectator at the
fight and enters his body.

Taking control of the man's VOICE and possessing him, he SHOUTS
obscenities at the giant that killed him.

This causes that giant to pick up the man and bite off his head.

This "demon" spirit leaves the man's dead body and enters another.

NARRATOR (V.O.)

And thus, the giants' war on mankind began.
Man and animal alike would remain vegetari-
ans no more.

Subtitle: "c.2578 BC, 336 years later."

INT. HOLY MOUNT/CAVE—NIGHT

All of the children of Seth are gone from the mountain except four:
Jared, Methuselah, Lamech, and NOAH.

NARRATOR (V.O.)

Noah was 365 years old here; the same age
Enoch was when he was taken alive to Heaven.
It would be on this night that they would be
taken to their new home.

Jared is lying on his deathbed. He gives his final instructions.

> JARED
>
> Bury Adam, our father, in the center of the Earth...the place where you are to be taken soon by God's chariots. Bury all the firstborn righteous sons there as well. And do not forget Eve.

A flickering lamp lights their wrapped, mummy-like bodies.

Jared closes his eyes as tears stream down from them.

> JARED
> (barely breathing)
>
> Forgive all the children of Seth, who fell in my days.

He dies.

FADE TO: BLACK.

FROM BLACK, the darkness of Jared's death, we SEE a LIGHT.

EXT. HOLY MOUNTAIN—NIGHT

It's the cherubim coming to take them to their new home.

The fiery cherubim leave the now uninhabited Holy Mountain.

We HEAR Satan LAUGHING as he now descends upon the once Holy Mount.

> NARRATOR (V.O.)
>
> This would become the future Temple Mount in Jerusalem. Evil sought its control.

Subtitle: "2450 BC, approx. 128 years later."

INT. TIAMAIT'S MOON—DAY—THRONE ROOM (IN COLOR)

Giants are everywhere. They've taken over the throne room along with many of the fallen angelic third.

> NARRATOR (V.O.)
>
> Tiamait's moon became home to evil as well. Satan transported giants here. Their destructive, evil nature caused much upheaval.

Satan is observing the wickedness here and on Earth, via his oval-shaped monitor.

> SATAN
> (laughing)
>
> Let's see the Redeemer come through their seed now.

EXT. GIZA PLATEAU (EGYPT)—DAY

The three remaining righteous men are in their new home. One huge river, the Nile, passes nearby and then splits into four smaller rivers as it dumps into Eden's river, the present-day Mediterranean.

> METHUSELAH
>
> This place has a great river with four heads, like the river from Eden. It is in the very center of the Earth as Eden was the center of all that was good.

INT. METHUSELAH'S TENT—NIGHT

Methuselah, Lamech, and Noah are holding an unusual brass-like object with many gears and wheels. They calibrate it.

NOAH

Adam knew of a flood and fire destruction in Earth's future. He passed this knowledge to Seth.

METHUSELAH
(referring to
the object)

Seth used Adam's knowledge and invented this…an analog computer, capable of showing the position of stars at any date in the past or future.

LAMECH

The stars tell the story of God's redemption plan for man. Stars or angels were the reason a plan was needed.

NOAH
(demonstrating)

Four points of the zodiac represent the four cherubim: Aquarius the man, Taurus the bull, Leo the lion, and Opheocus the serpent holder or eagle. These four points make a cross, or God's mark, in the heavens.

METHUSELAH

We'll leave our knowledge of the heavens, showing God's plan so future generations won't forget.

LAMECH

But how? What can survive water or fire?

METHUSELAH
(getting an idea)

We'll build two types of monuments, huge monuments, one of stone and one of brick. Hopefully one or both can withstand fire and water.

NOAH

But how will we construct such monuments? They would be bigger than anything we've built before and now, there are only us three.

METHUSELAH

Adam could command any object to get up and move itself. This is how God made the heavens, by His word. He spoke and it was done; He commanded and it stood fast.

LAMECH

Methuselah is right. We can build these monuments this way.

METHUSELAH

And we'll do as Jared commanded by burying our forefathers in them so they too are safe from the waters and the fires to come.

EXT. GIZA PLATEAU—DAY

The three men are now surveying the region and looking at its relation to the Nile. Methuselah holds a lute. Noah holds the analog computer. Lamech holds several measuring devices.

METHUSELAH

Ready to carve out the lion?

LAMECH
(to the limestone
bedrock)

Form a block 360 inches long by 144 inches wide by 120 inches tall.

Suddenly, a huge block of stone cuts itself, with laser-like precision, from the ground.

Methuselah plays a musical instrument causing the freshly cut stone to lift and move itself through the air.

This process continues as one by one, they stack themselves on the ground nearby. These stones are forming a foundation.

NOAH
(computing)

First, we cut out the monument of stone...a lion...the lion from the future tribe of Judah, from which the Redeemer will come.

NARRATOR (V.O.)

They decided to build three monuments of brick, mirroring the belt of Orion, the first three stars ever created. They chose the pyramid shape because it's the basis of three-dimensional geometry.

EXT. MIDDLE PYRAMID/LION—DAY—WEEKS LATER

We SEE the pieces removed from the stone lion forming the foundation for the middle pyramid, right beside the lion.

NARRATOR (V.O.)

This represents Jesus as the foundation, the very soul of the Divine Trinity. The ROCK or stone cut without hands that will someday destroy all other kingdoms when He establishes His kingdom on Earth.

EXT. BASE OF FIRST PYRAMID—DAY

The base of the first pyramid has been laid and is slightly larger than the middle pyramid's base, which was laid earlier beside and from the lion.

NARRATOR (V.O.)

This represented God's pyramid. It compares to the third or lowest star of Orion's belt and the physical part of the Trinity after Its separation.

The three masons are now holding a measuring rod, the length of a cubit divided by 25 equal measurements.

NOAH

The sacred inch is 1/25th of a cubit. Let's use it inside the corridors, passageways, and chambers of the pyramid to show God's redemptive plan for man...mankind's story of hope.

EXT. BASE OF FIRST PYRAMID—DAY—YEARS LATER

The construction of the Great Pyramid is nearly complete. Noah measures each of its four sides.

NOAH

Exactly 36,524 inches. Move the decimal and you get the number of the days in one year...365.24.

EXT./INT. FIRST PYRAMID—SUPERNATURAL 3-D VIEW

NARRATOR (V.O.)

Through these measurements, the grand gallery shows man's ascent through time until the end.

INT. FIRST PYRAMID—CLOSE ON—ADAM'S BODY

They place it inside the King's chamber sarcophagus.

METHUSELAH

As my grandfather Jared commanded us, we

place his body in the center of the Earth, exactly where this place is located.

INT. KING'S CHAMBER CEILING

NARRATOR (V.O.)

Over the last high point in the King's chamber are five levels illustrating the final five judgments by God and man's last chance during the great tribulation. The two slabs angled above the five, forms the chamber's roof and represent the wrath of God as the sixth and seventh final judgments, which will come together and complete man's time.

EXT. SECOND PYRAMID—NEXT DAY

We now SEE the second pyramid being built on top of the foundation laid first. It compares to the second star of Orion's belt.

NARRATOR (V.O.)

This represented Jesus' pyramid, which is why it's built beside the stone lion.

METHUSELAH

Eve, our mother, shall rest in the pillar we've dedicated to our Redeemer since He shall come from the seed of the woman.

INT. MIDDLE PYRAMID—YEARS LATER

We SEE them placing Eve's wrapped body in the burial chamber.

EXT. THIRD PYRAMID—DAY

With the first two almost equal-sized pyramids complete and looming in the b.g., the three men begin work on the third and much smaller pyramid.

> NARRATOR (V.O.)
>
> They build the third pyramid representing the Holy Spirit. It compares to the first star of Orion's belt. Inside this one they make three chambers representing the Holy Trinity completed by the spirit. It also represents the body, soul, and spirit of man.

EXT. GIZA PLATEAU—MORNING—LOOKING EAST

Finally, we SEE the two completed pillars of brick with the third one almost complete but still open.

The pillar of stone, the lion, looks very majestic as it gazes towards the rising sun.

Subtitle: "June 21, 2349 BC."

Subtitle: "One hundred years after construction began."

INT. LION'S TEMPLE

Lamech has died and his body lies inside the Temple.

EXT. LION'S TEMPLE/NEAR LION—SUNSET

Methuselah, Noah, his wife, three sons, and three beautiful young girls stand in front of the Lion with Lamech's body in the f.g.

NOAH

Lamech lived 777 years. He leaves behind three beautiful daughters, which my three sons will make their wives.

METHUSELAH

The setting sun represents death. Each year at this time, the sun sets between the two pillars for three days, representing the three days our Redeemer will spend in the Earth in order to restore man to God as promised in the Garden of Eden.

We can SEE the summer solstice sun setting on the horizon. As the mourners look to the western sky, they SEE the setting sun lining up exactly in the center of the large first and middle pyramids.

METHUSELAH

Adam, in God's image, rests in the pillar we've dedicated to God. This pillar shall be covered with 144,000 white pieces of limestone. These represent the resurrection of the first fruits to God *and* the remnant, which will cover the four corners of the Earth that God will spare in the end days. They are clothed in white to represent their righteousness.

METHUSELAH

In the pillar dedicated to God's Holy Spirit is where we'll place the six firstborn male bodies of Seth, Enos, Cainan, Mahalaleel, Jared, and now Lamech. When I die, place my body within the same pillar. Our seven bodies are to symbolize the seven spirits of the Holy Spirit, the seven lamps of fire, which burn like...the menorah.

NARRATOR (V.O.)

The seven spirits of the Holy Spirit...the Spirit of the Lord, Wisdom, Understanding, Counsel, Might, Knowledge, and the Fear of the Lord.

Subtitle: "Three days later."

EXT. CAIN'S CITY—NIGHT

Dozens of bonfires burn across the land surrounding the city. Giants are killing men and women, who are also killing each other.

NARRATOR (V.O.)

The wickedness of man was great.
Every thought was evil continually.

Giants and behemoths are making holes in the city's walls as they kick through them, on a destructive rampage.

A giant T-Rex enters through a hole in the wall into the city.

The stampeding giants and behemoths cause the ground to shake, like the tremors of an earthquake.

INT. CAIN'S HOUSE

Cain and his family are hiding here. The TREMORS shake their house.

Cain's roof begins to SHAKE, crumbling at the edges. It comes TUMBLING DOWN on top of Cain, killing him.

> NARRATOR (V.O.)
>
> Cain murdered the first righteous man when he lowered a stone, formed without hands, down upon Abel's head. It is ironic that a stone, raised without hands by a righteous man, came down upon the first murderer's head.

EXT. TOWN SQUARE

The group of people who sacrificed the little girl when we first arrived in Cain's city are now being chased and killed by the T-Rex.

Lilith and her two male companions stumble upon the T-Rex as the two male giants chase him off.

Lilith sees the girl's parents; they are the only ones still alive. She picks up a large tree limb and impales them both. She places them over a burning house like a shish kebab.

Lilith looks at the couple she's cooking.

> LILITH
>
> Dinner is about to be served.

INT. CAIN'S HOUSE

Cain's surviving daughters and the male Sethite are on their knees praying.

SETHITE

Lord, I know I disobeyed you...but please...hear my prayer...stop these giants from wiping the seed of man from the Earth.

EXT. CAIN'S CITY

We SEE many people on their knees praying for deliverance. Many of the giants are now eating the fleshly remains of the dead.

Lilith takes a bite from her human shish kebab, MOANING with an almost orgasmic expression of pleasure.

The SMOKE from the burning human bodies, along with prayers by the remaining people, RISES into the air where

EXT./INT. HEAVEN—GOD'S THRONE (COLOR)

It reaches God's nostrils. His face shows great displeasure.

The angel of the altar carries a golden censer with burning incense. The smoke mixes with the prayers and smoke from Earth.

The remaining archangels Raphael, Uriel, Michael, and Gabriel stand before God's throne.

They are joined by three other angels, Raguel, Seraqael, and Haniel.

RAPHAEL

Glory to God, the throne of Your glory is forever. You have made all things and have power over all things. Nothing can be hid from You.

URIEL

You have seen what Azazyel has done, how he

has taught every species of iniquity upon the Earth and has disclosed to the world all secret things that are done in the heavens.

MICHAEL

Samyaza and those associated with him, have gone together to the daughters of men, lain with them, and have become polluted.

GABRIEL

The women have brought forth giants. Thus has the whole Earth been filled with blood and with iniquity. And now the souls of those who are dead cry out.

God is silent. No one makes a sound. He finally speaks.

GOD

I have seen the wickedness upon the Earth. As the serpent's birthday draws near, I've decided to send him a most appropriate gift. His rebellion caused this chain reaction. I have a chain reaction of My own to begin.

God turns to Raguel, Seraqael, and Haniel.

GOD

Your rank is changed to archangel to replace the three that were lost in the rebellion, Yekun, Kesabel, and Gadrel. The three of you shall join the remaining four to complete the seven.

106 Revelations

God turns to address the other four original holy archangels.

GOD

Uriel. Go to the son of Lamech in a dream and tell him of the deluge I will send to destroy the wicked from the Earth. Teach him how he may escape and how his seed may remain on Earth.

While looking into the oval-shaped monitor of the cherub resembling a man, God SEES the archangel Uriel speaking to Noah in a dream.

GOD

Raphael. Go to Azazyel and bind him hand and foot and cast him into darkness. Bury him under the river Pison where the rocks shall be hurled upon him and cover him with darkness.

While looking into the oval-shaped monitor of the lion cherub, God SEES the archangel Raphael binding Azazyel and throwing him into the river.

GOD

Gabriel. Go to the children of fornication and destroy the offspring of the Watchers among men. Incite them to fight one against the other, that they might perish by mutual slaughter.

While looking into the oval-shaped monitor of the cherub resembling a flying eagle, God SEES the archangel Gabriel in the midst of the giants in Cain's city.

GOD

Michael. Go to Samyaza and those that are with

him, who have associated with women and polluted themselves, and bind them underneath the Earth.

While looking into the oval-shaped monitor of the cherub resembling a calf, God SEES the archangel Michael with a chain as

DISSOLVE TO:

EXT. CAIN'S CITY—NIGHT (BLACK AND WHITE)

Michael and other holy angels are escorting the twenty bound chiefs to the city's gate.

The giantess Lilith is hiding from the angels and witnesses them taking Lililea, her angelic mother. Lililea's S-shaped bracelet falls to the ground, unnoticed by her jailers.

After they've left, Lilith picks up her mother's bracelet displaying her S-shaped crest. She shakes her fist at the sky.

LILITH

One day...I will avenge my mother!

INT. UNDERNEATH THE EARTH—DARK CAVERN

The holy angels are individually placing the fallen chiefs deep in the ground, leaving them bound in chains and darkness.

INT. NOAH'S BEDROOM/GIZA—NIGTH

Noah suddenly wakes from a dream, startling his wife.

NOAH

God plans the global flood.

EXT. PYRAMID COMPLEX/GIZA—NIGHT

The third pyramid is still left open and incomplete.

Our VIEW SHIFTS from the pyramids to the night sky as we SEE the similarities between the pyramids and Orion's belt in the stars.

Our VIEW FOLLOWS an imaginary line drawn from the belt of Orion to the brightest star in the heavens, Sirius.

> NARRATOR (V.O.)
>
> The Dog Star that nips at the heel of Orion. Known as Sirius, it was the first star created after Orion's belt. It symbolized the creation of Lucifer, the bright morning star and the first angel created.

Upon CLOSER inspection, we SEE a tiny dwarf companion star orbiting the star Sirius.

> NARRATOR (V.O.)
>
> The white dwarf star that orbits Sirius every fifty years, making it a binary star.

As we're LOOKING at Sirius, we SEE Satan's face REPLACE the star.

INT. TIAMAIT'S MOON—THRONE ROOM (COLOR)

Satan watches the events on Earth through his oval-shaped monitor.

INSERT—MONITOR

Which shows all of the giants fighting and killing each other.

BACK TO SCENE

Apollyon looks like a dwarf as he stands beside the cherub. He never morphed to adult-height because he really is...a dwarf!

While Satan observes the capture of his high-ranking, fallen comrades, Apollyon keeps grabbing at his wrist to feel the bracelet that's just not there.

EXT. GIZA PLATEAU—NIGHT (BLACK AND WHITE)

God is descending from the sky atop the four cherubim. His VOICE BOOMS above the LOUD WINGS of the cherubim.

> GOD (V.O.)
>
> Noah, you've impressed Me with your ability to build large things capable of withstanding floodwaters. You and your full-grown sons are now going to build an ark. I've come to show you how.

EXT. LEBANON FOREST—NEXT DAY

Noah and his family are standing in the center of the woods. All the men SHOUT in unison and command the trees to fall. Hundreds of trees fall perfectly in rows.

EXT. NOAH'S FAMILY IN FOREST—LATER

We SEE one tree at a time being formed into planks of wood for building the giant ship. This cutting and moving operation is being performed to the SOUND of MUSICAL INSTRUMENTS played by Noah's sons.

EXT. TIAMAIT'S MOON—DAY—PALACE COURTYARD (COLOR)

Wickedness is everywhere as we SEE all kinds of filthiness being performed by the fallen angels. It's still one big party, just as when Lucifer started the rebellion here.

INT. THRONE ROOM

Apollyon is with Satan in the throne room where he's moving a golden pedestal while PLAYING a FLUTE.

> SATAN
>
> Why are you installing a pedestal?

> APOLLYON
>
> I have a surprise for you. I could tell you need-
> ed some cheering up. You didn't think I forgot
> your birthday, did you?

Subtitle: "2344 BC"

EXT. ARK CONSTRUCTION/GIZA—DAY (BLACK AND WHITE)

Noah's family is admiring the now completed ark.

Animals come towards the ark from all directions.

They are being herded TELEPATHICALLY by several female holy angels. Laurianna leads a lion and lioness. Just behind them are two lambs.

EXT./INT. SMALL PYRAMID/GIZA—LATE AFTERNOON

The sun is setting as Noah's sons place Methuselah's body in the main sarcophagus of the smallest pyramid. They seal it. All three pyramids are sealed with white outer casing stones.

Michael APPEARS to Noah and his family here.

MICHAEL

It's time to enter the ark now. Remain there for seven days. Then, the flood will come.

EXT. OUTER SPACE—OUR SOLAR SYSTEM

Planets are aligned in an almost straight row.

From the northern parts where Heaven is located, a BRIGHT shaft of LIGHT originates and heads right TOWARD US at an incredible speed.

INT. TIAMAIT'S MOON—THRONE ROOM (COLOR)

Apollyon has put the finishing touches on the pedestal.

APOLLYON

It's time for your surprise.

Apollyon claps his hands and four giants come in, carrying a large covered object. They set it upon the pedestal.

Apollyon uncovers the object revealing…a beautiful golden statue of the flying serpent cherub.

APOLLYON

Happy birthday.

EXT. TIAMAIT'S ORBIT

The fast-moving, bright object from Heaven is arcing along the gravity of the outer planets and like a slingshot, is now headed straight for Tiamait.

INT. TIAMAIT'S MOON—THRONE ROOM

Satan walks around admiring the image of himself made from gold. The serpent statue has four golden calves carrying it.

The mechanical-looking STATUE seems to come to life.

The fallen archangel Yekun becomes concerned for some reason.

> YEKUN
>
> Where did that statue come from?

> APOLLYON
>
> It was left in the courtyard as a gift. I discovered it outside the temple doors.

> STATUE
> (to Satan)
>
> Happy birthday.

Suddenly, a HUGE EXPLOSION is HEARD and felt from Tiamait below.

EXT. TIAMAIT'S ORBIT—OUTER SPACE

Tiamait is destroyed! Its moon is swept away by a huge BLAST WAVE.

Satan flies through space at incredible speed, along with the moon as they're being pushed to the outer limits of our solar system.

This force causes a huge volcanic eruption from within the moon.

EXT. JUPITER'S ORBIT—OUTER SPACE

A large fragment from Tiamait POUNDS nearby Jupiter, creating a large, red storm cloud swirling over the impacted area.

EXT. SATURN'S ORBIT—OUTER SPACE

Saturn gets its ring as a huge fragment from Tiamait IMPACTS this light, rapidly rotating planet.

EXT. URANUS' ORBIT—OUTER SPACE

Uranus gets HIT so hard by large chunks of Tiamait that it TILTS the planet violently to its present-day ninety-eight degree tilt.

EXT. NEPTUNE'S ORBIT—OUTER SPACE

Small EXPLODING fragments POUND into the icy blue planet.

Then, PASSING US by quickly, is Tiamait's moon. It's heading out past Neptune where it settles into an orbit seventeen degrees off the orbital plane of all other planets.

Volcanic activity on the moon now spits out a blob of molten lava, about one-third the size of the badly damaged moon. This blob begins to orbit the damaged moon, now Pluto.

NARRATOR (V.O.)

> This would become the planet known today as…Pluto and its companion…the moon Charon. Like their counterparts in mythology, both are forever doomed to spend eternity facing the deep, with Charon circling the God of the abyss. In another myth, this moon's name was changed to mean "one who shows the way," or "opener of the ways."

EXT. CAIN'S CITY—DAY (BLACK AND WHITE)

Men on Earth LOOK UP into the sky and SEE two suns.

EXT. NOAH'S ARK—DAY

As the bright object gets closer, some men are afraid now and begin to POUND on the closed doors of the ark but to no avail.

EXT. MARS' ORBIT—OUTER SPACE

Mars is hit by Tiamait's fragments! Much of its atmosphere is loosened with some of it slipping into outer space.

EXT. EARTH'S ORBIT—OUTER SPACE

Mars barely misses Earth as it's hurled towards the Sun's gravity.
Lightning bolts arc between the two planets, searing Mars' surface.
Electricity hits Earth's water, charging it, causing disruptions.
A huge asteroid is now heading towards Earth.

EXT. CAIN'S CITY—PEOPLE

LOOKING UP, SEE one of the two suns in the sky is getting brighter.

EXT. EARTH'S ATMOSPHERE—HIGH ANGLE

The huge meteorite IMPACTS Earth near the Garden of Eden.
This splits the single continent down the middle.

MONTAGE

A)   The flood begins as the water canopy begins to collapse.

B)   We SEE the first LIGHTNING and RAIN in human history as the electrically charged water canopy interacts with the meteor showers.

C)   Some evil men and giants are SEEN drowning.

D)   Mothers of giants, wives of the fallen angels, also drown.

E)   Volcanoes form and erupt around the edges of the huge landmass.

F)   Violent EARTHQUAKES cause buildings in Cain's city to collapse.

G)   Dinosaurs are being fossilized.

H)   Burial of vegetation forms the coal layer.

I)   Dinosaur footprints are filled with the green plants and mud.

END OF MONTAGE

EXT. WATERS NEAR THE ARK—STORMY

Lilith's fat, male, giant friend drowns. Lilith uses his buoyant body to stay afloat. She shakes her fist at the ark and sky. Rabeelalia, invisible, is watching this with tears in her eyes.

LILITH

Revenge! Revenge upon the seed of all men…and anything holy!

Unable to stay afloat, she slips below the surface. Her fist, clenching her mother's bracelet displaying the S-shaped crest, remains above water.

EXT. GIZA PLATEAU—RAINING

Rain drenches the lion statue until it is submerged underwater.

The largest two pyramids are only half covered by water.

We SEE Noah's ark floating between the pyramids in the rain as we

FADE TO: BLACK.

We SEE the GLITCH again. It BLACKS OUT as if we lost power. FROM BLACK, we FADE INTO:

EXT. NYC HARBOR—DAY—RAINING (COLOR)

We SEE a huge modern ocean liner in the midst of a rainstorm. **Subtitle**: "July 4, 1947. New York City."

EXT. UPPER DECK—SHIP'S BOW

Katy stands here. Her hair has grown a little but is mostly hidden underneath her hat. By her side is Eva, her one and one-half year-old daughter.

KATY'S POV—STATUE OF LIBERTY

Katy's attention is drawn to the landmark. She studies the torch.

BACK TO SCENE

Pointing in the statue's direction, she shows it to her daughter.

KATY

> This is where your daddy was from. His best friend lives nearby. He's coming to pick us up today.

Eva becomes more interested in a stack of brochures on a counter nearby. She toddles over and grabs a handful.

This goes unnoticed, as Katy can't take her eyes off the statue.

While looking at the statue, she remembers...

FLASHBACK—ONBOARD THE "SAINT LOUIS"—DAY

...being a little girl herself, standing beside her mother.

She HEARS the other passenger's AD LIBS interpreting the bad news that "America would not permit them entry."

END FLASHBACK

BACK TO SCENE

Katy LOOKS at her daughter and forces a smile.

Eva holds a brochure for Liberty, "Enlightening the World."

INT. SPACECRAFT—ROSWELL—MEANWHILE

We SEE the VIDEO GLITCH again. This time it's from a monitor inside a wrecked UFO as the power FADES IN and OUT.

An alien's body is lying in a pile of debris near the monitor, obviously from the crashed spaceship.

Subtitle: "Roswell, New Mexico."

We SEE more of the wrecked UFO. Fiber optic cables are everywhere.

GREY'S POV—OUTSIDE SHIP

He's crawling out and we SEE the world THROUGH HIS high-tech VISION just as he passes out, apparently from his injuries.

FADE TO: BLACK.

FROM BLACK, we find WE are inside someone's head as they are blindfolded and taken through some kind of ritual.

> GRAND MASTER (O.S.)

In your present, blind condition, what do you most desire?

> JOHNNY (O.S.)

Light.

> GRAND MASTER (O.S.)

What's more dazzling than light?

> JOHNNY (O.S.)

An exchange of ideas. The goal here is to gather what is scattered and reach farther.

> GRAND MASTER (O.S.)

Are you a Royal Arch Mason?

> JOHNNY (O.S.)

I am, that I am.

> GRAND MASTER (O.S.)

You are enlightened.

FADE INTO:

INT. NEW YORK CITY—MASONIC LODGE

As the blindfold is removed, we discover it's Johnny Rockwell! The room is decorated like the inside of Solomon's Temple.

A broken pillar has "ADHUC STAT" inscribed on it.

His father, JOHN ROCKWELL SR., forty-three today, a five-star General, appears to be the Head Mason.

John moves towards his son and places a sword on his shoulder.

> JOHN
>
> I give you the title of thirty-third degree Mason, the highest degree you can attain.

> JOHNNY
>
> Thanks Dad. Happy birthday!

Johnny looks at his watch.

> JOHNNY
>
> Sorry, now I'm really late.

> CUT TO:

INT. LIMOUSINE—LATE AFTERNOON

Johnny sits beside Katy as Eva sleeps beside her. Both are uncomfortable as they stare into open space. Johnny senses Katy is upset with him for being late and tries to break the silence.

> JOHNNY
> (explaining)
>
> David used to be late for everything too.

Johnny can see Katy's forgiveness now in her eyes. He pushes forward.

JOHNNY

Traffic is really bad for a holiday. Everyone comes for the parade and the fireworks.

We can tell Johnny is fond of Katy by the way he looks at her. He NOTICES the Statue of Liberty brochure next to Eva and gets an idea.

JOHNNY

Did you know the same guy who built the Eiffel Tower made Liberty's framework? France presented it to the US on July 4, 1884. It was dedicated on October 28, 1886. The statue commemorates our alliance with France during the Revolution.

Eva wakes up. She looks at Johnny and starts to CRY.

KATY
(laughing)

I see you have a way with women.

JOHNNY

I hope I'm not boring you.

KATY

Oh no, please tell me more about your home.

EXT. CENTRAL PARK

They are now passing through a section of Central Park.

INT. LIMOUSINE—EVA

Takes up more of the back seat, forcing Katy to sit closer to Johnny. Looking out the window, Johnny SEES an obelisk.

> JOHNNY
>
> That's one of Cleopatra's Needles. It once stood in front of the Temple of the Sun at the time of the Jewish exodus.

Katy raises her eyebrows as she listens more intently now.

> JOHNNY
>
> It came to the US in 1880 when my great grandfather, then the Grand Master of the New York Masonic Lodge, conducted the dedication ceremony for its pedestal. The Secretary of State back then said empires fell after erecting obelisks in their lands. I think we've been around long enough now to prove him wrong.

Katy looks at Johnny, wanting to say something, but she stops herself. She looks out the window, embarrassed. The uncomfortable silence returns. They both stare out opposite windows.

EXT. ROCKWELL'S ESTATE—LATER

Subtitle: "Tarringtown, New York."
A limousine pulls through security gates and into a huge estate.

INT. ROCKWELL'S ESTATE/DINING ROOM—THAT NIGHT

Johnny, his parents, Katy and Katy's daughter, who's wearing a birthday hat, all sit at the dinner table talking AD LIBS about the war.

KATY

They were burning the ovens night and day as news of the Allied advance reached our camp. Fortunately, the Germans fled before it was my time to die.

JOHN

The Allied British troops rescued you...on April 15, 1945?

KATY

Yes.

JOHN
(eyeing his son)

The world and its people are far from being perfect.

JOHNNY
(joining in)

When was the world ever perfect?

KATY

In the Garden of Eden.

JOHN

Atlantis.

JOHNNY

My father heard about Atlantis from a television report about Ed Cayce, some psychic healer they called the "sleeping prophet."

Johnny points to Eva, who has fallen asleep.

KATY

There's your sleeping prophet.

Everyone LAUGHS.

INT. ROCKWELL LIVING ROOM—LATER THAT NIGHT

We SEE an early attempt at television in BLACK and WHITE. It's a news program showing short reels about each topic.

JOHN

Would you believe someday, these things might be in color?

Everyone LAUGHS at this bold statement about the future.

The first show we find is a sports reel showing wrestling bouts.

KATY

I've never liked those matches. They're just so barbaric.

As the sports reel ends, a newsreel begins.

ANNOUNCER (V.O.)

Making news headlines today…

JOHN

The very first newscast was by NBZ in 1939. NBZ sits in one of our Manhattan buildings.

ANNOUNCER (V.O.)

...John D. Rockwell has just donated millions for the future United Nations building, which the 1947 General Assembly just approved for construction.

KATY

Now I'm impressed, Mr. Rockwell. I'm glad someone is trying to stop dictators like Hitler from coming to power again. I hope this organization will help Israel become a nation again by gathering those that have been scattered.

John gives Katy a dirty look, unseen by her.

Johnny notices it though.

ANNOUNCER (V.O.)

And finally, from the first UFO story from last month, June 24, 1947, to something just breaking today in Roswell, New Mexico.

JOHN

"WAR OF THE WORLDS" again?

The PHONE RINGS, interrupting. A servant enters and motions to John.

JOHN

Excuse me…the military doesn't take holidays.

He takes the call in his private study, closing the door behind him.

INT. JOHN'S STUDY

He is disturbed by the phone call.

We SEE many artifacts on shelves. Most notably, a tape entitled "PROPAGANDA RADIO EXPERIMENT." 1938 Broadcast "WAR OF THE WORLDS."

INT. NEVADA—UNDERGROUND MILITARY BASE

A SCIENTIST in a white lab coat looks at a computer chip and what APPEARS to be a fiber optic cable from the wrecked UFO.

SCIENTIST
(to someone O.S.)

What is this?

The O.S. person hands him a phone receiver. While he listens, we SEE underground tunneling all around the area.

EXT. ROCKWELL ESTATE—STORMY NIGHT

It's THUNDERING and LIGHTNING but not raining yet.

INT. GUEST BEDROOM

Eva is asleep as Katy tucks her in and kisses her on the forehead.

Johnny stands in the doorway of the poorly lit bedroom. He is admiring Katy, who's dressed only in a nightgown.

JOHNNY'S POV—KATY

His GAZE MOVES DOWN, admiring the fact she has a very nice body.

BACK TO SCENE

Katy turns around and pretends not to notice Johnny staring. She doesn't seem to mind the attention, by the glow in her face.

> KATY
>
> Could you get me a glass of water? My mouth is dry from all that salt air on the boat.

Johnny smiles and nods, then heads down the hall.

Katy starts admiring herself in the mirror, when she HEARS something. The SOUND is coming from an air duct overhead.

She stands on a chair, moving closer. She hears two men TALKING.

INT. KITCHEN

It's Johnny and the SERVANT, who's pouring a glass of water.

> JOHNNY
>
> I heard a new joke at the temple today, want to hear it?

> SERVANT
>
> I love your jokes. Please do.

> JOHNNY
>
> Why did the Nazis burn so many Jews?

INT. GUEST BEDROOM

Katy's face becomes concerned and she stands on her tiptoes now.

SERVANT (O.S.)

I don't know...why?

JOHNNY (O.S.)

Because they were too skinny to become fertilizer.

The SOUND of two men LAUGHING can be HEARD O.S. as Katy sinks down in shock! She can't believe what she has just heard.

She HEARS Johnny's FOOTSTEPS and quickly climbs off the chair.

Johnny comes back to the door with the glass of water.

Katy takes it, gulping it down while looking out the window. LIGHT-NING FLASHES illuminate her almost see-through gown.

Unable to control his impulses any longer, he makes a pass at her.

Katy pulls away, an emotional 180-degree turnabout from before.

JOHNNY

What's the matter?

KATY
(stalling)

I...I...I guess I'm...still in love with David...David's memory, you know...

She breaks down in tears. Johnny moves closer but she pulls away.

KATY

Technically...we were married. Well, we did it

ourselves…but it counted. We performed our own ceremony…we exchanged vows…I gave him one of my hair braids…when I had long hair…he gave me his watch.

Johnny now noticeably backs away from her.

JOHNNY

I didn't know. But…I understand now. You know Katy…he's…you know what I'm trying to say.

KATY

Yes, I know he's gone but…

There's more silence between them. Johnny becomes disturbed now.

JOHNNY

He's still number one, even in death. I've always walked in his shadow. It was true then and it's true now.

He realizes all is lost now. He steps back.

JOHNNY

Hey…I want to give you something.

He leaves the room momentarily, returning with a WWII Air Force hat.

JOHNNY

It's David's hat. He left it at the base before our last flight.

Katy takes the hat slowly as she bursts into tears again.

KATY
(sobbing)

I don't know what to say…thank you.

JOHNNY

I've got something else for you.

He reaches in his pocket, takes out a small box, handing it to her.

JOHNNY

It was recovered from a concentration camp
and sent to my division since the information
was engraved on the back. David had no family, so my senior officer gave it to me.

She opens the box as he's explaining. It's David's watch! She bursts into
tears again. RAIN FALLS HARD on the windowpane.

EXT. BEDROOM WINDOW—NIGHT—RAINING

OUR VIEW SHIFTS to the rainy skies over NYC where fireworks are
exploding over the Statue of Liberty.

We CLIMB higher into the sky until we are above the Earth's atmosphere. A glint of a rainbow can be SEEN along some clouds as the sun's
reflective rays hit the precipitation.

Song "SOMEWHERE OVER THE RAINBOW" begins.

EXT. HEAVEN'S GATE—CLOSE ON—MAN'S ARM

He's wearing a braided hair-wrap bracelet, revealing as our VIEW

WIDENS that it's on David's wrist!

David is in his uniform. He's wet, dirty and disheveled. He stands before Heaven's huge gates. Bright light comes from the city.

David walks through the gates and towards the light. A huge rainbow becomes visible over the city.

Chorus of SONG repeats.

The COLORS of the rainbow over Heaven slowly

DISSOLVE TO:

EXT. THE OCEAN—NOAH'S ARK—DAY (BLACK AND WHITE)

The ark is floating on a never-ending stretch of water.

Subtitle: "2343 BC"

Above the ark in the b.g., clouds are forming in the sky where we HEAR God's VOICE.

GOD (O.S.)

> It's time for another chain reaction…mountains to come from the sea.

EXT. CONTINENTS UNDERNEATH OCEAN—OVERHEAD VIEW

Eastern and western hemispheres split and move apart.

South America moves west, pulling Antarctica westward too. Since most of Antarctica is directly east of Africa, they COLLIDE!

This BOUNCES Antarctica off the east coast of Africa, pushing it on a southeastern course, now heading under Africa.

On its way down, Antarctica SMACKS India just to the northeast, BUMPING India northeasterly into a collision course with south Asia.

Still on its way DOWN, the southeasterly moving TAIL of Antarctica CLIPS Australia, which was just south of the Asian coast on its southeastern side, separated by the former Pison River.

This DRAGS Australia to its current position with Antarctica ending up south of Africa but still attached to South America.

These collisions cause mountain ranges to form, pushing up above the water's surface.

Moving westward, the entire western hemisphere develops mountain ranges along its west coast as resistance slows the drift.

Further buckling creates mountain ripples, the Rocky Mountains, and as the westward drifting stops, the Appalachian Mountains form.

EXT. SOUTH ASIA—AERIAL VIEW

India's IMPACT into Asia forms the Himalayas. This closes the Pison River, pushing Azazyel closer to the top of the newly formed range.

This impact also closes up the former Hiddekel River gorge through Asia, forming mountain ranges bordering modern-day Russia and China.

Finally, this collision creates the mountains of Turkey just below Noah's ark, where it comes to rest.

EXT. MT. ARARAT—NOAH'S ARK—DAY

Subtitle: "October 28, 2343 BC. A few months later."

The ark rests atop Mt. Ararat and we SEE God in the clouds riding atop the wings of the cherubim.

EXT. SKY—GOD'S CHERUBIM

The COLORS of the RAINBOW surrounding His throne EXPAND in

the sky.

God is seated on His throne in the midst of the cherubim. He sniffs the air, noting a pleasant, aromatic smoke.

EXT. ALTAR—OUTSIDE NOAH'S ARK

NOAH, now 601 years old, is offering one of every clean beast and bird as a sacrifice and burnt offering. All other animals are dispersing into the land with an empty ark in the b.g.

The first RAINBOW gets larger in the sky as God talks from there.

> GOD
>
> Be fruitful and multiply, and replenish the Earth. You may now eat the flesh of every moving thing, but its blood is sacred. It is not to be eaten for it is the life. The life of man in My image is sacred and not to be shed by any. As a token of My covenant, this bow in the sky is a reminder that when it rains, the waters will never again cover all the Earth.

The rainbow is complete. Suddenly, the entire world is in COLOR.

> NARRATOR (V.O.)
>
> COLOR will remain from here on.

After Noah's sacrifice is complete, he tastes flesh for the first time. A chicken runs in front of Noah, crossing the tiny road leading from the altar to the ark.

> NOAH
>
> Hmmm…I wonder what chicken tastes like?

EXT. REMAINS OF EDEN—DAY—OVERHEAD VIEW

Much of Earth is still under water. WE DESCEND, landing on an island near the Sargasso Sea, where Eden used to be located.

We DISCOVER our descent POV was that of SATAN and APOLLYON.

> SATAN
>
> We'll have to rebuild here in the middle of the Atlantic since there is no more Eden.

> APOLLYON
>
> I've got the perfect name for our new home…Atlantis.

EXT. ATLANTIS—DAY

Subtitle: "Atlantis. 310 years later."

A beautiful, blue-eyed, blonde, female angel stands with the fallen angels admiring their new home. She's Lililea's twin, RABEELALIA.

INSERT—HER WRIST

She's wearing her sister's bracelet with the S-shaped crest, now combined with her own. The two overlapped S's create a SWASTIKA!

BACK TO SCENE

> SATAN
>
> Rabeelalia, God is planning to send man's Redeemer soon. You must become a wife of Cush, from the seed of Ham, and create the

134   Revelations

first giant in the New World.

APOLLYON

It's time we sent a little present of our own…up to God.

RABEELALIA

I'm ready to avenge my sister…and her only daughter.

EXT. MEDITERRANEAN COAST—DAY

A multicolored light DESCENDS from the sky like a modern-day UFO. The egg-shaped object lands in the water and floats to shore.

SATAN (O.S.)

Her son will rule the Babylonians. They're expecting the Redeemer to come from the seed of the woman. We'll give them OUR Redeemer…first.

EXT. SHORE

As the egg-shaped craft opens, revealing light from inside, it reminds us of the serpent's egg, hatching in Eden's opening scene.

Rabeelalia emerges from the light as a full-grown, naked woman with long blonde hair and blue eyes. She has a very hard, toned body.

NARRATOR (V.O.)

And Semiramis was born. Many would believe she was carried safely upon the waters from the

Old World into the new one. Some called her the Lady of the Lake. Others believed she came from Heaven. But everyone called her...the Queen of Heaven.

INT. ANCIENT ASSYRIA—CLOSE ON—SEMIRAMIS

Is in labor with her husband Cush by her side, obviously the father of the dark-skinned, almond-eyed baby being born.

Subtitle: "One year later."

NARRATOR (V.O.)

And they named him Nimrod. He was destined to become the New World's first giant...and king.

MONTAGE

A) We SEE the city of Babel in its formative stages, complete with fortifications being built to protect men from wild animals.

B) Reptiles are larger now, but still small compared to pre-flood days.

C) Baby Nimrod in his carriage. A huge python comes in to wrap around the baby. Nimrod chokes the snake barehanded.

D) Wild animals are becoming plentiful. A pack of wild dogs and wolves attack a small group of men outside the city walls.

E) A large black man dressed in leopard skins rescues a man that is about to be killed by a lion. It's Nimrod as an adult giant now.

F) Holding the lion, we SEE a tattooed SWASTIKA on the back of his right hand.

G)   We SEE him hunting a leopard and being victorious.

H)   The unicorn or rhinoceros is no match for Nimrod as he wrestles it to the ground. He places the horn on his own head for a crown.

END OF MONTAGE

> NARRATOR (V.O.)
>
> He was popular and athletic. The mighty hunter customarily wore the slain animal's skin as a trophy. People got used to seeing their leader wearing the lower half of the bull, along with its horns. This made Nimrod...the first centaur.

EXT. BABYLON—MARKET AREA—DAY

Nimrod's name and symbol, the SWASTIKA, are embroidered and printed on all kinds of merchandise being sold in his kingdom.

INT. NIMROD'S CASTLE—DAY

Subtitle: "Nimrod's wedding day."

Nimrod is being crowned king and wed all on the same day. As his bride's veil is lifted, we see it's Semiramis! She is as young and beautiful as the day he was born.

The newly crowned king starts to kiss his bride and queen on the lips, but she turns her head. He settles for a kiss on the cheek.

SEMIRAMIS
(to herself)

That's all your ugly self is ever going to kiss. My cheeks…any one of the four.

EXT. MIDDLE EAST—DAY—OVERHEAD VIEW

Subtitle: "City of Babel, c.339 years after the flood."
People are working all along the banks of the Euphrates.

NARRATOR (V.O.)

Without the water canopy, man's life shortened as the sun's harmful radiation took effect. The first post-flood generations lived 400 to 500 years. Japeth's descendants were spreading to modern Turkey and south Russia with Shem's people locating just south of them. Ham's children occupied land along the Nile. The cities along the Tigris and new Euphrates were Nimrod's kingdom. The largest city was Babel. Everyone feared being scattered and separated.

EXT. WESTERN HEMISPHERE—CORNFIELD—SUNRISE

We SEE corn growing wild in the fields. Satan and Apollyon pick an ear of it and look at each other. Evil is plotting something.

SATAN

Look at us…struggling to survive against man…made of clay. We're made of fire…billions of hydrogen atoms constantly fusing to sustain our light. It's time we strike God where it hurts. We'll teach man the secrets of hydrogen fusion...and have him send a red-hot package right up to...Uranus.

Satan makes a thrusting motion with the ear of corn, then twists off the kernels with his other hand. His left hand is still gloved.

APOLLYON

Into Heaven itself?

SATAN

Where else?

EXT. CITY OF BABEL—DAY

SERIES OF SHOTS

A)   Four horsemen ride hard, carrying banners. Upon one is Nimrod's symbol, the swastika.

B)   Upon another is a winged bull with the face of Nimrod. Its head has two bullhorns and a unicorn's horn in the middle, thus three horns.

C)   Another banner shows Nimrod killing a unicorn, or rhinoceros.

D)   The fourth banner shows him killing a lion.

E)   One of these four HORSEMEN introduces Nimrod to the eagerly awaiting crowd that has gathered.

HORSEMAN

And now I present to you, the lion killer and

champion over behemoths and leviathans and...your Redeemer and King...Nimrod.

The bald-headed Nimrod, clothed in the skin of a leopard and standing roughly eighteen feet tall, prepares to give a speech to all his loyal subjects. One of the horsemen hands him a torch.

Nimrod holds a torch in one hand and a crosier in the other.

NIMROD

We've been taught that the sun is the servant of the great, unseen creator. But notice that it is the bright revolving orb that provides the bounty of the Earth for its inhabitants. Without the sun there can be no crop.

Several more people are gathering now and forming a larger crowd.

NIMROD

I say the sun is not the servant, but is instead the master. For *it* is the minister of the bounty, not the unseen God.

He holds the flame of his torch under water. The torch somehow continues to burn underwater to the amazement of the crowd.

NIMROD

But the sun is made of fire, which gives us heat and light!

He pulls the torch out of the water and lets it burn brightly.

Everyone is amazed by this miracle, murmuring among themselves.

NIMROD

It is not the unseen God that deserves our worship but instead the sun and its minister of fire, the moon that reflects it, and the stars, which are the true gods of fire and light.

Semiramis smiles as she joins her husband now.

NARRATOR (V.O.)

Men now regard the stars as gods. Since Nimrod is a giant, he associates himself with the giant in the sky, Orion. Thus, setting himself up as a God.

Nimrod wears a belt or sash with three stars on it symbolizing the belt of Orion, as our VIEW SHIFTS to constellations in the sky.

NIMROD (O.S.)

In the heavens, the stars of Orion kill the bull Taurus with his club. He then prepares to kill the lion, Leo. I have been sent to you as this giant from the sky, to kill the wild bull and conquer the lion.

Our VIEW SHIFTS back to the crowd surrounding Nimrod. A little white dog, apparently wild, makes its way through the legs of the crowd. It runs up and starts nipping at Nimrod's heels.

NIMROD

Oh yes, and the brightest star in all the heavens, Sirius, the Dog Star nipping at Orion's heels.

The crowd LAUGHS. Another little dog watches through the legs of some men standing in front. It's a smaller dog and appears to be the wild companion of the dog nipping at Nimrod's heels.

The crowd begins CHANTING Nimrod's name.

He grabs a banner from one of his men, holding up the swastika.

> NIMROD
>
> And with this symbol, a combination of the Old and New World, I'll personally avenge the blood of my giant brothers and sisters, killed before the flood.

> NARRATOR (V.O.)
>
> This became the symbol for all giants, offspring of evil.

> NIMROD
>
> Choose the god of light, the bringer of life, and follow me. With me, you can do whatever you want. If it feels good, do it. Or choose the God of Seth, the bringer of rules and laws.

He holds up his long, wooden crosier now.

> NIMROD
>
> As the sun renews itself each year on the shortest day of the year, a serpent renews itself by shedding its old self.

He holds up the dead skin of a snake for illustration.

NIMROD

(continuing)

And becomes a new creature.

His crosier magically turns into a serpent now. The snake slithers up the base of the torch and HISSES at the crowd.

NIMROD

The serpent was the giver of eye-opening knowledge to mankind back in the Garden of Eden. And now, I alone possess the keys that unlock the secrets of the sun and its flame. I can create this flame that the unseen God sent to destroy us with.

EXT. CITY'S OUTSKIRTS—BEHIND CROWD

A fire-breathing dragon suddenly appears on the outskirts of town. Clouds of smoke rise as the dragon incinerates the countryside.

The crowd turns its attention to the dragon.

NARRATOR (V.O.)

The children of Pride had already revered the watery leviathan or dragon as a god since it could breathe fire underwater.

EXT. NIMROD'S CROSIER—CLOSE ON—SNAKE'S EYES

Which look like the eyes of the first-born serpent after the fall.

The snake stares into the crowd, where his EYES meet Noah's gaze.

EXT. THE CROWD

CHANTING Nimrod's name and AD LIBS for him to "slay the dragon." Noah shakes his head and turns away, followed by Shem next to him.

Nimrod moves through the crowd carrying some sort of grenade-like device. He throws it at the dragon where there's a HUGE EXPLOSION!

Everyone turns to look at all that remains of the dragon.

> SHEM
>
> What on Earth did he throw at the dragon, father?

> NOAH
>
> He truly understands the power of the sun...my son.

Semiramis OVERHEARS Noah's comment and smiles.

> SEMIRAMIS
> (to crowd)
>
> That's right...the power of the sun and stars belong to mankind now. And with that knowledge, you can harness that power and send it to God's throne room.

Nimrod makes his way through the crowd and rejoins his angelic wife.

> NIMROD
>
> Yes, we will take the sun's energy and place it atop a tower, which we shall build here. We'll send it to Heaven and destroy this god that seeks to scatter us upon the face of the Earth.

SEMIRAMIS

We first must build a ziggurat along the Euphrates and divert its waters through the tower. From this water, we'll make fire.

The crowd CHEERS, heading towards the river to build the tower.

NARRATOR (V.O.)

The sun and stars get their energy from fusion of hydrogen atoms…something a fallen angel, bent on revenge and loyal to another bent on preventing his own demise, was more than capable of teaching to mankind.

EXT. EUPHRATES RIVER—THAT NIGHT

The full moon reflects upon the Euphrates, along Babel's shores.

Something comes to the water's surface. Supernaturally we SEE it's the soul of LILITH, joined by her two male companions.

NARRATOR (V.O.)

The souls of dead giants became demons. Never again to be joined with their own bodies, they sought other bodies to inhabit.

They SEE the city's lights and head towards them, LAUGHING evilly.

NARRATOR (V.O.)

Can your hear your thoughts? They're silent, of course. You can't hear them audibly. Did you know spirits could prompt your mind with these same silent thoughts?

EXT. CITY STREETS—NIGHT—TWO MALE DEMONS

ENTER the MINDS of two drunken men stumbling across the street. Noah and Shem walk past the men as Lilith ENTERS Shem's MIND.

SHEM
(to himself)

That was disgusting...I can't believe I even thought that.

NARRATOR (V.O.)

But if you resist evil, it will flee from you.

INT. SHEM'S MIND—A WRESTLING ARENA

A male demon becomes the ring ANNOUNCER.

ANNOUNCER

Let's get ready to rumble! In this corner...Shem!

A crowd of demon spectators surrounds the ring, "BOOING."

Shem's THOUGHTS are represented by IDENTICAL TWINS, which resemble Shem. One is skinny and dressed in black with the word "FLESH" tattooed on his forehead. Likewise, the other is very muscular and dressed in white with the word "SPIRIT" on his forehead.

ANNOUNCER

And the returning champion, straight from the watery deep...Lilith!

The demon audience is hysterical with SHOUTS of encouragement as the BELL RINGS.

Lilith dives on top of the white-clad Shem, holding him to the mat. As the referee starts to COUNT, Shem struggles free.

> NARRATOR (V.O.)
>
> Holding an opponent for a count of three began here...in the mind. It's necessary to break into the mind and take control of ones thoughts. Dwell on a tempting thought for more than three counts...it becomes sin.

EXT. CITY STREETS—NIGHT

Noah's spiritual eyes are opened as one of the drunken men SHOUT obscenities at him. Noah LOOKS around at the men in the city, noting their strange behavior. Noah prays silently.

MONTAGE

A)   We SEE demons invisibly ENTER the minds of several men.

> NOAH (O.S.)
>
> God let your grace be upon my sons, and let not wicked spirits rule over them.

B)   Two demons have caused two men to start fighting.

> NOAH (O.S.)
>
> You know how the Watchers, the father of these spirits acted in my day. As for these spirits that are living, imprison them. Hold them fast in the place of condemnation, and let them not

bring destruction.

C)   The battle between the two men has intensified and now
        includes other men from opposing sides...a real street fight.

                        NOAH (O.S.)

        For they were created in order to destroy. Let
        them not rule over the spirits of the living.

D)   Many of the men are now savagely killing each other.

END OF MONTAGE

INT. HEAVEN—GOD'S THRONE ROOM—DAY

God is WATCHING Noah via the monitor of the man cherub. The
seven archangels stand at attention facing God's throne.

                        GOD

        Archangels...do as Noah has petitioned and
        bind them all.

Satan and Apollyon plead with God as they appear on the monitor.

                        SATAN (O.S.)

        Leave us a tenth to help fulfill our mission of
        leading astray.

                        APOLLYON (O.S.)

        Let them hearken to my voice.

> GOD

> I'll grant this. But the rest of them shall be bound to the abyss.

EXT. BABEL—WALL CONSTRUCTION—NOON

Men are making bricks out of mud and placing them in the sun to dry.

Alongside the Euphrates River, the foundation for the tower is being laid. It measures roughly 300 feet square.

Nimrod stands OVERLOOKING the construction, smiling.

The righteous men, under Shem's leadership, WATCH the construction.

> SHEM

> We must kill Nimrod to prevent further apostasy.

EXT. NIMROD'S CASTLE—MIDNIGHT—A FULL MOON

Shines on Nimrod leaving his queen to go on a hunting trip.

INT. NIMROD'S CASTLE/BED CHAMBERS

Several white males sneak into his bedchambers with his queen.

While Semiramis is making love to one of the men...

EXT. OUTSKIRTS OF BABEL

...Nimrod is ambushed. He's killed by Shem, who beheads him.

His body is cut into fourteen pieces and WE SEE them being sent to all sections of his kingdom to serve as an example.

EXT. TOWER OF BABEL—NEXT MORNING

A crowd is visibly disturbed SEEING Nimrod's dismembered body. Shem stands atop the highest brick, getting their attention.

> SHEM
>
> This is what will happen to all those that openly rebel against the one and true God!

While holding the head of Nimrod, Shem gives a speech to the crowd.

> SHEM
>
> I beg you, return to the ways of God and abandon this rebellion. Abandon this unholy project.

This is most effective as we SEE almost all the men walking away.

EXT. BABEL'S WALLS—NIGHT

Men with spears LOOK over the city walls, watching for wild animals. Beside the city's main gate, Nimrod's head is atop a tree there.

INT. NIMROD'S THRONE ROOM—LATER

Semiramis has locked herself in her chambers. She's very angry.

> SEMIRAMIS
>
> I'll have revenge on Shem's seed!

She motions for her black servants to gather around.

> SEMIRAMIS
>
> Go quietly and invite anyone that will listen.

I'm conducting a secret meeting tonight on top
of the incomplete ziggurat.

As the servants turn to leave, one SERVANT turns back.

SERVANT

May we attend?

SEMIRAMIS

Women and anyone with dark skin are not
allowed.

The servants leave, obviously disappointed.

SEMIRAMIS

Women will be jealous of me. And besides, they
won't allow what I have planned. I'll include
them later as protectors of the light.

EXT./INT. INCOMPLETE ZIGGURAT—NIGHT—THE FULL MOON'S

Light shines on Semiramis, wearing Nimrod's three-horned crown.
The men she slept with the night Nimrod was killed are dressed as high
priests. She shaves the sides of one man's head…the one she made love
to while Nimrod was killed.

SEMIRAMIS

Keep the sides of your head shaved to show
your allegiance to me. Single men remain celi-
bate. I'll take care of ALL your needs.

The man she's shaving looks at her with a gleam in his eye. Then he

LOOKS at the other men. They all know she means SEX.

> SEMIRAMIS

> We must gather that which has been scattered.
> Gather Nimrod's body parts back together.

The men look puzzled now. The MAN she's shaving looks up at her.

> MAN

> But all the king's men could never put him
> back together again…and cause him to live.

> SEMIRAMIS

> If you can find all of his body parts, I can give
> him life.

EXT. BABEL'S GATES—NIGHT

At each of the city's thirteen gates, the men gather Nimrod's body parts from the pikes atop each gate.

EXT. BABEL'S MAIN GATE—NIGHT

Two MEN are cutting down the tree with Nimrod's head.
As the tree falls, the head rolls under the back hooves of a donkey.
The donkey kicks the head away, sending the men chasing after it.
They pick up the head covered with dirt, twigs and other debris.

> MEN
> (together)

> We should wash it off first.

INT. BABEL'S TOWER—SECRET MEETING—LATER

The men return with Nimrod's body parts, which are badly mauled.
The men, overcome with sadness, start cutting their own flesh.

> MAN ONE
>
> We're missing the heart, the intestines and...his penis.

> SEMIRAMIS
>
> I'll have to make substitutions.

LATER THAT NIGHT

Semiramis is SEEN sculpting a penis out of clay. Its uncircumcised head has a pointed top, resembling an obelisk.

> SEMIRAMIS
>
> This phallic symbol will represent the god of light's male member. As the sun covers and mates with the fertile mother Earth, their union creates the harvest each year and deserves our worship. We will now worship this symbol...

She holds up the clay sculpture for all to see.

> SEMIRAMIS
> (continuing)
>
> ...the symbol of the sun god's masculinity. Even the sun tower we shall send to God shall be patterned after this shape.

We SEE Satan INVISIBLY observe this. He smiles.

SATAN

God wanted me to worship man made of clay. Now man will worship his own penis made from clay.

His GAZE mysteriously meets OURS, as if he's LOOKING at US.

SATAN

Up yours!

Satan makes an upward motion with his arm as he DISAPPEARS.

BACK TO SCENE

A pig is placed before the queen. She cuts its throat.

SEMIRAMIS

These innards will replace the ones lost to the dogs. Someday, the blood of a pig will defile the walls of all that Seth's seed shall call sanctified.

She cuts open the pig and removes the guts, stuffing them inside Nimrod's corpse.

SEMIRAMIS

Now, seal up his body. Place his body into an ark and let it float upon the waters. As the great patriarch did survive atop the waters from the Old World to the new one, so shall our great king. He will come back from the world of the dead and live again.

EXT. BANK OF THE EUPHRATES—LATER THAT NIGHT—STORMY

The SOUND of THUNDER ECHOES as several men place Nimrod's body in a boat. Eight men, four on each side, man the oars of the boat as a living sacrifice.

Nimrod's body is SEEN floating away, lit up by FLASHES of LIGHTNING.

> NARRATOR (V.O.)
>
> Someday, the legend of taking a man's body, sewing it together and giving it life on a stormy night would inspire Mary Shelley's "FRANKENSTEIN, OR THE MODERN PROMETHEUS."

> SEMIRAMIS (O.S.)
>
> Nine months does it take for man to come from the womb, so shall it be for our great king. In nine moons, he'll be reborn.

> DISSOLVE TO:

INT. UNDERGROUND CHAMBERS—NEXT NIGHT

She holds her stomach with one hand and an ear of corn in the other.

> SEMIRAMIS
>
> As the seed is placed in the ground and we harvest its fruits, so shall Nimrod be reborn and resurrected from the Earth through the seed of the woman.

Semiramis picks up a golden cup. She pours in it some wine.

> SEMIRAMIS

> From the fruit of the vine.

She adds some water.

> SEMIRAMIS

> Necessary for plants and animals.

Next, she adds some honey.

> SEMIRAMIS

> Representing the sweetness of every word from my mouth.

Finally, she adds some flour made from the corn.

> SEMIRAMIS

> The symbol of Nimrod's crushed and broken body.

She gives a sip of this drink to each new member. Soon, all of them are very drunk and rowdy. She disrobes as a drunken orgy begins.

> NARRATOR (V.O.)

> Over the next nine months, the Queen of Heaven taught men the skills needed to complete the building project. They learned advanced building techniques and the secrets of electrolysis…a process necessary to separate hydrogen from ordinary water.

MONTAGE

A)   Semiramis wears a crown with a pagoda-like tower on top. She also wears an apron. Knots border the apron.

B)   Men around her lust after her beauty. She rarely wears much clothing and here, we SEE she is wearing ONLY the apron.

C)   She introduces new tools: a compass, a square, a gauge, a lever, a plumb rule with 24 equal measurements, a plumb line and a trowel.

D)   Semiramis shows them how to make brick faster and stronger by baking them in fire-heated ovens instead of sun-drying them.

E)   Sculpting clay on a potter's wheel, she forms a jar.

F)   She demonstrates how to make a small battery from the jar by inserting a galvanic rod into liquid.

END OF MONTAGE

INT. SECRET UNDERGROUND MEETING—A BLINDFOLDED INITIATE

Is led by three other men. Each man is portraying a different element. The three represent Earth, wind and fire.

> NARRATOR (V.O.)
>
> Now simply known as the Mysteries, new recruits to this first pagan religion were being initiated every day. The new initiate would fast, then go on a symbolic journey to commemorate Nimrod's present journey. The powers of nature were confronted: sun, moon, fire and

wind.

One man fans air in the initiate's face.

Another man passes a torch around the initiate's body.

The third man trips the initiate, causing him to land in a sandpit.

> NARRATOR (V.O.)
>
> The final element was water. Each man was held underwater. If he lived, his first breath was that of an enlightened man.

EXT. BANKS OF EUPHRATES—NIGHT—FULL MOON

Semiramis, dressed only in a thong with a short skirt wrap, holds a bound initiate under water, almost drowning him.

There's almost a perverse pleasure in her torch-lit eyes as she watches the man writhe under her.

We now SEE the demon Lilith witnessing what is happening.

> SEMIRAMIS
>
> You must pass through the trial of death by water in order to reach the New World. Janus or Dagon did it, now you must do it.

> NARRATOR (V.O.)
>
> Janus was the pagan name assigned to Noah since he lived in both the Old World and the new. He was represented by a man with two faces—one looking back and one looking forward. Dagon, synonymous with Janus, was the fish god capable of living underwater. It was

another name for leviathan—now worshipped as bringer of light and wisdom, like the serpent in Eden.

The initiate does not survive as we SEE he has drowned. Since he's dead, she simply sits on him, her butt slightly out of the water.

NARRATOR (V.O.)

But not all make it into the enlightened world.

LILITH

I want some of this action. It's payback time for that flood.

We HEAR her enter the mind of the next initiate, who's afraid to be initiated now. Lilith whispers to his mind telepathically.

LILITH (O.S.)

Look at that beautiful woman. We all have to die. Wouldn't that be an exciting way to go?

The initiate relaxes now, but is slightly aroused. He proceeds.

We SEE the initiate under Semiramis. Lilith and Semiramis are both smiling wickedly at his body struggling underwater.

NARRATOR (V.O.)

Sadly, news of this initiation ritual spread as did the demonic forces that encouraged weak-minded men to gamble with their lives this way. Their goal, to destroy mankind and his seed. Hopefully, averting their fate.

INT. CAVE—ONE MONTH LATER

Even more men are assembled now for another initiation ceremony.

Semiramis' pregnancy is beginning to show slightly. A new blindfolded initiate waits for the ceremony to begin.

> SEMIRAMIS
> (rubbing her belly)
>
> Since you are united as brothers with my unborn son, the future reincarnation of Nimrod, whose death has left me now a widow, you are all sons of the widow.

She takes the undergarments from one of the men and holds them up.

> SEMIRAMIS
>
> We must continue the tower project. For protection from others during your work on the tower, I'll place a spell on your clothing, to be worn secretly.

> NARRATOR (V.O.)
>
> Since angels spoke in a tongue unknown to man, it appeared that their simple commands over matter were magic. This resulted in man's belief in witchcraft and incantations.

She places the swastika as a good luck charm on their undergarments.

> SEMIRAMIS
>
> Wear it secretly and no one else will know you worship the sun.

One MAN has a puzzled look on his face.

MAN

But how do we know a brother of the Mysteries
if we all wear the symbol on our underclothes?

She thinks long and hard on that one. She studies her own hand.

SEMIRAMIS

Since the middle finger is longer than the rest,
it must represent the sun god Nimrod, as does
the obelisk. All other fingers bowing as subjects
for their king…this shall be the secret sign.
Make this gesture to someone, if they don't
return the sign, they're not enlightened men.
Keep making the gesture 'til someone returns
it…you'll know then that you both worship the
one true god of light.

All the men stand around flipping each other off, LAUGHING.

SEMIRAMIS

As sons of the widow, if you are in trouble and
fear for your life, look up and utter these words:
'Is there no help for the widow's son?' If a
brother is in a position to give assistance, he
will hear your plea and help you.

EXT. TOWER OF BABEL—DAY

The construction is back up now in full swing. Men are using bitumen
to waterproof the ziggurat's oven-baked bricks.

Subtitle: "Eight months later. The Winter Solstice."

Other workers are refining petroleum products from the bitumen. Primitive fuel cells store highly flammable, yellow-colored liquid.

Others refine a clear gas substance from the ground.

NARRATOR (V.O.)

> The area was naturally rich in petroleum products...gasoline, natural gas, helium, and oil. Perfect for man's first...tower.

EXT. NEARBY HILL

Noah and Shem observe this from afar, shaking their heads. The number of the men working on the tower exceeds the righteous men.

INT. ZIGGURAT—MEN

Are separating heavy hydrogen from water diverted from the river.

EXT. TOP OF ZIGGURAT

Several silversmiths are constructing parts for the tower itself. The work all around is interrupted as we HEAR some men SHOUTING.

Someone from the Queen's tower is CRYING OUT in pain. Semiramis is in labor.

INT. UNDERGROUND CAVE—SECRET MEETING—NIGHT—LATER

Semiramis holds up her baby boy to thundering APPLAUSE from the men, all on their knees showing respect for their newborn king.

A master silversmith displays a statue of Semiramis holding a child.

NARRATOR (V.O.)

The first mother and child icon. Since the child was regarded as Nimrod reborn, as the Sun is reborn on the Winter Solstice, he was given the title of 'the Sun incarnate.' His birthday would be celebrated with the sun on December twenty-fifth.

Semiramis lights a candle marked by twenty-four equal measurements.

SEMIRAMIS

Every year on this day, we'll light a candle to celebrate the sun reborn. We'll dedicate the first day of the week to the sun, calling it Sunday. The following day belongs to the moon. Since I reflect the sun's radiance, I'll be known as the Moon Goddess.

All priests kneel before the babe, each holding a candle. Semiramis lights their candles from her candle.

NARRATOR (V.O.)

The custom of worshipping the sun god by lighting a candle on his birthday began. Soon men would adopt this custom for their own birthdays.

INT. THRONE—LATER—CLOSE ON—THE QUEEN

Sits upon her underground throne. She wears a crown that has seven rays of light shooting out. There's a star on top of each spike.

NARRATOR (V.O.)

Claiming the influence of the seven stars of the Pleiades, she made this crown. But these seven stars 490 light years away, or seven times seventy, represent the seven spirits of the Holy Spirit. Later, legends would call these seven spirits the seven sisters or muses that inspire. This Queen, a.k.a. Juno, symbolized by a dove, associated herself with the Holy Spirit's most divine symbol.

EXT. BABEL'S MAIN CITY GATE—NIGHT

We SEE the word "GATEWAY" over the arch.

Satan and Apollyon, invisible, overlook the city at its entrance.

A tree stump remains of the tree where Nimrod's head was placed.

INSERT—TREE STUMP

With wild holly and bright red berries growing around it.

BACK TO SCENE

SATAN

If we are going to cash in on OUR redeemer, we should get people used to celebrating his birth with this season.

APOLLYON

How are we going to do that?

SATAN

Oh, I don't know.

He picks some of the holly and studies it carefully.

SATAN

Perhaps we'll symbolize the divine branch with a branch of our own. The holly wood is interesting…and a holly tree grows green and red. We'll start with that color scheme.

APOLLYON

Can we start with the color red?

He squeezes the berry, making a BRIGHT RED stain on his hand.

EXT. TOWER CONSTRUCTION—NEXT MORNING

Men from the previous night work on the nearly complete tower.

Noah walks up, inspecting the work. He drops to his knees before all the men and begins praying to God.

NOAH

Lord, the children of my children hearken not to my voice. United, they openly rebel after secretly worshipping the god of light, who teaches them the secrets of the sun and stars. They plan to send this firepower up the angel's stairway to Heaven next time it is opened.

NOAH'S POV—THE SKY

Opens up like the iris of a camera lens. God comes through the opening on the wings of the cherubim. He inspects the tower.

> ### GOD (O.S.)
>
> People are united with one language and this is what they do. Anything they imagine in their minds can be done.

EXT. TOP OF TOWER—MEN

Are putting final touches on the tower's top. It's here where the mechanics of the hydrogen bomb rest.

"GODS OF THIS WORLD" is written boldly across the nose.

They load the final piece…the warhead, which shows that it's ARMED!

> ### GOD (O.S.)
>
> I'll confuse their language so they cannot understand one another. They'll be forced to scatter from here.

A mighty WIND begins to BLOW all around the workers. They look around to see where this storm could be coming from.

The men along the top of the tower who armed the missile lose their balance, falling to their deaths.

EXT. BASE OF TOWER—WORKERS

Run to their aid, discovering they can't understand one another. Everyone is AD LIBBING in a different language now. There is great confusion as the work comes to a stop and pandemonium ensues.

INT. QUEEN'S CHAMBER

Semiramis HEARS a commotion and looks out her window to investigate. She turns to her servant for an explanation.

He answers in an unknown tongue, much to the queen's frustration.

> SEMIRAMIS
>
> Oh, stop babbling!

EXT. TOWER OF BABEL—LATER

The workers abandon the tower. It appears that everyone is splitting up into small groups that understand each other.

> NARRATOR (V.O.)
>
> Finally, with man's language confused, each family was forced to obey God's command to spread out across the face of the Earth.

EXT. TOP OF TOWER

God inspects the workmanship of the tower. He reads the words written on top.

INSERT—TOP

"GODS OF THIS WORLD"

BACK TO SCENE

Gabriel and Michael join God. They begin looking over the tower.

MICHAEL

How much firepower does it have?

GABRIEL

Enough to destroy God's throne room.

GOD

Reprogram it. Send it to theirs.

EXT. ATLANTIS—MINUTES LATER

Satan and Apollyon sit in the golden throne room they've constructed. Apollyon notices something bright in the sky.

APOLLYON

The men of Babel wouldn't launch the tower without first letting us open the gateway, would they?

SATAN

No. Why do you ask?

He looks up and sees the rocket. He and Apollyon take to the air just in time as a HUGE EXPLOSION replaces Atlantis.

NARRATOR (V.O.)

And the legend of the destruction of Atlantis was born.

EXT. EUROPE—DAY—HIGH ANGLE—YEARS LATER

We SEE the tribes and clans of Japeth's descendants heading even farther north into Russia and west into Europe.

NARRATOR (V.O.)

The seed of Noah spreads out and separates
from each other.

EXT. PALESTINE REGION—DAY—OVERHEAD VIEW

We SEE the tribes of Shem's descendants as Caucasoid with dark hair
and dark eyes. The crest of one tribe displays a lion.

EXT. FUNERAL

An old man has died. Upon closer inspection, we SEE it's Noah. Beside
his grave is another man's tombstone, which reads, "PELEG."

EXT. PALESTINE—OVERHEAD VIEW

NARRATOR (V.O.)

While most of the seed of Canaan settled nearby in Canaan land, many of them went east.

We SEE the dark-skinned Canaanites just north of modern-day Israel.
Others head east and settle into modern day India and China. They
have distinct features and their eyes are almond-shaped.

NARRATOR (V.O.)

As these tribes mixed, certain features emerged
that are still apparent today.

Now we SEE this group has almond-shaped eyes mixed with slight Mongoloid features. Their tribal banner displays the crest of a dragon.

NARRATOR (V.O.)

> Advancing sheets of ice, which had not receded from the time they were formed by Noah's flood, became a bridge for tribes expanding eastward. This is how the dark-eyed, dark-haired peoples arrived in North America, later to be known as Native American Indians.

EXT. EARTH—DAY—HIGH ANGLE

People migrate across the ice bridge into the Americas. They migrate from North to Central to South America.

Various groups split into different Indian tribes.

EXT. INDIA—(HARRAPA AND MOHENJO-DARO)—DAY

Tribes of almond-eyed people are constructing buildings here made from oven-baked bricks.

EXT. GIZA PLATEAU—DAY

Mizraim has dark-colored skin, eyes and hair. He looks out over the pyramids. His tribe inhabits upper Egypt near the future city of Abydos.

NARRATOR (V.O.)

> Ham's seed remained on the African continent with Mizraim, in upper and lower Egypt.

Floodwaters haven't completely receded around the pyramids or lion.

EXT. PILLARS OF HERCULES—DAY

Semiramis, her son Ninus, his real white father, and the other male priests are rowing a boat west through the Straits of Gibraltar.

EXT. TIAHUANACO—ANDES MOUNTAINS—DAY—MONTHS LATER

Many ships filled with Semiramis' men approach the large Lake Titicaca nestled high upon the Andes. Semiramis SCANS the coast.

> SEMIRAMIS
>
> We'll build here on this, the highest point in the west. We need to produce fire from water again, but how can I get these men to understand me?

Satan APPEARS from out of nowhere. He hovers above the coast.

> SATAN
>
> I've been thinking about this latest curve from God. My internal processor is the finest computer ever made. With it, I've created a language of my own. We'll teach this language to our followers. We'll then use it to bridge the other languages so this can interpret them...

He holds out a small mechanical device. It's apple-shaped with a chunk missing, slightly bigger than a human bite.

> SATAN
> (continuing)
>
> A computer translator device I've created.

SEMIRAMIS

But how can you teach these idiots a new language? I can't motivate them to do anything.

SATAN

There grows a bush here in these mountains. The leaf from the tree is most intoxicating and satisfying. They'll learn anything you have to teach them once they become dependent on the leaf. You'll have them literally eating out of your hands.

EXT. TIAHUANACO—DAY—YEARS LATER

The beginnings of a port city overlook Lake Titicaca. We SEE several giants moving huge stones into place.

Several fallen angels are playing trumpets, causing stones to cut and shape themselves and move into the air until landing in their final resting place as part of a wall.

Many giants are chewing on a green leaf. They seem very satisfied from whatever the plant is giving them and have boundless energy.

Men are speaking AD LIBS in the same artificial language now.

NARRATOR (V.O.)

This skillfully designed language was easily transformed into a computer algorithm to translate one language into another...a bridge language. This language is still spoken by the Aymara Indians still living in this region even to this day.

EXT. TIAHUANACO—AKAPANA PYRAMID—DAY

Dozens of fallen angels and giants are SEEN working on a huge pyramid. Water from the lake is being diverted through several stone sluices winding throughout the pyramid.

> NARRATOR (V.O.)
>
> This became known as the Akapana Pyramid, which means 'people perish' in the Aymaran tongue. It would soon become obvious why.

NINUS, now fully-grown, watches the work. He has very LARGE saucer-shaped eyes and HUGE eyebrows. He's over fourteen feet tall.

A small boy comes up to him and tugs on his cloak. He turns and picks the boy up, setting him upon his own shoulders.

> NINUS
>
> Ah, my young Thouros...soon you'll be as tall as your father.

One of the GIANTS working on Akapana approaches Ninus.

> GIANT
>
> The city is almost complete. We are putting the final touches on the docks now.

> NINUS
>
> Good. Any problems?

> GIANT
>
> Only with some slaves we picked up from the north.

NINUS

Behead them all. Shrink them and make a belt from them. I'll wear the belt as a reminder to them of the price of rebellion.

EXT. LAKE TITICACA—TIAHUANACO'S DOCKS—DAY

Giants are pouring molten metal into an I-shaped groove, which is cut into the stones where they meet. As the iron cools, it holds the huge stones together. Semiramis is overlooking the work.

SEMIRAMIS

Excellent. Now, let's take the Huanuco coca leaf back to our Egyptian friends and begin trading with them. Once they become addicted to it, we'll be able to name our price and their allegiance is guaranteed.

EXT. ELEPHANTINE ISLAND/UPPER EGYPT—DAY—MONTHS LATER

Mizraim and other descendants of Ham have settled here. Most of lower Egypt at the mouth of the Nile is still a marsh.

Boatloads of Tiahuanacans arrive at the island of Elephantine.

As they pull into the port docks, we notice that the stones there are joined together with the same I-shaped iron piece.

As soon as the first bale comes off the ship, men tear it apart and begin chewing on the leaves. A peaceful look returns to their face.

As the Egyptians speak their native tongue, the apple-like translating device converts their AD LIBS.

NARRATOR (V.O.)

Uniting that which has been scattered. And so trading between the Old World and the New World had begun. Soon, giants helped them construct a huge dike, diverting the Nile. This soon dried up the marsh.

EXT. GIZA PLATEAU—PYRAMIDS—DAY

The water that surrounded the pyramids and lion has dried up.
Subtitle: "Several years later. Ninus' 100th birthday."

EXT. HIMALAYAN MOUNTAINS—DAY

We are atop the highest mountain range in the world now.

NARRATOR (V.O.)

A protective layer in the upper atmosphere allowed man to live almost 400 to 500 years. This layer, although starting to deteriorate, still kept upper elevations from getting cold. It was here that Ninus had begun building a home for his son, Thouros. Legends would refer to this place as…Mount Olympus.

A huge castle has been constructed here. We SEE Semiramis, Ninus and THOUROS atop a castle wall. They're enjoying the VIEW.

SEMIRAMIS

I'm proud of you, my son. You are truly the son of a great king. Your father, the New World's first king, lifted the burden of the Heaven's rule from the shoulders of men. Your title as his successor shall be the father and King of the Gods. Ninus shall rule in the west...and Thouros shall rule from here, this mountain in the sky. You shall rule all that you see.

Ninus and Thouros LOOK UP at the sky, then each other.

NINUS

But we can see the sky.

SEMIRAMIS

Both of you will rule that as well. You will fly with condors and hawks. As children of the sun, your weapons shall be fiery.

THOUROS

But when do we get our wings?

SEMIRAMIS

Both of you shall glide upon the wind this very day.

She points to two condor-like gliders behind them.

SEMIRAMIS

Happy birthday, my sons.

EXT. HIGH ABOVE MOUNTAINS—NINUS AND THOUROS

Are inside their primitive gliders, soaring higher than any bird.

NINUS

This is the best present ever!

NINUS' POV—THE GROUND BELOW

Overlooking Tibet, we SEE the Gobi Desert is still an inland sea.

Trade ships filled with giants travel down the expanded rivers of the Ganges, Yangtze, and Indus to the Arabian Sea.

EXT. MOHENJO-DARO/PAKISTAN—DAY

The trade ships wind along the Indus to this river town inhabited by giants. A bath and initiation pool is being built out of oven-baked bricks and lined with bitumen.

EXT. HARAPPA/PAKISTAN—DAY

Upstream from Mohenjo-Daro along the Ravi River, a tributary of the Indus, Harappa is also being built by giants with oven-baked bricks.

EXT. SOUTH ASIA—OVERHEAD VIEW

WE FOLLOW some of the ships as they stop through other giant cities on the island of Sri Lanka, off the coast of India.

NARRATOR (V.O.)

This was the beginning of the Raman Empire.

EXT. ABYDOS/EGYPT—THE OSIREION—DAY

Huge stones glide through the air as the Osireion Temple in Abydos is being built.

EXT. CUZCO/PERU—DAY—NINUS AND SEMIRAMIS

Are atop their temple covered with sheets of gold.

> **NINUS**
>
> Reports indicate that floodwaters are receding. Some cities can't be reached by boat anymore.

> **SEMIRAMIS**
>
> All this has been foreseen and will be taken care of.

> **NINUS**
>
> And what about the weapons of fire you promised?

> **SEMIRAMIS**
>
> We are ready but we must test this power first. The fusion of hydrogen generates much heat.

EXT. SACSAYHUAMAN/PERU—DAY

Fallen angels assist giants in building a fortress in stone using many interlocking and multi-angled jigsaw-puzzle patterns.

EXT. CUZCO/PERU (JUST SOUTH OF SACSAYHUAMAN)—DAY

Ninus and Thouros OVERSEE construction of the Temple Coricancha. Its foundation stones and walls use interlocking polygonal blocks.

In the center of a rectangular stone courtyard sits an octagonal stone platform. This is where an obelisk sits.

NARRATOR (V.O.)

Their first rocket...sits here as an object of worship.

EXT. MACCHU PICCHU/PERU (NEAR CUZCO)—DAY

Semiramis, Ninus, and Thouros observe the construction of the Intihuatana. A giant, ENGINEER, supervises the actual cutting.

NARRATOR (V.O.)

Intihuatana means "hitching post of the sun."
This giant was referred to as...the Engineer.

NINUS

The hitching post is complete. When do we
give the sun wings?

SEMIRAMIS

When the sun has set in the west, we'll send
up...our sun.

From the sky, a bright fire unfolds as Satan lands upon the recently completed hitching post. Apollyon accompanies him.

SATAN

We are finally ready for a test flight. I've waited
a long time for this day. Is the flying cylinder
assembly complete?

SEMIRAMIS

We've attached the top to the body of the tower.

The top is armed and ready to be tested.

NINUS
(bowing to Satan)

It's ready to deliver the power of a bright star as her payload. With this new fire, we'll rule the world!

THOUROS
(holding a device)

Can I push the button?

Everyone looks at the eager young giant holding the firing switch to the golden missile, which is tethered to the upright stone.

SATAN
(laughing)

Why not? I believe a countdown is in order.

EVERYONE
(counting down)

Three, two, one, ZERO!

EXT. CLOSE ON—ROCKET

The golden rocket lifts off. Instead of heading out to sea, it veers southeast and heads straight for Lake Titicaca.

EXT. CROWD

Everyone LOOKS UP with shock as they realize the rocket is headed straight towards their booming water town.

EXT. LAKE TITICACA/PERU—MINUTES LATER

The rocket nosedives directly into the northern end of the lake, right between a fleet of ships carrying more processed hydrogen.

Suddenly, there's a HUGE EXPLOSION underwater. This sets off a terrible chain reaction as the ships now EXPLODE from the heat.

Shock waves create a terrible earthquake. The waters of Lake Titicaca spill over the northern banks until breaking off, causing huge amounts of water to spill, and dropping the lake's level.

EXT. TIAHUANACO—ALONG THE SHORE

People along the banks of the lake are overcome by water and drowned.

EXT. CITY OF TIAHUANACO

The violent tremors cause the huge megaliths at Puma Punku or "Puma Gate" to become strewn about like matchsticks.

The huge Gateway of the Sun gets its crack.

DISSOLVE TO:

EXT. TIAHUANACO—SEVERAL DAYS LATER

We can SEE the lake is much lower. City docks can't be reached.

INT. PERU—CUZCO TEMPLE—DAY

Semiramis, Ninus, Thouros, Satan and Apollyon are all LOOKING at the destruction through Satan's monitor.

SATAN

We'll have to work on the guidance system. Not to worry. But we'll have to abandon Tiahuanaco soon...radiation fallout is deadly to flesh. Keep producing hydrogen isotopes at Akapana until we can build new pyramids elsewhere.

EXT. SOUTH AMERICA—OVERHEAD VIEW

We SEE various images of construction all over the land.

NARRATOR (V.O.)

Ziggurat construction all over South America began. The Pan American Highway was built right through the Nazca plains. Suspension bridges were erected and tunnels were carved through solid rock. The Nazca plain was very dry and its key position through the region made it the ideal place for landing strips for...new condor planes.

EXT. SOUTHERN PERU—NAZCAN PLAINS—DAY

Laborers are making lines on the plains under the supervision of a whirlybird, which hovers just high enough to observe the patterns.

INT. HELICOPTER

The tail rotor is in front of the giant pilot so he can watch the smaller blade, which controls the craft from turning against the large overhead blades. The blades seem to run off a primitive compression engine utilizing refined bitumen.

The SOUND of the beating WIND causes the laborers to cower below.

> LABORER ONE
>
> Huitzilopochtli is a bloodthirsty hummingbird god. He beats down on us with his mighty wings as we work in the hot sun with no water to drink…again.

> LABORER TWO
>
> Careful, they have ears that hear from great distances. You could lose your head.

> LABORER ONE
>
> If we're lucky, we'll get transferred to Akapana. I hear you don't survive long against the invisible sickness that causes your teeth, hair and nails to fall out…but you have plenty of water to drink.

Along the horizon, we SEE some kind of vehicle arriving to the area along the Pan American Highway. It's some kind of hovercraft as it glides across the surface along a cushion of air.

> NARRATOR (V.O.)
>
> Helicopter wings led to the invention of an amphibious boat using fan-like wings underneath to create the cushion of air. Local legends called these serpent rafts. Similar Norse legends claimed Thor had a boat like this and could

even fold it up into his pocket, which was true of the inflatable variety. This explains how the Incans inherited a sophisticated road system but didn't even have the wheel.

EXT. NAZCA DESERT—DAY—WEEKS LATER

From the horizon, a BRIGHT OBJECT approaches. It DESCENDS and begins its landing approach on the now completed Nazca airport.

> NARRATOR (V.O.)
>
> The Nazca lines were finished, paving the way for these flying condors. But these weren't gliders. These metal birds had a propulsion system similar to a modern pulse-jet engine.

COCKPIT POV—AIRPORT BELOW

We SEE the triangular appearance of airport landing strips below.

> NARRATOR (V.O.)
>
> The seed of the woman was again mixed with fallen angels. This produced a new batch of demigods or giants with large eyes and cone heads, genetic mutations from mixing their seed with mankind's seed.

EXT. AIRPORT STRIP—FLYING VEHICLE

Taxies along the runway towards the step pyramid complex. The primitive hover jet comes to a stop. A small man climbs out.

He has a high forehead and a very pointed conehead.

He walks towards the step pyramid as several slave laborers attend to his iron chariot, now resting on the ground.

INT. STEP PYRAMID—MINUTES LATER

Satan, Apollyon, other giants, and a CONEHEAD surround a table.

Satan's appearance is as a serpent. He wears a wig made from dozens of tiny snakes, giving the illusion of having braided hair.

> GIANT
>
> We are gods of the air now, capable of soaring higher than the mighty condor, swifter than the hawk and capable of moving in the air like the hummingbird.

> SATAN
>
> We are ready to implement our next phase to take over all lands surrounding the Mediterranean. We must prevent this redeemer by completely inhabiting the area prophesied as his birthplace.

> APOLLYON
>
> We must pollute the seed of the woman any way we can. Even if radiation poisoning is our last resort, we will annihilate the entire region of Canaan.

> GIANT
>
> We must address the continuing rebellion of

our laborers in the hydrogen pyramids. They are aware of radiation and its effects. Some choose the penalty of instant death rather than the slow death caused by radiation.

CONEHEAD

We have hundreds of these rebels in detention and labor camps.

SATAN

Let's make an example of them.

APOLLYON

The ball games?

SATAN

Yes...let the games begin.

EXT. COPAN (HONDURAS)—DAY

Several giants and coneheads are playing together as a team in some sort of soccer game. They are playing a team of condemned slaves. Large groups of slaves in chains are being forced to watch.

EXT. LATER—NEAR END OF GAME

A giant kicks the rubber ball to a conehead teammate.

The ball bounces off his pointed head, and then soars into a round goal made of stone, roughly 23 feet above the ground.

The CROWD of attending giants ROARS with approval.

Satan and Apollyon are in the crowd and rise, APPLAUDING.

SATAN

Give them my sword of fire.

Apollyon takes the golden-handled instrument from Satan's belt and enables the device as a bright rod of fire emerges.

NARRATOR (V.O.)

This was the legendary device known as the Xiuhcoatl, or Fire Serpent, the rod of revolving fire used by angels. Stone carvings found in Palenque show a Mayan ruler holding one.

As he HANDS it to a conehead, we NOTICE the conehead has six fingers. He begins cutting off the heads of the losing team with it.

NARRATOR (V.O.)

Satan was the legendary Moche god, Aiapaec...the winged decapitator. A.K.A. the god Tezcatilpoca, whose name means smoking mirror, which described an object enabling him to observe from afar the activities of men and gods...his monitor.

EXT. TEOTIHUACAN—DAY (VERNAL EQUINOX)

Two large ziggurats come into VIEW. The larger one, the Pyramid of the Sun and the smaller one, the Pyramid of the Moon, are almost complete.

Subtitle: "Teotihuacan, Mexico. The vernal equinox."

NARRATOR (V.O.)

Tezcatilpoca's first temple still remains in Central America. It became the foundation of what became the Temple of the Moon.

The city is a bustle of activity as giants, coneheads, Native American slaves, and others are busy working.

The Pyramid of the Moon, sitting at the northern end of the Street of the Dead, is where water begins flowing from.

We SEE water flowing down past the Pyramid of the Sun on its way to the Citadel, where the Pyramid of Quetzalcoatl sits.

The water then FLOWS another two kilometers PAST the Citadel.

NARRATOR (V.O.)

Teotihuacan, the City of the Gods, lies at exactly 19.5 degrees N. latitude. The same axis the Osireion was built at Abydos in Upper Egypt. Here the energy of the sun was again harnessed by separating the isotopes of hydrogen from water. After separating the heavy water from the ordinary water, the Pyramid of the Sun performed a very important function.

INT. PYRAMID OF THE SUN—UPPER ROOMS

Here we SEE several giants installing a thick and extensive layer of mica into the floor between the pyramid's two upper levels.

NARRATOR (V.O.)

Mica…used in the construction of capacitors and is valued as a thermal and electric insulator.

It is also opaque to fast neutrons and acts as a
moderator in nuclear reactions.

INT. CAVE UNDERNEATH

Where a subterranean passageway LEADS to a natural cave running
eastward towards the pyramid's geometrical center.

The cave opens into a second and much larger cave that's been carved
out into a four-leaf clover shape.

Each of the four 'leaves' or chambers is roughly sixty feet in circumference. A high-tech circular machine sits inside each room.

> NARRATOR (V.O.)
>
> These atom smashers allowed them to produce
> atomic weapons and hydrogen bombs. They
> needed these iron thunderbolts or flying serpents for global domination.

Water and hydrogen filters into the rooms through a complex system of
interlocking segments of carved rock pipes.

Men wearing iron gloves safely handle the radioactive materials. They
observe their work using highly polished, angled mirrors.

> NARRATOR (V.O.)
>
> Iron gloves had to be worn by those who made
> Thor's hammer…

EXT. CHICHEN ITZA—DAY

A snake-like SHADOW slithers up the northern side of a step pyramid.

NARRATOR (V.O.)

This pyramid was named after Kukulcan and Quetzalcoatl. Another name for Nimrod was Vulcan, which comes from Khukhold, or King of the World. The legend of the Cyclops comes from Kuclops, Kings of the Flame. Three horns and three eyes, with one of them in the fore-head, represented them. Legends of Cyclops with ONE eye in the forehead came from this.

We SEE a missile with an eye surrounded by rays of light painted on the nose. The missile is launched!

NARRATOR (V.O.)

Legends say Vulcan was the forger of the thunderbolts said to have wreaked havoc among the enemies of the gods. His symbol was placed upon his weapons.

We FOLLOW this missile all the way to...

EXT. ABYDOS (UPPER EGYPT)—DAY

...where it falls harmlessly on the ground. Several Egyptian priests run towards it upon realizing the missile isn't going to explode.

NARRATOR (V.O.)

Success...takes time.

EXT. THE NILE—THIRTEEN BOATS

Are rowing up the Nile. Each boat carries a different son or daughter of

Thouros, who's leading the procession in his own boat.

All twelve sons and daughters have large saucer-shaped eyes and huge eyebrows. The men have braided hair and beards.

> NARRATOR (V.O.)
>
> Thouros had five sons and seven daughters. His youngest son was named...Saturn.

EXT. OSIREION—MINUTES LATER

The boats are moored in the background. The twelve giant children follow their father towards the Temple. Thouros makes his way to the top.

> THOUROS
>
> Today, we bury our boats in the sand. We leave behind this mode of transportation as we've been given flying chariots from our brothers in the heavens...where we shall fly with the hawk.

EXT. HELIOPOLIS (SUN CITY)—DAY

Several PRIESTS are watching other dark-skinned Egyptians construct small pyramids here. One priest holds a disk-shaped calendar.

INSERT—CALENDAR

Divided into twelve sections. There are thirty dots representing days within each of the twelve sections.

BACK TO SCENE

> NARRATOR (V.O.)
>
> The Egyptian calendar based on the helical rising of the star Sirius. This disk-shaped, yearly renewing wheel was the forerunner of the satanic wheel of Paganism, devoting eight sections to its eight pagan gods. It was the basis for the Buddhist Wheel of Life and finally evolved into the symbol of the double cross.

> PRIEST ONE
>
> Sirius has not yet risen on the horizon. We cannot celebrate the New Year until then.

> PRIEST TWO
>
> Our calendar ends soon. If the Nile doesn't send its annual flood, I'm afraid we're due a most severe famine.

> PRIEST ONE
>
> Sirius will reappear and the New Year will begin and the Nile will give us its abundant waters. You must always be watching for Sirius to rise on the horizon.

EXT. GIZA PLATEAU (LOWER EGYPT)—LATER

A group of Egyptians LOOK along the horizon towards the rising sun. A bright, multicolored star is CLIMBING above the horizon.

CROWD'S POV—SKY

The object looks like a bright fireball, twinkling as it comes down.
As it gets CLOSER, its brightness dwarfs the sun directly overhead.

EXT. VALLEY TEMPLE (GIZA)—MINUTES LATER

We now SEE that the fireball is some kind of golden space ship, utilizing a fiery propulsion system to light up the sky.

Helicopter blades stabilize the descending craft, easing it to an upright position alongside the Valley Temple's water-worn walls.

EXT. CLOSE ON—SHIP

We SEE it's the flying serpent himself, Satan. His snake-like appearance is accented by the cobra-look of multicolored stones covering over his head...the look of future Egyptian pharaohs!

His six golden wings drop to his side as he LOOKS OUT at the crowd, members of which have fallen to the ground in obvious reverence and fear.

From within his midsection comes the dwarf Apollyon accompanied by a conehead from Peru. His cone-shaped head is covered by an Atef or dome-shaped gold crown.

The crowd stares at these three unusual creatures in fear.

> APOLLYON
>
> Greetings from the Dog Star Sirius and your first king, Ra.

> NARRATOR (V.O.)

Named after Nimrod, known as the ROD that

ruled, or Ra, for short.

EXT. GIZA PLATEAU—DAY—SEVERAL WEEKS LATER

OUR VIEW of the lion starts at the base, RISING until we SEE the finished product: our modern-day sphinx!

Satan's freshly carved serpent-shaped head bearing a man's face out of the lion's head, contrasts the older water-worn lower section.

Our VIEW INCLUDES the remodeled Valley Temple. The ENGINEER giant carves out the last granite block that conforms to the water-weathering patterns on the old wall originally built by Seth's line.

The dwarf-sized Apollyon PLAYS his TRUMPET, lifting the stone into its final resting place, neatly fitting into the weathered patterns and interlocking jigsaw puzzle wall.

> APOLLYON
> (to Engineer)
>
> We'll tunnel through here and meet you in Abydos.

INT. UNDER PAW OF SPHINX—UNDERGROUND TUNNEL

We see some underground tunneling in the b.g. as Apollyon enters the tunnel. Satan follows, holding a round tablet made from an unknown metal with mysterious writing upon it.

Satan looks at the tablet and adds a few more glyphs and markings.

> SATAN
>
> Divide this into three sections. Bury one in the tunnel, which leads here under the Sphinx. Bring the second with us. We'll bury it in the

New World. Give me the third piece. I have special plans for that one.

INSERT—METAL DISK-SHAPED OBJECT

With strange markings resembling hieroglyphs. Another set of glyphs resembles our DNA strand with pairs of chromosomes lined up.

BACK TO SCENE

> SATAN
> (referring to
> tablets)

One day, that which has been scattered will be united again.

> APOLLYON

It's time for our fallen comrades to help us now. We must again intervene in the affairs of man and impart our divine wisdom.

> SATAN

After we've tunneled in Egypt, go to the plateau of Tibet. We must start tunneling there. With any luck, we'll find where Samyaza and Azazyel are buried.

EXT. HELIOPOLIS (EGYPT)—DAY

Two hundred fallen angels stand around a recently completed temple, the Mansion of the Phoenix. Apollyon stands before them with their two highest-ranking captains by his side, YEKUN and KESABEL.

APOLLYON

Comrades, you've been chosen by lot to fulfill a most important mission. To lead men astray from God with knowledge that will puff up their pride. Soon they'll think of themselves as gods.

YEKUN

And as if that's not going to be enough fun, some of you get to mate with their women. We need many races of giants to inhabit the Promised Land.

KESABEL

We'll cast lots for the privilege of fathering nations. The rest of you have your assignments.

The angels split up into groups as they eagerly cast lots and head off in different directions, based on the result of the lottery.

NARRATOR (V.O.)

Yekun and Kesabel, two of the original archangels, were the two leaders who convinced the others to mate with women.

EXT. ATHENS (GREECE)—DAY

Another fallen archangel, GADREL, instructs a group of men gathered in a secret meeting. He's showing them how to make instruments of death such as knives, swords, shields, etc.

He also instructs them how to make a coat of mail.

> GADREL
>
> Now, to make a sword, you need iron ore. This process is what I'll show you today. But before I demonstrate this, Kasyade is going to teach you the art of focusing all your spiritual energies to deal a deathblow without the need of weapons.

The crowd of men AD LIB their excitement and approval.

> KASYADE
>
> The wicked strokes of spirits and demons, the stroke of the embryo, you must learn to focus all your energies. Let us demonstrate.

The angels begin fighting using advanced martial arts techniques.

> NARRATOR (V.O.)
>
> And the game known as Pancratium, or Thunderbolt Fists, began its popularity among the lovers of violence. Using only their feet or fists as weapons, the only rule was…in the end, only one man could be left standing. It evolved into martial arts. Indian Yogis added the spiritual aspects to these invading Aryan games. Pearl diving Chinese Daoists added breath control when this style of fighting entered into Shao Lin Ji's walls. Pure choreographed fluid

movements became known as Gong Fu, or Kung Fu, the Masterful Art.

EXT. SUMERIA (ASSYRIA, MODERN IRAQ)—DAY

Several scribes, holding soft and wet clay tablets, are sitting around the fallen angel Penemue as he's teaching them how to write.

> NARRATOR (V.O.)
>
> Ever wonder why writing appeared overnight? Satan knew God would soon make a written covenant with man so he wanted to write his story first. The fallen Prince Penemue would become one of seven earthly princes by becoming the Prince of Assyria, the second of seven kingdoms. Since the voice of an archangel is like a trumpet sound, he was able to teach the secret wisdom of writing using the shape of a trumpet.

INSERT—CLAY TABLET

Penemue's hand is making cuneiform, wedge-shaped writing in the moist clay. Each of these wedges resembles a miniature trumpet.

BACK TO SCENE

> PENEMUE
>
> Now, today I'll be dictating the Epic of Gilgamesh.

All the young scribes look at each other in confusion.

PENEMUE

It's a collection of myths and legends with our hero Gilgamesh covering a great span of time…going back to the beginning and ahead…into the future.

We SEE several small gypsum statues resembling the wide-eyed giants with their large brow bridges. Some of them are shaved bald; others with braided hair and beards. Most wear long skirts.

NARRATOR (V.O.)

Satan's leaders encouraged mankind to make idols from clay.

On a wall in the b.g. is a relief carving of a man wearing the head of a fish, which forms a mitre above the man's head. The fish continues as a scaly cloak on the man's back.

NARRATOR (V.O.)

Penemue's stories made Noah into the fish god Dagon with his two-horned mitre. The original eight Pagan gods represented the eight people on the ark. Noah also became Janus, the two-faced man with one face looking into the Old World and the other into the new one after the flood. Janus later became the god who could open and shut the doors of heaven with his key, representing the many incarnations of Nimrod. Semiramis became Cybele, the other deity holding a key opening Heaven to men on Earth. Pagans prayed THROUGH these two false mediators with their two keys.

EXT. ATHENS (GREECE)—NIGHT—LATER

All men previously seen learning how to fight are sitting around a campfire, listening to Gadrel. The men are bruised and bandaged.

> GADREL
>
> Tonight, I'll tell you where giants come from. When the blood of Uranus falls into the lap of Gaea, this produces giants.

All of the men are scratching their heads, confused.

> GADREL
>
> Oh good grief, do I have to start with the birds and the bees?

> NARRATOR (V.O.)
>
> The blood of Uranus, which means Heaven, was the life or seed of fallen angels. It fell, because the angels fell, into the lap of Gaea, which means Earth in the feminine. The lap was the reproductive organs of a woman, which are made from the Earth or clay. These legends survived unto the days of Rome.

EXT. HERMOPOLIS MAGNA (EGYPT)—DAY

Several scribes, holding a quill and papyrus, sit around the fallen angel Penemue as he teaches them how to write.

NARRATOR (V.O.)

He taught the use of ink and paper. They deified him as Thoth, the Egyptian god of learning, letters, and wisdom.

INSERT—PAPYRUS

Penemue dips the quill in the ink and makes hieroglyphs for a phonetic picture language. He circles the glyphs with an oval-shaped cartouche, resembling the shape of Satan's monitor.

BACK TO SCENE

PENEMUE

Today, I'll be dictating the story of Osiris, Isis, and Horus.

He holds up a drawing of an Egyptian mother holding a child.

NARRATOR (V.O.)

The images remained the same, only the names were changed. Nimrod became Osiris, Semiramis was Isis, and Ninus was Horus, the hawk god because of his flight capabilities. The story of Seth killing his brother Osiris was really a rehashing of the true story about Shem, a descendant of Seth, killing Nimrod. Horus avenged his father's death by unleashing the powers of nature, actually…giants…on his murderers, or the righteous seed of Seth. Osiris' name came from Sirius.

Penemue now holds up a drawing of two jackals.

> PENEMUE
>
> In the Book of the Dead, Anubis and Upuaut are two jackal gods. Anubis was the jackal-headed guardian of the secrets and god of the funerary chamber. He was the "opener of the ways" of the dead and also the guide and companion of Osiris. Upuaut, companion of Anubis, was also "opener of the ways."

> NARRATOR (V.O.)
>
> Jackals were wild dogs in Asia. Sirius, the Dog Star was represented here as Anubis. Apollyon, his companion, represented Upuaut. Remember the gods Pluto and his companion Charon? You're catching on...

INT. FUNERAL CHAMBERS

Two priests are showing long, sad faces as they pray over a dead man's body. His widow gives them large sums of money.

> NARRATOR (V.O.)
>
> Since Penemue also possessed magical powers of healing, he became the patron of physicians. As students of life and death, they charged great amounts of money for their services. Even for long prayers for the dead.

EXT. ANCIENT MOHENJO-DARO (PAKISTAN)—DAY

Iron flying machines now look like modern jets complete with tail rudders and capable of carrying several people at a time.

Penemue makes notes detailing the accounts of these flying machines.

> NARRATOR (V.O.)
>
> He wrote an instruction manual for these advanced flying machines and also technical manuals for building them. They survive today in Sanskrit as…the Veda's.

EXT. PLATEAU OF TIBET (CHINA)—DAY

Satan joins several fallen angels, giants, and slaves tunneling.

> SATAN
>
> Samyaza and Azazyel are under here somewhere…keep digging.

Apollyon joins them, running up to Satan with urgency.

> APOLLYON
>
> If we are to succeed in our mission to the red planet, we should act now or be forced to wait another hundred years.

> SATAN
> (looking around)

Here…we'll resurrect the past. Our past.

EXT. PALENQUE, NEAR LA VENTA (CENTRAL AMERICA)—DAY

A huge rocket ship sits on the stone platform atop a ziggurat. We HEAR someone O.S. counting down to "zero" as the ship lifts off.

In the f.g. is a stone carving of a man sitting inside a feathered serpent. His headdress is huge. To its left is something square with two X-shaped crosses. It's an artist's depiction of a man inside a flying serpent. The square object is a monitor.

> NARRATOR (V.O.)
>
> Not only did the Prince of the Air teach men to fly, he allowed them to boldly go where no man had gone before.

EXT. EARTH'S ORBIT—OUTER SPACE

The rocket ship BLASTS past us. As it does, it loses its main section revealing that it's a multistage rocket.

> NARRATOR (V.O.)
>
> Passengers were carried inside the *third* section. Every 108 years, alternating in the spring and fall, Earth's orbit crossed paths with Mars—a lingering condition from Tiamait's explosion. This caused hail mixed with fire to fall and lightning to arc between the two planets. But while this close to Earth, these demigods went to build a fortress of safety.

EXT. CYDONIA REGION (MARS)—DAY

The red planet has little oxygen; therefore giants roam around in space suits with oxygen packs strapped in front.

Satan and Apollyon survey the undeveloped region. Apollyon looks into Satan's monitor, where we can SEE the Giza pyramids on Earth.

> SATAN
>
> We'll build pyramids of our own here. We'll carve out a face like the one now on the Lion. This way we'll carry out my plan of deception...the big lie...in the final days.

> APOLLYON
>
> Anything God's people make, we'll make a counterfeit. In time, people will forget who really started what. With time on our side, we can tell future generations whatever we want.

> NARRATOR (V.O.)
>
> And so the Cydonia region on Mars was patterned after Giza in many ways. However, the pyramids were made from glass to function as oxygen-producing greenhouses.

EXT. CYDONIA—DAY—PYRAMID CONSTRUCTION

They're keeping oxygen trapped under their pyramid-shaped canopies.

The engineer who carved the lion's face on Earth carves a face from stone while looking at his Giza handiwork through Satan's monitor.

Apollyon admires the resemblance both carvings have to Satan's man-like face, which he used to make when combined with other cherubim.

APOLLYON

Excellent! We should send him back before the
launch window closes and our orbits separate.

EXT. FAR SIDE OF EARTH'S MOON—BARELY LIT

We SEE a secret base with glass domes enclosing it. Plants are growing
in greenhouses, producing oxygen for these domed cities.

NARRATOR (V.O.)

These giants needed reassurance that when
God did purify Earth with fire, they could get
to your moon and then, safely to Mars.

EXT. ABYDOS (EGYPT)—DAY

Advanced flying machines fill the sky now, including helicopters that
look amazingly like our modern Apaches.

One FIRES an iron thunderbolt, OBLITERATING its target.

INT. HELICOPTER

The pilot wears an Atef crown, which is somehow attached to the
weapons directional firing system. As his head turns, so does the turret
holding the iron thunderbolts.

INT. PHOENIX MANSION (HELIOPOLIS)—DAY

A scribe sits inside the temple. He draws hieroglyphs on papyrus. He
draws an object in front of him.

INSERT—PAPYRUS

He's drawing pictures resembling many of the aircraft we've seen in India, Central America, and here in Egypt. He puts final touches on the drawing of an Apache-type helicopter.

> NARRATOR (V.O.)
>
> These images would be placed on a stone beam in a future temple built in Abydos by Seti I honoring Osiris. Flying serpents were depicted in Egyptian art as snakes with two legs and two wings. Historian Sanchuniation wrote in 1250 BC: "The snake has a speed that nothing can exceed because of its breath...its energy is exceptional...it has illuminated everything with its gleam." Does this sound like an ordinary snake...or a rocket?

BACK TO SCENE

In front of the scribe, sits a rocket standing upon a stone.

> NARRATOR (V.O.)
>
> Located here in the City of the Sun, this missile would be remembered as the Benben stone. It didn't explode when it fell from the sky and became an object of reverence, surviving unto Hitler's day. It was once balanced upon a pillar of stone resembling the pad used to launch them. It was well known that the sun's energy was harnessed in its top, causing people to revere its pyramidal shape. This started the tra-

dition of naming the apex stone, the Benben, which was placed on top of pyramids.

EXT. NAZCA PLAIN—FOGGY—THE AIRPORT

Is very quiet due to the foggy conditions.

INT. NEARBY CAVE—A NATIVE NAZCAN SLAVE WOMAN

HEARS her baby CRYING and takes off her papoose. Upon taking the baby out, we SEE planks tied around its head.

> NARRATOR (V.O.)
>
> Natives imitated the look of their demigods by using planks to sculpt the skull of their babies. Anything to get better treatment.

The woman's husband draws pictures on their cave walls in the b.g.

INSERT—WALL

He's drawing men in space suits, like the ones we saw on Mars.

INT. MAIN ZIGGURAT

There seems to be mass hysteria as coneheaded demigods and giants are busily moving about, exchanging heated words.

> CONEHEAD
>
> Nobody has heard from him? He left the red planet weeks ago!

GIANT

My flight arrived on schedule…after his!

DEMIGOD

The Master won't be happy. Organize a search party immediately!

GIANT

But the fog hasn't lifted for days. We can barely see the end of the runway for takeoff.

CONEHEAD

The Master returns to his island in the Atlantic tomorrow…I'll let you explain your incompetence.

GIANT

I'll search the coastline. But we'll need a more advanced Vimana from Mohenjo-Daro.

CONEHEAD

One is being repaired as we speak and will join your fleet of Condors, Hawks, and Hummingbirds.

The giant grabs his flight helmet and is escorted by several other giants as they storm out of the building.

EXT. EASTER ISLAND—FOGGY

The engineer has apparently become shipwrecked in the fog as we SEE his badly damaged ship in the b.g.

He's writing on wooden tablets and is making various notes to himself as if recording his thoughts in a journal.

INSERT—WOODEN TABLETS

Show picture writing using strange glyphs.

INT. MOHENJO-DARO—ENGINEER'S HOME—SAME TIME

Where several giants are helping his WIFE look through several of his manuscripts written with the same glyphs.

> WIFE
>
> I can't find anything indicating he had plans to stop anywhere before returning to Nazca.

> GIANT
>
> We've organized a search party. The latest Vimana capable of sensing heat should be repaired soon and joining our search.

EXT. TULA (NEAR TEOTIHUACAN)—DAY—FOGGY

Tensions here are being taken out on the playing field where the demigods challenge slaves to the dreaded games.

EXT. PLAYING FIELD

Two teams, represented by puma and condor emblems embroidered on their colorful jerseys, take turns playing against teams of slaves.

As slaves are defeated, they're beheaded and their flesh eaten. Some victors flay the dead men and wear the skin over their own bodies, parading in front of spectators.

EXT. NAZCA CITY—DAY—FOGGY

A coneheaded PRIEST wears a headdress of Quetzal feathers, hiding his cone-shaped skull. He drills a hole in a dead conehead's skull.

> PRIEST
>
> This frees your spirit brother.

> NARRATOR (V.O.)
>
> Since they knew they'd never be resurrected, they felt this was the only way to separate their spirit from the dead flesh.

EXT. NEAR SODOM AND GOMORRAH (CANAAN)—DAY

Abraham is on his knees praying to God.

> ABRAHAM
>
> You have helped me before in battles against the giants to save my brother's son, Lot. I pray to you on his behalf again.

INT. GOD'S THRONE ROOM (HEAVEN)

God watches all the events on the monitors of all four cherubim.

> GOD
>
> Man was scattered and his language confused for building towers of destruction but the fallen Prince has united them again. Satan tries to force my hand and avert his own destiny. We must intervene…again.

The seven holy archangels magically appear before God.

> GOD
>
> Incite warfare among the giants and demigods. They will destroy themselves. Make sure every weapon of advanced technology is removed from the Earth. Let them destroy their bases on the moon and Mars. I'll take care of the two most-wicked cities myself. Cherubs, prepare for flight.

EXT. EGYPTIAN SKIES—DAY

Demigods are pawns in a war where most of them kill each other off.

> NARRATOR (V.O.)
>
> Egyptologists would call this…the end of the first time.

As we SEE the souls of the newly slain giants and demigods become disembodied spirits or demons, they shake their fists at the sky.

DEMON

We'll have our revenge on man this same way. We'll provoke them in their minds and hearts, causing them to hate one another and constantly fight each other 'til they're all dead!

EXT. MOHENJO-DARO'S SKIES

There is much warfare in the air over India by the demigod factions.

NARRATOR (V.O.)

"They hurled against the cities a single projectile, known as Indra's dart, charged with all the power of the universe. A column of smoke and fire, as brilliant as ten thousand suns, rose in all its splendor." Translated from Sanskrit, this account was found in an ancient Indian poem, the Mahabharatra. Other accounts were recorded in the Rigveda, the Ramayana, and the Chaldean Sifrila.

EXT. MOHENJO-DARO'S CITY STREETS

Many dead bodies are lying all over the ground.

NARRATOR (V.O.)

Like the mummies of Egypt, when these bodies were excavated, they were highly radioactive. The Mahabharatra explained that entire races were reduced to ashes. Those that lived soon died from radiation poisoning as their hair and nails fell out. Only those dwelling in caves underground survived.

INT. MOHENJO-DARO—UNDERGROUND TUNNEL

The repair shop where the super-advanced Vimana was being worked on is where we find the youngest son of Thouros, SATURN.

A dark-skinned Canaanite and several giants are with him. Lights flicker as they lose power in the tunnel.

> SATURN
>
> We've got to get out of here. We'll head through the northeast tunnel back to Tibet and Gobi.

> NARRATOR (V.O.)
>
> Their large eyes allowed them to see well in total darkness.

EXT. OUTER SPACE—ABOVE MARS

Mars continues its erratic orbit, passing VERY CLOSE to Earth.

Suddenly, LIGHTNING BOLTS cover the sky.

The bolts of lightning are being created by the closeness of the passing Martian planet and Earth. The bolts arc between the two planets. The path of lightning sears the surface of Mars.

A large battle ensues near Pyramid City. Giants destroy each other.

Underground bases EXPLODE, causing oxygen domes to collapse. Domes shatter into millions of molten glass droplets.

EXT. EARTH'S MOON—FAR SIDE—MOON BASES

Are destroyed in similar fashion, killing all giants here.

Their bodies float into outer space with most of the debris.

EXT. EASTER ISLAND—DAY

Dozens of stone statues now line the shores facing towards the sea. Statues in fields look up at the sky.

The engineer lies dying next to his disabled ship.

> ENGINEER
>
> They'll see these statues from the sea or air and rescue me.

EXT. BABEL—ZIGGURAT REMAINS—DAY

Earthquakes from nearby explosions break up the hydrogen-producing ziggurat in Babel, erasing Nimrod's greatest feat.

EXT. DEVIL'S ISLAND (NEAR SARGASSO SEA)—DAY

The remaining island of the former Atlantis breaks up, causing most to sink into the blue abyss of the Sargasso Sea.

What's left splits into three smaller islands.

This commotion upsets a school of eels migrating here from afar.

Satan's followers leave in boats, witnessing the destruction of their island home. People wail their CRIES for the fallen city.

They are rowing in the general direction of the Mediterranean Sea.

EXT. SODOM AND GOMORRAH—AERIAL VIEW

God rains down fire and brimstone on these cities from his cherubim.

EXT. CITY'S OUTSKIRTS—PILLAR OF SALT

Shaped like a woman, faces the city under siege. A man and two young girls run past, escaping the expanding fallout.

EXT. NAZCA PLAINS—GIANTS

And cone-headed demigods litter the landscape, all dead.
Liberated slaves castrate and deface statues of the giants.
They begin burying the radioactive cities that made them slaves.

NARRATOR (V.O.)

Thanks to strict government controls, less than one-percent of these pyramid cities have been uncovered…under the cover of native religious superstition.

Flying machines are being burned, along with all weapons of war.

NARRATOR (V.O.)

History will repeat itself when Jews burn weapons of Armageddon.

As we move in CLOSE on the FIRE, we

DISSOLVE TO:

EXT. ISRAEL (NEAR BETHLEHEM)—AN OPEN FIELD—NIGHT

Where several shepherds are sitting beside a FIRE as they tend to their sheep.

Subtitle: "Near the city of David. Circa 3 BC."

Suddenly a BRIGHT LIGHT appears overhead above them. An ANGEL'S VOICE is HEARD from the light. The men fall to their knees.

> ANGEL (O.S.)
>
> Fear not: for, behold, I bring you good tidings of great joy, which shall be to all people. For unto you is born this day in the city of David a Saviour, which is Christ the Lord. And this shall be a sign unto you; Ye shall find the babe wrapped in swaddling clothes, lying in a manger.

EXT. BETHLEHEM—INN COURTYARD—SAME TIME

We see the baby boy, Jesus, lying in a manger being attended to by his mother and father, Mary and Joseph.

> NARRATOR (V.O.)
>
> Glory to God in the highest, and on Earth peace, good will toward men. Mankind's Redeemer had arrived right on schedule.

EXT. THE ABYSS—CLOSE ON—SATAN

As he starts LAUGHING hysterically. Demons and fallen angels outside of the abyss are also LAUGHING.

Subtitle: "Thirty-three years later."

INT. THE ABYSS

More demons are LAUGHING from their underground prison. They're watching video monitors hanging from above, arranged in a way that resembles a sports bar.

Our VIEW WIDENS as we see what they're laughing at.

EXT. GOLGOTHA—NOON

We SEE three crosses on the hill of Golgotha.

Subtitle: "Jerusalem, circa 30 AD. Golgotha."

JESUS CHRIST hangs on the middle cross.

> NARRATOR (V.O.)
>
> Golgotha...the place of the skull or calvaria. Christians look upon this place with great reverence. But the devil, always quick to combine evil with good, associated pornography with the sign of the triple cross...triple X.

Satan is SEEN watching this. Jesus is in much pain.

> SATAN
> (laughing)
>
> Look at the promised one now. Some redeemer...

Thousands of God's holy angels INVISIBLY surround Jesus, CRYING.

Demons and fallen angels join in with LAUGHTER again, making fun of the crying angels. The sky becomes very dark now, concerning all.

Subtitle: "Three hours later."

The skies are very dark now.

DISSOLVE TO:

EXT. CENTRAL AMERICA—STORMY DAY—HIGH ANGLE

A huge storm brews in the Atlantic. It originates at 19.5 degrees south latitude where warm waters flow off the coast of Peru.

The four angels who hold back the winds unleash the first hurricane, which blows across NEW Atlantis, a large island southeast of Florida.

NARRATOR (V.O.)

Evil men began rebuilding on Eden's remains. Satan always tried to control the region where his mortal enemy began. There arose a great storm, such a one as never known before.

EXT. TIAHUANACO—DARK AND STORMY—NATIVES

WATCH with wonder as their human sacrifices are interrupted by the darkness and approaching hurricanes. The WIND picks up more.

One native stops eating the flesh of a sacrificed victim.

Many priests are naked and covered with the blood of their victims. Some wear the skins flayed from their victims.

Some men, dressed like women, are *with* other men.

INT. GOD'S THRONE ROOM (HEAVEN)—CLOSE ON GOD

His eyes well-up with tears. SOUNDS from Earth ECHO all around.

JESUS (O.S.)

My God, My God...why hast thou forsaken me?

God sheds a tear. As the tear drops, we FOLLOW it all the way to

EXT. GOLGOTHA—3:00 PM—CLOSE ON JESUS

The teardrop FALLS, becoming the first raindrop to LAND on Jesus' forehead. He takes his final breath.

> JESUS
>
> It is finished.

His head drops as he exhales and dies.

RAIN begins to POUR as an EARTHQUAKE shakes everything. The SOUND of THUNDER booms while FLASHES of LIGHTNING light up the area.

INT. JEWISH TEMPLE—HIGH PRIEST

Cuts the throat of the sacrificial lamb before Passover.

> HIGH PRIEST
>
> It is finished.

The tall veil separating the inner court TEARS from top to bottom.

> NARRATOR (V.O.)
>
> Access to God by Jew and Gentile alike was now available.

EXT. NEW ATLANTIS—SAME TIME

The earthquake is felt here, combining with the first hurricane to sink the entire island known as "New Atlantis."

NARRATOR (V.O.)

The great city did sink into the depths of the sea, and the inhabitants thereof were drowned. Book of Mormon.

EXT. SOUTHERN TIP OF SOUTH AMERICA

Where Antarctica is still attached, FEELS the effects of the EARTHQUAKE. Separating, Antarctica drifts to its current position.

EXT. GOLGOTHA—RAINING

LONGINUS, a Roman centurion from Germany, has one eye that's completely white. It looks blinded from a war injury.

He LOOKS UP as he pierces Jesus' side with his spear.

Some of Jesus' blood splatters into his bad eye, healing it!

As sight returns, he looks at the Redeemer's lifeless body.

LONGINUS
(kneeling)

I see! I can see! Truly this man was the Son of God!

Longinus holds the spear while rain washes the blood from its tip.

NARRATOR (V.O.)

This became known as the Sword of Destiny. Whoever held it held the power of the world's governments. All world leaders sought this great sword. Hitler took his own life just hours after he lost possession of it.

EXT. SARGASSO SEA

Nothing remains of New Atlantis, only eels and seaweed.

NARRATOR (V.O.)

It came to pass that when the thundering, the lightning, the storm, and the quaking of the Earth did cease—for behold, they did last about the space of three hours...

EXT. JESUS' TOMB—SUNSET—JESUS' WRAPPED BODY

Is in the b.g. as a stone rolls over the opening, sealing it.

FADE TO: BLACK.

EXT. CENTRAL AMERICA—DARKNESS

FROM BLACK: A single torch lights scared faces of survivors.

NARRATOR (V.O.)

...then there was darkness upon the face of the land...and it did last for three days. Mormon.

INT. PARADISE CHAMBER—IN THE EARTH

Jesus is preaching to the fallen angels bound in the abyss. These angels were bound before the flood by the holy archangels.

He also comforts the souls being held captive here by Satan.

NARRATOR (V.O.)

Paradise moved from Heaven to below the

surface of the Earth after the fall. Heaven, now
sanctified by His blood, made it possible for
Paradise's return.

The thief that was on the cross beside Jesus is among them.

We also SEE Abel and others, including Adam and Eve's spirit.

EXT. JESUS' TOMB—SUNRISE

Subtitle: "End of third day."

A great earthquake shakes the tomb, causing the stone to roll away.

A bright light from within is REVEALED to be Jesus as he walks out
past guards who've passed out from fear.

EXT. GRAVEYARD (JERUSALEM)—SUNRISE

We SEE graves emptied as dead saints come out and appear to people.
They are the 144,000 first fruits of the resurrection. We SEE the resurrected bodies of Noah and Abel.

> NARRATOR (V.O.)
>
> And the Earth did quake, and the rocks rent,
> and the graves were opened, and many bodies
> of the saints, which slept, arose and came out of
> the graves and went into the Holy City and
> appeared unto many. Matthew 27:51-53.

EXT. GIZA PLATEAU—SUNRISE

This earthquake causes the 144,000 white outer casing stones on the
Great Pyramid to come loose. One stone covering the airshaft over the
northern end of the King's Chamber falls off.

INT. GREAT PYRAMID—KING'S CHAMBER

Adam's dust comes from the sarcophagus and OUT the airshaft.

EXT. GREAT PYRAMID

His dust joins with his spirit, which hovers just outside the pyramid's airshaft. He's reunited with his resurrected body.

INT. SECOND PYRAMID

The lid atop Eve's sarcophagus quickly slides off and falls to the floor, breaking it. The dust of her body exits an airshaft exposed by the removal of its outer casing stones.

EXT. SECOND PYRAMID

Eve's spirit and body now join as we SEE her resurrected body.

EXT. THIRD PYRAMID

We see the resurrected bodies of Seth, Enos, Cainan, Mahalaleel, Jared, Lamech and Methuselah, the firstborn righteous sons.

NARRATOR (V.O.)

The legends that the pyramids transformed a soul after death, then shot them up into the heavens where they became stars, or like angels…were true. John, the author of "REVE-LATION," would even confuse these last seven men…with angels.

EXT. THE SPHINX

A bolt of LIGHTNING strikes off the nose of the sphinx.

EXT. CENTRAL AMERICA—DARK

Out of darkness, we SEE a light approaching from across the water.

The coastline becomes visible, revealing huge amounts of foam along beaches, caused by strong winds pounding waves onto the coast.

As the light gets closer, we SEE it's Jesus and the 144,000 saints.

Some NATIVES SEE the outline of Jesus coming through the foam.

> NATIVE ONE

Quetzalcoatl!

> NATIVE TWO

Viracocha!

> NARRATOR (V.O.)

Viracocha…whose name *means* foam of the sea…was Jesus.

EXT. MEXICO CITY—DAY

Jesus is SEEN teaching good things to many people and tribes.

> NARRATOR (V.O.)

Local legends state he wore a long, white robe. He condemned human sacrifices and was known as the god of peace, teaching couples to live together as husband and wife.

EXT. ATLANTIC OCEAN (AMERICA'S COASTLINE)—SUNRISE—
DAYS LATER

Jesus is leaving with the 144,000 by boat, the same way he came…towards the rising sun in the east.

JESUS

I'll return someday.

NARRATOR (V.O.)

He witnessed for forty days to the four corners of the Earth before his ascension into Heaven. On the fiftieth day, the day of Pentecost, the Holy Spirit would come like a rushing wind.

EXT. SARGASSO SEA—WINDY

As they leave, several hurricanes are brewing and passing over the sea where Atlantis and New Atlantis used to be.

NARRATOR (V.O.)

Hurricanes would now keep Satan from ever rebuilding there.

Satan and Apollyon are looking out over the area near the Bahamas. Satan is obviously displeased with this unexpected turn of events.

APOLLYON

The redeemer has come, fulfilling God's promise. What now?

Apollyon is scared. It's the first time he's shown fear. Satan tries to reassure him.

SATAN

Since we've failed to prevent his first coming, we'll have to prevent his Second Coming. He can't come back as a Messiah if there are no Jews left to save.

Apollyon's face begins to show a glimmer of hope.

APOLLYON

To insure victory after finishing off the Jews, Christians must be dealt with as well.

SATAN

That's easy. I'll twist my pagan religions into their new church. I'll sow my tares with the good seed. Eventually, they'll choke the very life out of them. I'll take the breath of life He breathed into their clay frames and toss it to the winds.

He looks at all that remains of the islands where he's rebuilt so many times. Eels are all along the surface where his GAZE is fixed.

SATAN

I'll rebuild my throne where God can never destroy it again.

He RISES up and walks upon the water now. He stoops down and picks up an eel, holding it in his hands.

> SATAN
>
> Ah, a serpent that lives in the water. If one day I'm to be the highest-ranking member of the underworld, then that's where I'll rebuild my kingdom.

Storm WINDS suddenly pick up, causing him to fall in the water. Bobbing in water surrounded by eels, he shakes his fist at the sky.

EXT. PARADISE—BELOW GOD'S THRONE

Jesus, holding two keys in his hands, arrives in Paradise with the 144,000 resurrected first fruits and all the righteous souls.

> NARRATOR (V.O.)
>
> Jesus defeated the grave and now possessed the keys to Hell and Death. He was truly the one mediator, or hinge, with the keys that could open and shut the doors or gates to Heaven or Hell. Paradise would no longer be in the bowels of the Earth. It moved below God's throne room.

Jesus sits at His Father's right side. He looks out at the saints.

> JESUS
>
> As a man, I was a carpenter by trade. Now, I'll build all of you a mansion of your very own.

EXT. OUTER SPACE—LEAVING EARTH

Fallen angels are leaving Earth and heading out past our asteroid belt or

228   Revelations

the remains of Tiamait. They weep as they pass by.

Apollyon feels his wrist where the bracelet his sister Laurianna gave him used to be.

Satan and Apollyon head towards Jupiter and Saturn.

> SATAN
>
> I'll go and prepare a place for my children. I'll find a new place among the stones of fire facing the deep. Before I surrender to my destiny, I'll destroy mankind…

> FADE TO: BLACK

VIDEO GLITCH.

Then, a computer readout displays the following words as they are typed ONSCREEN:

> I will open my mouth in a parable. I will utter dark sayings of old, which we have heard and known and our fathers have told us. We will not hide them from our children…

> Psalm 78:2-4

INT. GOD'S THRONE ROOM—DAY—YELLOW LION CHERUB'S MONITOR

Is displaying the info we just read as our VIEW WIDENS.

> LION CHERUB
>
> I've shown you what happened before your

church history began. The Blue Ox Cherub will show you what happened next. Laurianna will continue to explain.

INSERT—CHERUB'S MONITOR

Subtitle:...to be continued in "REVELATIONS II OMEGA."

FADE OUT.

THE END

Revelations II Omega

◆

"John and Ezekiel were given a scroll with words written inside and out. Both were commanded to eat the words and in their mouths the taste would be as honey, but bitter in their belly. Such is a revelation of truth from God containing lamentations, mourning and woe. Divine words are sweet but can be hard on the stomach when full of dark prophecies. Such is this story..." *Laurianna*

The Ending and the Last

FADE IN:

EXT. JERUSALEM—SUNRISE

The city is quiet as the Sabbath is being celebrated by the nation of Israel. We SEE several Orthodox Jews praying at the Temple Wall.

A small group of Palestinian boys TAUNT some of them.

Subtitle: "May 1981. Jerusalem."

The SOUND of MUSIC can be heard in the distance along with the LAUGHTER of women preparing for a Jewish wedding ceremony.

INT. SYNAGOGUE—BRIDESMAID'S CHAMBERS

Several bridesmaids are attending to EVA, thirty-five. KATY, now fifty-two, admires her only daughter. Both are very attractive.

> KATY
>
> Your father would've been so proud to see you
> dressed in your wedding gown. God knows it
> took you long enough.

EVA

Mom...we've talked about this enough. You know the reason I held out this long.

KATY

I know...you didn't want to be heartbroken like your mother. I don't blame you, really. I'm just glad you found a good man.

EVA

Me too. Levi is a very good man.

One of the bridesmaids adds the veil to Eva's long hair.

EVA
(continuing)

You know...Johnny still has feelings for you. I can see it in his eyes.

KATY

Anyone can see that. I think he's just being dutiful to David's memory...taking care of us. Remember that he's paying for your honeymoon.

EVA

I know. I can hardly wait. I've always wanted to go the Bahamas.

Katy adds finishing touches to Eva's hair. She takes her own necklace off, which has David's old watch hanging from it. She dangles the watch from behind her daughter's veil.

KATY

There…something borrowed.

EVA

Mom, are you sure? I know how much that watch means to you.

KATY

David should be part of your special day, don't you think?

A tear rolls down Katy's cheek, noticed by her daughter.

Eva breaks down and CRIES as she hugs her mother.

INT. SYNAGOGUE SANCTUARY—MOMENTS LATER

Processional MUSIC PLAYS as a little girl tossing rose petals walks down the aisle. A little boy carrying rings on a heart-shaped pillow follows her.

Everyone stands as the bride enters.

JOHNNY, now fifty-seven, stands next to Katy.

LEVI stands in front under a canopy or chupah as he watches her.

As Eva joins her fiancé under the canopy, the RABBI begins.

RABBI

Blessed be you who come here in the name of the Lord.

Katy begins to cry as she is overcome with joy for her daughter. Through her tears, we

DISSOLVE TO:

LATER

The ceremony concludes as an empty wineglass is placed on the floor where the groom stomps on it, BREAKING it.

Everyone shouts "Mazel Tov" as they APPLAUD the newlyweds.

While Katy admires her daughter, she has a

FLASHBACK—1945—DAVID'S HIDEOUT

Katy, sixteen and DAVID, twenty, are exchanging their vows. He reaches for a braided hair-wrap in her hair. He breaks it off.

>   KATY

> Ouch!

>   DAVID

> Sorry.

He wraps it around both their wrists as they exchange vows.

>   DAVID

> Do you, Katy Ann Weiss, take me, David Adam
> Smith, to be your lawful wedded husband?

>   KATY

> I do. Now…do you take me for your lawful
> wedded wife?

DAVID
(pretending to
think twice)

Just kidding. Of course I do! And I've got an idea...

David takes off his military watch and places it on her wrist.

Katy reciprocates by tying the hair-wrap around his wrist.

KATY

Wait. We have to break something. It's traditional. It symbolizes the destruction of our temple...our sadness in this time of joy.

They both look around for something. David spots a piece of junk nearby and tosses it out a WINDOW, causing it to BREAK.

DAVID

There. That ought to cover it.

David leans towards Katy. He kisses her on the cheek.

David starts to kiss Katy on the cheek again but she turns towards him and this time their lips meet.

END FLASHBACK

BACK TO SCENE

Katy's teary VISION CLEARS as she SEES the watch adorning her own daughter's hair.

Johnny notices this and reaches out, taking her hand. They embrace.

INT. HONEYMOON HOTEL—THAT NIGHT

Eva is on the phone while her new husband GARGLES in the bathroom nearby. She wears only a sexy nightgown.

> EVA
>
> Mom, will you stop worrying? I'm fine. Yes, I'll call you as soon as we get to the airport tomorrow, okay?

She hangs up the phone as Levi enters their bedroom.

> LEVI
>
> I hope you're done gabbing for the night.

> EVA
>
> You better believe it. Now get over here and fulfill your marriage contract.

The room goes dark as SOUNDS of playful LAUGHTER fill the room.

INT. HOTEL LOBBY—NIGHT

Katy is sitting in the hotel lounge having a drink with Johnny.

> JOHNNY
>
> She looks just like him.

> KATY
>
> I know. Acts just like him too.

JOHNNY

You still miss him, don't you?

KATY

Is it a crime for a girl to carry a torch for the man she loves?

Johnny finishes his drink and motions to the bartender for another.

JOHNNY

Better than me...I'm on my third marriage. Seems I can't find that light. That's reason enough to hold on to its memory, if that's all you have.

KATY

Thank you for all your financial help on the wedding. She's really excited about the cruise.

JOHNNY

It's the very least I could do.

KATY

While I'm at it, thanks for all your help over the years too. If it weren't for you and your family, we would've never made it to our homeland back in 1948.

JOHNNY

You know I wouldn't have had it any other way.

(pause)

So, you think they'll have kids right away?

KATY

She'd better...she's running out of time. She say's she'll adopt if she has to though. She wants two boys.

He NOTICES David's old watch hanging from her neck.

JOHNNY

I see you keep it close to you.

KATY

I still have the hat too, but I think I'd look silly wearing it.

They both LAUGH. The BARTENDER brings Johnny his drink.

BARTENDER

Another one for the lady?

KATY

No thanks. I really should be turning in soon.

JOHNNY

Katy...there's something I've been dying to ask you...

Katy opens her purse and nervously takes out a cigarette.

JOHNNY
(lighting it)

You really should quit. Those things can kill you.

KATY
(exhaling)

You were gonna ask me something?

JOHNNY

Yes...you know, my marriage isn't working out...you're still single...

KATY
(smiling)

This is one hell of a proposal don't you think?

She turns to him with a more serious tone now.

KATY

Johnny, I've always thought you were a very handsome man. You're also very wealthy. A girl would be very lucky to have you and you know it. In fact, you could marry a beauty queen if you wanted. But, I'm done with that whole marriage thing. I had my one true love and I'm happy knowing that. Some people wait all their lives and never find what I had. So what if it didn't last? I'm happy. I have his child. She's all I need. Please tell me you understand.

Johnny manages to crack a smile as he struggles to regain his composure. He tips the bartender and looks at Katy again.

JOHNNY

David always did have exceptional taste. I do understand. Let's never let this come between us.

KATY

I never have.

Johnny rises, offering his hand. She gets up, walking out with him.

INT. HOTEL LOBBY—MINUTES LATER

Johnny waits with Katy in front of the elevator door. As he pushes the up button, we NOTICE a Masonic ring on his middle finger.

JOHNNY

I have to head back to New York. We'll keep in touch?

KATY

Always.

Johnny leans towards Katy, starting to kiss her on the cheek, but she turns towards him as their lips meet. Johnny is surprised and starts to pull away but Katy holds him tighter.

Finally, they separate. Katy looks into his eyes.

KATY

Finally, there's one more thing I can scratch off

my to-do list.

The elevator door opens as Katy walks inside. She turns around, facing Johnny. Johnny is still in shock. She just smiles as the door finally closes.

Johnny turns and slowly walks to the hotel's front door. He turns, looking back at the elevator door. He smiles and finally leaves.

EXT. HOTEL—SUNRISE—NEXT MORNING

The city is back to business as usual as the streets are crowded. From the distance, we SEE a delivery truck approaching the hotel.

INT. EVA'S HONEYMOON SUITE

Eva wakes up to the SOUND of her telephone RINGING. As she picks up, she can see Levi heading towards the door already dressed.

                    EVA

Where are you going so early?

                    LEVI

I'm just going down to the lobby to get a paper.
Need anything?

                    EVA

Just a bagel and lox. And some orange juice. I
love you!

                    LEVI

Love you too. Be right back.

Eva turns her attention to the phone now.

EVA

Hello?

INT. KATY'S HOTEL ROOM

Katy is looking out her penthouse window at the street below.

KATY

You're never going to guess what happened last night.

EVA (O.S.)

I thought that was my line.

KATY

As if I don't know what happened in your world. Just tell me that I'm going to be a grandmother in nine months.

EVA (O.S.)

Oh, I think that's a definite maybe. So what's this big thing you couldn't wait to tell me?

KATY

I kissed Johnny.

INT. EVA'S ROOM

She's getting up now and walks over to the window, opening it.

EVA

No way! Mom…I thought you said…

KATY (O.S.)

It was only a kiss…that's all.

Eva LOOKS out her window, enjoying the sunrise.

As she LOOKS DOWN, she SEES Levi purchasing a newspaper from a vendor across the street from the hotel.

INT. KATY'S ROOM

Katy is now LOOKING at the same thing. WE NOTICE the white delivery truck parking beside the street vendor in the busy shopping area.

KATY

I would never go any further and you know it.

EVA (O.S.)

I know…you're afraid if you get too close to someone that something will happen to them. Do you know how long I lived in fear of being cursed too?

As Katy stares at Levi below, her expression turns to one of fear.

EXT. HOTEL—THE WHITE TRUCK

Parked next to the vendor EXPLODES, apparently a suicide bomber! The vendor and Levi are completely obliterated!

INT. EVA'S ROOM

Eva is looking down in total shock. Katy's VOICE can be heard through her receiver, which Eva has dropped to the floor.

> KATY (O.S.)
> (screaming)

Eva! Eva! Answer me!

Her words hauntingly ECHO as we

> FADE TO: BLACK

VIDEO GLITCH.

FROM BLACK, we begin traveling through space with stars passing us.

> NARRATOR (V.O.)

I guess this is where I come in…again.

> (beat)

John and Ezekiel were given a scroll with words written inside and out. Both were commanded to eat the words and in their mouths the taste would be as honey, but bitter in their belly. Such is a revelation of truth from God containing lamentations, mourning and woe. Divine words are sweet but can be hard on the stomach when full of dark prophecies. Such is this story…

INT. GOD'S THRONE ROOM—DAY—BLUE OX CHERUB'S MONITOR

Displays the visuals from the last scene as our VIEW WIDENS.

> BLUE OX CHERUB
>
> The last time we met, you had finished learning your past before Christ's ascension. I'll show you what happened next.

EXT. TEMPLE COURT—9:00 AM

The disciples are among 120 men gathered and seated in prayer.

Subtitle: "Day of Pentecost."

Suddenly, a mighty rushing wind comes from Heaven above, like when the winds blew about the men working on the tower of Babel.

> NARRATOR (V.O.)
>
> When you combine the heavier isotopes of hydrogen, deuterium and tritium, you get fire. Now that the Son was seated at the right hand of His Father, they were united again. This created…fire!

FIRE appears above the heads of men as they begin speaking AD LIBS in various languages.

A crowd of people from the city has gathered and is amazed to hear these men speaking in their own native tongue.

> NARRATOR (V.O.)
>
> The same spirit that caused confusion at Babel now came to unite all men by giving them utterance and understanding of all tongues.

PETER, one of the twelve disciples, begins to prophesy.

> PETER
>
> In the last days, God will pour out his spirit among all flesh. He will show signs and wonders in Heaven above and Earth below: blood and fire and vapor of smoke. The sun shall be turned into darkness and the moon into blood, before that great and notable day of the Lord.

INT. LIBRARY—NIGHT—A CANDLE

Lights an old, bearded man who is writing in a huge book.

> OLD MAN (V.O.)
>
> They were the inventors of the peculiar wisdom concerned with the heavenly bodies and their order. And that their inventions might not be lost, upon Adam's prediction that the world was to be destroyed at one time by the force of fire, and another time by the violence and quantity of water, they made two pillars; one of brick, the other of stone. These remain in the land of Siriad to this day.

He signs the text, "Flavius Josephus." He closes the book, revealing the title: "JEWISH ANTIQUITIES."

> DISSOLVE TO:

EXT. CAIRO (EGYPT)—DAY

Various ANGLES of the pyramids emphasizing they are made from brick and the sphinx carved from solid stone.

FADE TO: BLACK.

Subtitle: "Rome, 303 AD"

From BLACK, we SEE an apparition appearing in a pool of light.

INT. BEDCHAMBERS—NIGHT—THE EMPEROR DIOCLETIAN

Is on his knees, trembling with fear as the apparition speaks.

APOLLO

Diocletian, I am the Sun God, Apollo. You are the emperor yet Christians refuse to bend even one knee to honor you. Their example will cause Rome to fall to her enemies unless destroyed.

DIOCLETIAN

What am I to do?

APOLLO

They claim to be the light of the world...so burn them.

EXT. ROMAN TOWN SQUARE—NIGHT

A great bonfire is blazing in the center of town.

Many men and women tied to stakes are being set on fire.

Subtitle: "Feast of Saturnalia"

We see hundreds of Christians being used as torches to light the night sky. Romans are using them for light.

NARRATOR (V.O.)

The city of Saturn…one day to be called Rome.

Pigs are being sacrificed on an altar in front of the Pantheon.

NARRATOR (V.O.)

This Pantheon was built to honor all gods and deities.

Here we SEE statues of a mother and child referred to as the "Queen of Heaven" and her "reborn king."

A painting of the Queen of Heaven shows a woman surrounded by rays of light. She has a crescent moon under her feet.

NARRATOR (V.O.)

Diana and Minerva of Troy, simply incarnations of Semiramis. These images of goddesses supposedly fell from heaven…or Jupiter.

Pagan prayers honor "Saturn, the hidden god and true light."

Romans and slaves alike are celebrating by eating and drinking.

Many orgies take place in pagan temples with temple prostitutes.

NARRATOR (V.O.)

Since they worshipped fertility, their services were often orgies.

Little clay images, "sigillaria," are being exchanged as gifts.

EXT. APOLLO'S TEMPLE—NIGHT

A priestess at the Oracle at Delphi mocks Holy Ghost Christians by speaking belligerent AD LIBS in a drunken manner.

EXT. ROMAN COLISEUM—NIGHT—CHRISTIANS

Speaking in tongues BURN as torches along the top of the arena. Several ANGELS invisibly watch, including MICHAEL and GABRIEL.

> GABRIEL
>
> It's time to stop this.

> MICHAEL
>
> Let's fight fire with fire.

A MAN

Is burning as we LOOK into the door of a hot oven.

INT. FLAMING HOT OVEN—THE MAN

SCREAMS in pain as he's on fire. It's Diocletian! Our VIEW WIDENS revealing we are actually in HELL.

EXT. ROMAN CAMP—NIGHT

Subtitle: "Rome, October 27, 313 AD"
Roman soldiers are preparing for battle.

INT. CONSTANTINE'S TENT

A soldier is announced. He brings a gift to CONSTANTINE. Constantine's GUARD opens the gift. It's a Roman spear tip.

> GUARD
>
> The legendary sword of kings. Carry it tomorrow.

Suddenly a mysterious light appears to Constantine. It's some kind of apparition. Constantine faints.

Unsure if dreaming or awake, Constantine hears a VOICE.

> VOICE (O.S.)
>
> Fight under this sign.

The bright light forms two letters: "X" and "P."

> VOICE (O.S.)
>
> You will be victorious tomorrow.

Our VIEW WIDENS to reveal Constantine now looking up into the sky where he SEES this unusual symbol.

> CONSTANTINE
>
> The first two Greek letters of Christ's name…chi and rho. It is his God who has promised me victory tomorrow.

EXT. BATTLEFIELD—NEXT MORNING

Constantine's soldiers carry shields displaying bright red crosses. Some exhibit the two Greek letters in Constantine's vision. Other shields have a double-cross and swastikas painted on them.

CUT TO:

The battle is now over and Constantine has been victorious.

CONSTANTINE

I've been given victory by the god of the Christians. Today, this twenty-eighth day of October marks the end of their persecution. To honor my victory over Maxentius, I'll build an arch. The Arch of Constantine. Through this arch, Romans can pass from the east to the west…a united Empire.

The crowd CHEERS.

NARRATOR (V.O.)

Ironically, the Saint Louis Arch, which also became a gateway to the west, would be completed on the twenty-eighth day of October in 1965 AD. Do you remember the date when God made the colorful arch in the sky for the first time? Or when the Statue of Liberty was dedicated?

DISSOLVE TO:

EXT. VATICAN HILL—DAY

A basilica is being built over a two hundred year-old shrine to St. Peter. Constantine admires the progress.

CONSTANTINE
(to a bishop)

The early popes of your church believe this is
where St. Peter was crucified?

BISHOP

Well…yes. As you know, this was once the site
of Nero's gardens. Many early Christians suffered martyrdom here. Tradition holds that
Peter was one of them.

CONSTANTINE

What about the critics who claim he was never
in Rome? Why did their apostle Paul never
mention him in his letters to Rome?

BISHOP

You know how traditions are sire…once they
begin; they have a life of their own…and only
grow with time.

CONSTANTINE

What do you believe?

BISHOP

Whatever the people believe.

CONSTANTINE

I see. These same people give you your office

and title?

BISHOP

Yes, sire.

Constantine walks away from the bishop, shaking his head.

CONSTANTINE

Apollo was the son of Jupiter. He is the god of light, purity and the sun. I worship him.

BISHOP

There are many religions and mystery religions in your kingdom. Therefore, there are many gods worshipped here. Which will you serve on your deathbed?

CONSTANTINE

I'll let you know on that day.

Subtitle: "Twenty-four years later."

INT. EMPEROR'S BEDCHAMBERS—NIGHT

Constantine is on his deathbed. The bishop, even more decorated now, is reading Latin phrases from a book.

CONSTANTINE
(to bishop)

Bury me in a tomb with twelve empty coffins, one for each of the disciples. Since I helped the Christians, I want to be buried as one of them.

Place my body in the thirteenth coffin.

We see a coffin with skull and crossbones on its side.

CONSTANTINE

Has anyone found the spear tip?

BISHOP

No sire, it's still missing from yesterday.

Constantine closes his eyes and dies.

FADE TO: BLACK.

From BLACK, we HEAR

VOICE (O.S.)

You, who have confessed your sins to me, go from darkness now and discover the light. Find the true light and be enlightened. Your journey through death will be complete when you are resurrected as light, reborn in the heavens. I command you, young Demasus, to rise.

Our sight returns from a bright, blurry light.

INT. ROME—PAGAN TEMPLE

As we FOCUS, we SEE many men looking at us.

We discover we are seeing the world through the eyes of a twelve year-old boy, DEMASUS. A PRIEST is holding an ear of corn.

PRIEST

You must now prepare for the second of seven

degrees. You'll learn about the death and rebirth of a seed. This ear of corn symbolizes Osiris. The burying of the seed symbolizes his death. When it rises out of the ground, it symbolizes the resurrection of Osiris, who is now Orion among the stars in the sky.

Demasus gets up, then RUNS out of the Egyptian-like temple. The other men dressed in robes LAUGH.

PRIEST

I told you he was too young to become a member.

EXT. ROMAN CITY STREET—DAY

Demasus is met by another boy his age, GRATIAN as they both walk through the market. They hungrily look at baskets of apples.

GRATIAN

Buy something. I'm starving.

DEMASUS

I can't. I'm broke. The initiation cost me everything I had saved.

GRATIAN

Initiation? To what?

DEMASUS

Mithraism. I'll tell you more later. Right now, my stomach's talking.

Demasus steals a couple of apples while a vendor isn't looking. They run off to a nearby alley.

GRATIAN
(panting)

Mithraism? Why did you go and join that bunch of stupid idiots?

DEMASUS

They're not stupid. They're gonna help me attain a higher wisdom. You'll see…

GRATIAN

What did they teach you?

DEMASUS

I'm not supposed to tell anyone. I took a blood oath.

He sits down beside Gratian. They begin eating the apples.

DEMASUS

All right. The first initiation rite is the most difficult. I had to face and pass through the forces of nature. Water was the hardest…I almost drowned.

(pause)

Did you know thousands of years ago all the Aryans almost drowned when their home sank into the ocean?

GRATIAN

Where was their home?

DEMASUS

Some island called Atlantis. You could only get to it by sailing through the Straits of Gibraltar.

GRATIAN

My mom told me the only right religion is Christianity.

DEMASUS

The Christian church is dull and boring. Mystery religions are exciting.

GRATIAN

You're gonna burn in hell.

Demasus takes offense to these fighting words and takes off, chasing his best friend down the street.

EXT. GRATIAN'S PALACE—DAY

Subtitle: "Rome, 378 AD, forty-one years later."

A church procession is arriving. Demasus, the bishop over all the church now, is led into the palace like royalty.

INT. THRONE ROOM

Gratian sits upon the throne as Bishop Demasus enters.

GRATIAN

Old friend, what honor do I owe this visit?

DEMASUS

As representative of the Babylonian Mysteries, I come to you, the new emperor of Rome, with a title. A tradition going back to Julius Caesar and beyond. You are now the Head Master of the Mysteries.

GRATIAN
(to his guards)

Leave us!

Everyone clears the room now, leaving only Demasus and Gratian.

GRATIAN

Demasus, old friend. You know how I feel about mystery religions. I cannot, in good conscience, accept the title.

DEMASUS

What am I to do? It would be an insult to refuse. Most of your guards belong to the Mysteries.

Gratian begins pacing back and forth. He picks up an apple from a fruit basket and walks over to a window, looking out.

GRATIAN

What if I bestowed the honor upon you, starting

a new tradition?

DEMASUS
(joining Gratian)

The Pope of the Christian Church, the Head Master of the Mysteries?

GRATIAN
(turning to him)

Yes.

DEMASUS

I suppose it could work. The public would never have to know.

GRATIAN

Then it's settled. You...are the new Head Master.

Gratian tosses the apple to Demasus, who takes a bite.

GRATIAN

You know you're going to hell.

DEMASUS

You know...I think I'm too old to chase you anymore.

EXT. ROME—DAY

We SEE the bishop Demasus now wearing the two-horned mitre of the fish god Dagon. He's being initiated as the Head Master.

NARRATOR (V.O.)

And mystery religions from Babylon and Christianity became intertwined. Mystery Babylon was born. From her, all future denominations of the church would come. Her seat of power, the city upon seven hills…Rome.

EXT. PAGAN TEMPLE—DAY

Several women are praying to various statues. The new church has adopted icons of the Babylonian mother and child.

A young woman prays to a statue of the Egyptian Isis and Horus. She CALLS them Mary and Jesus, but the statues are Egyptian.

NARRATOR (V.O.)

Demasus restored and beautified all heathen temples in Rome, encouraging their rituals. He restored the Pantheon in Rome.

Overlooking this is the invisible Prince of Rome, TURYAL.

TURYAL

Now, to complete my work. The Book of Enoch must go. The truth about giants must be buried in the past. Our future depends on this truth being forever lost.

INT. CHURCH COUNCIL MEETING

Bishop Demasus sits around a table of men in a heated debate. One of the men is drawing a picture of an angel.

> CHRYSOSTOM
>
> It would be folly to accept such insane blasphemy, saying that an incorporeal and spiritual nature could unite itself to humans!

> FILASTRIUS
>
> He who thinks that angels, having been transformed into flesh, sinned in such a way and remained in this flesh or thus did such carnal deeds—this one discerns history with a convoluted logic.

> AUGUSTINE
>
> Sons of God in Genesis Six refer to the righteous sons of Seth who married the daughters of Cain. These sons of God could not have been angels. Angels fell from pride, not lust.

The man drawing an angel draws a circle around its head, giving the first halo to an angel in art.

The yellow circle resembles the golden sun in the sky, which the artist SEES just outside a nearby window.

> MAN ONE
>
> If you argue that giants came from the sons of Seth and the daughters of Cain, how do you account for giants AFTER the flood? Cain's

seed was gone!

MAN TWO

By giants, do you refer to Anakims and Rephaims?

MAN ONE

In Deuteronomy 3:11, the bed of a giant measured eighteen feet, nine inches long!

FILASTRIUS
(interrupting)

Teaching from the book of Enoch should be considered heresy!

MAN ONE

What about the Book of Jude? Jude quotes Enoch in verses fourteen and fifteen!

MAN TWO

Jude was the half-brother of Christ. We can't throw Jude's book out of the Bible.

MAN ONE

That's my argument—if the man grew up with our Messiah, he ought to know something of Enoch's authenticity!

All of the men start arguing and SHOUTING loudly.

> DEMASUS
> (rising with anger)

If a priest takes a vow of celibacy and never breaks it his entire life, then how could angels? The Book of Enoch is HERESY and that's final!

EXT. ROMAN STREETS—NIGHT

There's a great bonfire in the Town Square. People are SEEN throwing Enoch scrolls into the fire.

> NARRATOR (V.O.)

Scribes were forbidden to copy the Book. Enoch's words almost became lost to man.

EXT. ROME—NIGHT

Subtitle: "Feast of Saturnalia, a few years later."

Roman pagans we saw setting fire to the Christians are playing the role of Christians. "When in Rome…" someone AD LIBS.

Several women kneel before a statue of Mary and the baby Jesus. A PREGNANT WOMAN is praying to a statue of Isis and Horus.

> PREGNANT WOMAN

Oh mother Mary, bless the child in my womb…

> NARRATOR (V.O.)

Jesus said it was more blessed to hear and obey God's word than to have been his mother.

Conversion of pagans into the fold demanded the mother be worshipped also.

Many new Christians are seen praying to statues and relics.

> NARRATOR (V.O.)
>
> Jesus said no one could come to the Father except by Him. Paul said there is one mediator between God and men. Pagans always had more than one mediator and now…so did the new church.

EXT./INT. ROMAN HOMES—NIGHT

Subtitle: "December 25th. Feast of Saturnalia ends."
People are exchanging gifts and lighting the last candle of the season. Someone AD LIBS "Saturn is the light of the world."

> NARRATOR (V.O.)
>
> The Sun God's birthday had always been celebrated on this day. Recruiting more pagans into Christianity meant one final compromise. Jesus would have to share his birthday. As the new church gathered in Mass on this day, it would be called Christ's Mass, becoming…Christmas.

EXT. ROMAN MARKET SQUARE—DAY

Merchants are selling goods, which are all packaged as gifts.
Various moneychangers in front of pagan temples are sitting on benches

in the courtyard leading into the temple.

As some of these gifts are brought in, paper notes denoting the value of the gift are given in return.

> NARRATOR (V.O.)
>
> People were allowed to borrow from the wealth stored in pagan temples. But the wealth was left in the temples and only a paper promissory note was needed to borrow on this new wealth. World banking began…

INT. TEMPLE

Several men lounge around the temple. One man removes his robe. Dozens of women are entertaining these traveling male merchants.

> NARRATOR (V.O.)
>
> Ancient Babylonian rules of paganism forced all unmarried women to serve as temple prostitutes for one day. Merchants gave their wealth to the temples to enjoy the services of these women.

A man lies in the middle of these women. It's Demasus!

INT. FRANCE—NIGHT—LARGE CASTLE

Where an elderly WIDOW is on her deathbed. Several church officials, including Demasus, surround her.

Subtitle: "Feast of Saturnalia. One year later."

DEMASUS
(whispering)

If you leave all your wealth to the church, I can promise you forgiveness of all your sins and guarantee your place in Heaven upon your death.

WIDOW

What about my husband who died earlier this year? Will you pray to get his soul out of purgatory?

DEMASUS

I'll personally pray until the sun rises in the east.

The widow smiles, nodding her head.

WIDOW

You may have everything.

She dies as Demasus begins chanting in Latin.

EXT. WIDOW'S CASTLE—SUNRISE

Several church officials are SEEN leaving her estate with valuables in hand. We FOLLOW their procession to...

INT. WIDOW'S CASTLE—CLOSE ON—DEMASUS

SNORING LOUDLY in the widow's bed, her body obviously long since removed. Several other bishops are busy removing paintings.

                    BISHOP ONE

Should we wake him?

                    BISHOP TWO

He's been asleep for hours.

                    BISHOP THREE

Let him sleep. Another widow lives just down
the road.

EXT. TURKISH TOWN—NIGHT

People are still exchanging clay statues as gifts.

INT. POTTER'S WORKBENCH—A DWARF-SIZED MAN

Creates clay statues. His muddy hands hold his latest statue up for better inspection in the lamplight.

                        MAN

        I'll call this one…Adam.

EXT. POTTER'S SHOP—SUNSET

The midget potter leaves his shop, heading towards a church with a sack
full of the clay statues.

INT. CHILDREN'S BEDROOM—LATER THAT NIGHT

A bishop leaves the toy statues for children as they sleep.

> NARRATOR (V.O.)
>
> You guessed it...the bishop was named...Saint Nicholas.

Satan invisibly observes this. His bulbs LIGHT UP!

> SATAN
>
> Now, that gives me an idea.

INT. HAPSBURG FAMILY ESTATE (AUSTRIA)

Subtitle: "The Middle Ages, 1273 AD."

Subtitle: "Hapsburg Estate, Austria."

A man of nobility is standing in front of several relics. He SEES a Roman sword tip and picks it up to examine it.

> NARRATOR (V.O.)
>
> Excalibur...the sword drawn from a stone, making Arthur a great king. Jesus was referred to as the stone cut without hands and the ROCK. The sword taken from his side would make a ruler a great king. So the legend goes.

The man studying it has a big, red nose. A SERVANT enters.

> SERVANT
>
> Rudolph...you shouldn't keep other heads of state waiting.

EXT. PARIS STREETS—DAY

Thousands of knights are returning to the city upon horseback. Their shields display red crosses, double-crosses and swastikas.

Subtitle: "1307 AD. Paris, France. The Crusades."

INT. FRENCH PALACE—LATE AFTERNOON

The French KING PHILIP IV and a French ARCHBISHOP are receiving a report from the leader of the Templars, JACQUES DE MOLAY.

> JACQUES DE MOLAY
>
> We have returned with more treasures, Your Majesty. But we need more men.

> KING PHILIP
>
> I believe the Pope is capable of granting more pardons in exchange for service.

> ARCHBISHOP
>
> Indeed, Philip the Fair. All who die in battle against these pagans shall have immediate remission of sins.

Jacques de Molay nods, bows and leaves.

> KING PHILIP
>
> I don't like this. The Templars have become the wealthiest group in the entire known world.

> ARCHBISHOP
>
> Paris has become the center of the world's

money market where Pope's and kings alike deposit their revenues. The Templars protect all financial transfers.

KING PHILIP

They've become a secret society practicing witchcraft. Our spies report this. Templars victimize the very pilgrims they protect. These Crusades are causing Jews to be persecuted now because they blame them for killing Jesus.

ARCHBISHOP

What are we to do?

KING PHILIP

I have a plan.

Subtitle: "Friday, October 13, 1307."

INT. WIDOW'S CASTLE—NIGHT

A young man dressed in armor sits alone in a small room. He is preparing for his initiation. Above his head is a sign.

INSERT—SIGN

"If curiosity brings you here, then leave. There's still time."

INT. DINING ROOM/CASTLE—CLOSE ON—A SKULL

Sits in front of De Molay, who is seated at a round table with eleven other Templars. They are obviously in a secret meeting.

DE MOLAY

All men are brothers and must be judged according to their good works, and not the religion they belong to. Humans can be redeemed only through knowledge.

EXT. WIDOW'S CASTLE—NIGHT

The King's armies are riding towards the castle holding torches.

INT. DINING ROOM

De Molay holds the skull while addressing the others. We can SEE there is a silver dollar-sized hole carved in the side of the skull.

DE MOLAY

Jesus was never crucified. He married Mary Magdalene. His descendants are the Merovingians, the true nobility in France.

EXT. WIDOW'S CASTLE—NIGHT

The king's armies secretly take positions all around the castle.

INT. DINING ROOM

DE MOLAY

The Merovingians believed one must drill a hole in the skull to release the spirit. On our most recent Crusade, we found this on the Hill of the Skull. Some claim it belongs to Adam...

Suddenly, there's a KNOCK at the DOOR.

EXT. CASTLE

Dozens of French soldiers escort the Archbishop to the front.

> ARCHBISHOP
>
> You are under arrest by the King of France, charged with witchcraft and heresy.

> CUT TO:

LATER

The Templars, including De Molay, are led away in chains.

> NARRATOR (V.O.)
>
> The Templars' wealth was divided between the Catholic Church and the French King.

EXT./INT. WIDOW'S CASTLE—DAYS LATER

Church officials are moving into the widow's castle.

> NARRATOR (V.O.)
>
> The Papacy moved from Rome to Avignon, France where it remained seventy years. Referred to by some as the Babylonian Captivity.

EXT. NOTRE DAME CATHEDRAL (PARIS)—DAY

Gargoyles along the cathedral become masked by smoke drifting upwards.

We FOLLOW the smoke to its origin, where Jacques de Molay is being burned at the stake.

> DE MOLAY
>
> Oh Lord, my God...is there no help for the widow's son?

> NARRATOR (V.O.)
>
> The last Grand Master of the Templars was burned at the stake for heresy in 1314.

INT. SECRET MEETING—NIGHT

Subtitle: "June 27, 1555. France."

A group of Templars conducts a secret meeting. They AD LIB how to avenge their leader. They make a secret sign by slashing their hands across their chests.

> OLD MAN (V.O.)
>
> Rain, famine and war in Persia will not cease. A trust too great will betray the monarch. For the end was planned and conceived in France, a secret sign for one to be more sparing.

INT. NOSTRADAMUS' STUDY—NIGHT

Nostradamus is sitting at his desk writing.

OLD MAN (O.S.)

Until the beginning of the seventh millennium, at the revolution of the great number seven. Will bring a time, joyous sacrifice of war. Not far from the millennium age, the buried shall come out of their graves.

He signs, "Nostradamus." We SEE the book's title, "CENTURIES."

CUT TO:

EXT. BAVARIAN CASTLE—NIGHT

Subtitle: "Ingolstadt, Bavaria. 1777."

INT. CASTLE

ADAM WEISHAUPT and several MEN are in a secret meeting.

ADAM

We must rid the world of its monarchies. We'll get our members in every office of education and the press.

He holds up a manuscript for all to see.

ADAM

This contains my plan for the future. Study it well.

Several of the men gather around the opened book.

ADAM

We'll encourage strife among men and let them destroy themselves. We'll pick up the pieces and begin our reign of peace.

One MAN has found something in the book, which causes concern.

MAN

Why is Masonry dropping the Tower of Babel and replacing it with Solomon's Temple?

ADAM

We must continue to hide our true allegiance. Most men would never openly commit to pagan worship, so we must disguise it…make it easier to swallow. By changing Nimrod to Hiram, men of conscience will join us.

MAN
(referring to book)

Who will finance all this?

ADAM

The International Bankers, keepers of the Templars' wealth, will finance all. Every war from the French Revolution…to Armageddon!

EXT. PARIS STREETS—DAY

Subtitle: "Paris. January 21, 1793. The French Revolution."

A huge guillotine blade is being hoisted up.

Released, it chops off the head of French King Louis XVI.

EXT. WASHINGTON, DC—DAY

Subtitle: "September 18, 1793. Washington, DC"

GEORGE WASHINGTON conducts a Masonic ceremonial dedication of the cornerstone being laid for the US Capitol building.

We SEE a drawing showing a serpent "Don't Tread on Me" and a divided serpent into thirteen pieces "Unite or we die!"

> GEORGE WASHINGTON
>
> We must preserve the sacred fire of liberty…If
> we lose that sacred fire, if we let it be smothered
> with doubt and fear, we will reject our destiny.

> DISSOLVE TO:

INT. NATIONAL CONVENTION (PARIS)—NIGHT

We SEE torches and candles lighting a room with eleven men seated around a table. Two of the men are engaged in light conversation.

> MAN ONE
>
> I remember well his rallying cry, ECRASEZ
> L'INFAME.

> MAN TWO
>
> Yes, of course…"Crush the evil thing." Voltaire
> was referring to religious superstition. But, I'm
> referring to his book, "MICROMEGAS."

MAN ONE

Yes, also penned during the Age of Reason.

MAN TWO

But, my point is this: in the story, giant visitors came from a distant star and from the planet Saturn...

MAN ONE

I've read the book, monsieur. It discusses man's insignificance...

The two men are interrupted as MAXIMILIEN ROBESPIERRE, leader of the Public Safety Committee, enters carrying a small closed crate.

ROBESPIERRE

We've raised an army to defend France from her enemies from without...and from within. All rebels who oppose the National Convention have been rounded up and beheaded. But this Reign of Terror must go farther.

He opens the crate, revealing the French King's head.

ROBESPIERRE

Why stop with the king?

EXT. NOTRE DAME CATHEDRAL—DAY

Subtitle: "November 1793."

Hundreds of ROWDY patriots surround the town square in front of the cathedral. A bishop is on trial before a tribunal.

The tribunal unanimously gives a "thumbs-down" as the bishop is now being led to the guillotine located on the church steps.

The blade rises as the bishop is placed in the wooden stocks.

The BLADE then COMES DOWN and his head FLIES OFF.

Blood from his lifeless body spills into the street.

The two men from Robespierre's committee observe everything.

MAN ONE

Should we not clear away the blood of a priest?

MAN TWO

Why? It's the blood of a rebel. Let the dogs lick it up.

INT. NOTRE DAME CATHEDRAL

A revolutionary crowd has taken over the church. They are wearing priest's garments, robes, etc.

One man performs a mock service as a PRIEST.

PRIEST

The church represents the pillar of the old order. Today, we'll change the old order into a new order and forever change history. No more BC or AD marking the birth of Christ on our calendars either. We'll begin all calendars in France on the day the new French Republic was born…September 22, 1792!

The crowd becomes LEWD. Several patriotic maidens dressed in white dresses make their way to the altar.

> PRIEST
>
> All maidens will be enthroned as goddesses in this Temple of Reason, celebrating the New Age of Reason.

He disrobes as an orgy begins with the new temple prostitutes.

INT. FRENCH PALACE—NIGHT

The two men from the committee are watching crowds in the streets below where more citizens are losing their heads.

> MAN ONE
>
> Soon, there will be no more people to rule.

> MAN TWO
>
> We must hold a secret meeting with the others. I'm sure they will vote with us to stop this bloodletting.

EXT. NOTRE DAME CATHEDRAL—DAY

Subtitle: "July 28, 1794."

Using the same guillotine that beheaded the bishop earlier, we SEE Robespierre lose his own head.

His blood runs into the streets where a dog licks it up.

> NARRATOR (V.O.)
>
> Revenge for a man's death was carried out on

the anniversary of his death. One hundred and twenty years later, the length of a man's life as outlined by God after the flood; Robespierre would be avenged.

EXT. EUROPEAN BATTLEFIELD—DAY

Subtitle: "July 28, 1914. World War One begins."
An intense battle is taking place. Blood of soldiers on both sides runs bright red into the ground and into street gutters.

> NARRATOR (V.O.)
>
> The French Revolution helped create modern nationalism. Now, Germany and Italy united men with their campaigns of nationalism.

Subtitle: "1917."

MONTAGE

A)   The Czar of Russia is being executed with his entire family. One of the soldiers wears a Maltese cross around his neck.

B)   A female apparition wearing a white dress and veil APPEARS to three little girls in Fatima, Portugal.

C)   Moslem troops flee Jerusalem as Gen. Allenby enters with his troops. The British flag, the double-cross, leads the brigade.

D)   Congress of the United States votes to enter WWI.

E)   The Capitol building's ceiling murals show George Washington riding across the sky in a chariot drawn by four horses.

F)   We SEE an eleven-foot tall marble statue of Washington as the Greek god Zeus in the Smithsonian Institution.

END OF MONTAGE

EXT. CAPE CANAVERAL—(1969) DAY

A countdown is in progress as we HEAR MISSION CONTROL.

MISSION CONTROL (V.O.)

Five, four, three, two, one, zero...we have liftoff!

We SEE a huge Saturn Five rocket BLASTING OFF.

EXT. MIDWESTERN RANCH—NIGHT

A helicopter can be HEARD where a herd of cows are grazing.
Suddenly a LIGHT APPEARS over a cow.

EXT. SEVERAL MINUTES LATER—THE COW

Lies on the ground, lifeless. It appears that it has been surgically cut in various places.

EXT. RANCH—NEXT MORNING

A COWBOY is scratching his head. He's inspecting the cow.
He's last SEEN quickly riding his horse away from the cow.

EXT. THE MOON—LUNAR LANDING SITE

The lunar module Eagle is hovering over its landing site.
Subtitle: "July 20, 1969. Apollo Eleven lands at Tranquillity Base."
We HEAR one of the astronauts, NEIL ARMSTRONG.

ARMSTRONG (O.S.)

Roger. The Eagle has landed.

INT. EAGLE LUNAR MODULE (33 MINUTES LATER)

The two astronauts, Armstrong and BUZZ ALDRIN, are sitting in the cockpit. They LOOK out at the stars over the lunar horizon.

Subtitle: "Thirty-three minutes later."

ARMSTRONG
(pointing)

There it is.

The astronauts pour a small vial of wine into a silver chalice.

ALDRIN

She's at 19.5 degrees on the horizon…just as planned.

The star Sirius is precisely at 19.5 degrees latitude above the horizon, as indicated by a computer DISPLAYING the information.

NARRATOR (V.O.)

Apollo Eleven was the thirty-third mission to the moon.

Song "DARK SIDE OF THE MOON" by Pink Floyd begins.

EXT. EAGLE LUNAR MODULE—WIDE VIEW

As we PULL AWAY from the module, we DRIFT to the far side of the moon where we can barely SEE something in the darkness.

INT. RANCHER'S HOUSE—DAY

The cowboy is now on the phone to someone. He's very excited. While he's speaking, we SEE a newspaper lying on the floor.

INSERT—HEADLINE

"UFO Abductions on the rise…truth or fiction?"

> COWBOY (O.S.)
>
> That's right, the cow's blood is gone…all of it. Those cuts on its body were too precise to be done by kids. Somebody knew what they were doing…but what?

EXT. THE VATICAN—MIDNIGHT

A huge crowd has gathered in St. Peter's Square.

Subtitle: "Christmas Eve, 2003 11:59 p.m."

An ANNOUNCER for a news station begins commentating.

> ANNOUNCER (O.S.)
>
> The Vatican announced that an unfulfilled Fatima prophecy is about to be revealed. The Pope will unseal the last of the Fatima prophecies outlined by Our Lady of Fatima back on October 13, 1917 to three young girls. They promised to only reveal the last prophecy eight days before its fulfillment. Tonight marks the first of those eight days.

The Pope appears before the crowd. He unseals a scroll and begins to

286 Revelations

read. As he speaks in Latin, a female voice translates.

TRANSLATOR (O.S.)

My children, I come to you as a mediatrix between God and man. Soon, great chaos will come. Store canned food and water. Take candles and blankets too. But from this unrest will come a time of great peace. Like the peace between Arab and Jew allowing the rebuilding of the Jewish temple, ushering in the return of my Son.

ANNOUNCER (O.S.)

As you know, Saddam Hussein's son, Udai, authored the agreement. Jews were only allowed to rebuild the Holy of Holies, as the Dome on the Rock restricted room for their entire Temple. Since the Moslem faith denies the Jewish claim to Jerusalem, the peace treaty came from the Jewish belief that if they're allowed to rebuild their Temple, their Messiah would come after seven years. If He doesn't come at the end of seven years, then Jews must give all of Jerusalem to Palestinians...forever.

EXT. TIMES SQUARE—NIGHT

Subtitle: "DECEMBER 31, 2003."

Partying crowds are everywhere awaiting the New Year.

Some religious fanatics are carrying signs saying, "THE END IS NEAR," "OUR LADY OF FATIMA WARNED US."

EXT. MANHATTAN BRIDGE

National Guard troops surround NYC and are watching the crowds. Apache helicopters are BUZZING all around in the skies.

We HEAR a television ANNOUNCER talking about all the activity over several different TV sets and RADIOS in cars, houses, etc.

> ANNOUNCER (V.O.)
>
> Due to recent terrorist threats, the National Guard, along with FEMA's State Defense Forces, has taken up positions around every major city in the US.

EXT. PATTY'S HOUSE (ST. LOUIS)—NIGHT

We SEE the St. Louis arch in the distance behind a small house.

INT. PATTY'S HOUSE

The SOUNDS of a TV can be HEARD as someone is watching the New Year's Eve coverage from Times Square.

In the kitchen is PATTY, thirty-one, who's been doing dishes. She HEARS her two twelve year-old fraternal twins, J.J. and D.D., arguing over control of the TV in the living room.

> PATTY
>
> I told you two to share!

INT. LIVING ROOM

The kids have begun playing a video game as the boy takes his turn playing the Playstation game, "SPYRO THE DRAGON."

INSERT—VIDEO MONITOR

A fire-breathing dragon chases a lamb, burning him with fire.

BACK TO SCENE

A game box for "DOOM" sits beside the Playstation game. The box shows a sinister-looking devil with two large horns.

Patty enters the living room and observes her kids playing.

> PATTY
>
> Hey you two, I told you I want to watch the TV tonight.

Coverage of midnight Mass from Rome returns to the TV as the kids' game stops. Patty and the kids listen for a moment as the Pope's words are being translated into English.

> TV (V.O.)
>
> Our Lady has warned us of the great upheavals to come soon.

> PATTY
>
> I've got a better idea, how 'bout we watch a video?

She places the video to "FROSTY THE SNOWMAN" into the VCR.

INSERT—TV

Frosty comes to life after kids put a magic hat on his head. He speaks his first words.

FROSTY (V.O.)

Happy Birthday!

EXT. TOP OF EMPIRE STATE BUILDING—NIGHT

Reporters have set up a media headquarters here and are covering the celebrations live on their various stations.

REPORTER

Yes, it's true. As a precaution, the government has rounded up all known militia group leaders because of anonymous militia threats of a coup to take place tonight.

A different network's ANNOUNCER can be HEARD.

ANNOUNCER

Tonight's coverage sponsored by THIRD-UNION: The beacon of light in a confusing world of investments. If you can't come to the mountain, the mountain will come to you.

We SEE the commercial's video on a monitor. A man with tattoos, multicolored hair, and numerous body piercings acts as their stockbroker. He's showing an older couple how to invest online. A graphic disclaimer barely readable is displayed.

INSERT—CLOSE ON SCREEN

"Not FDIC insured. May LOSE value."

INT. SUBWAY CAR—UNDERGROUND, NEAR TIMES SQUARE

An old couple is sitting next to a man wearing a red beret and a white T-shirt with the words, "Guardian Angel" on the front. The elderly lady looks up at the Angel and smiles.

> OLD LADY
>
> I feel safe when you Angels are down here with us.

INT. DOLLAR MOVIE THEATER

We join a sci-fi film festival at a double-screen theater. Stanley Kubrick's "2001" and episode one of "STAR WARS" are on separate screens. We HEAR a line from "STAR WARS."

> V.O.
>
> A communications disruption can mean only one thing…invasion!

This is followed by the last line from "2001 A SPACE ODYSSEY."

> V.O.
>
> Oh my God, look at all the stars!

EXT. TIMES SQUARE—BALL DROPPING

ANNOUNCERS everywhere are ECHOING the crowds' CHANTS as they count down the incoming year. "Three, two, one, Happy New Year…2004!"

Right as the ball drops in Times Square, the whole city goes dark.

> **DICK CLARK**
> (several beats)

Well, it's normal for the ball to go dark before
lighting the sign, but something is wrong.

As the huge video screen in Times Square goes dark, the partying crowd
starts to panic now as chaos begins.

INT. NORAD HEADQUARTERS (COLORADO)—MINUTES LATER

We SEE radar monitor's track multiple incoming missiles from Russia,
China, and other countries.

EXT. VARIOUS US CITIES—VERY DARK

There's obviously no power for radio, television or EBS warning systems. Only FEMA guards with BULLHORNS are able to WARN people
in the streets of the impending disaster.
People are too drunk from partying to care and ignore the warnings.

INT. ELDERLY PERSON'S HOME

An old man kicks his electric heater while grabbing another blanket.

EXT. NEW YORK CITY—NIGHT

The "Jesus is coming…are you ready?" billboard lies on the ground. Its
owner has vanished.

MONTAGE

A)   Missiles hit areas of Wall Street in New York City. The World
       Trade Towers are engulfed in flames and come TUMBLING

DOWN.

B) Buildings near the United States Capitol in Washington DC EXPLODE!

C) Downtown Los Angeles gets HIT. The Hollywood sign is in flames.

D) Military bases and nuclear reactors also get BOMBED.

E) The subway car we saw earlier has derailed. Many passengers are dead including the old couple and the Guardian Angel.

F) Patty is searching her house frantically with a flashlight.

END OF MONTAGE

EXT. JERUSALEM—NIGHT

Crowds of angry Palestinians TAUNT Israelis praying at the Temple Mount. A rioter carries a Moslem flag displaying a crescent moon.

The shape of the CRESCENT MOON on an Islamic flag

DISSOLVES TO:

EXT. OUTER SPACE—EARTH'S ORBIT

BECOMES the ACTUAL CRESCENT MOON orbiting Earth. One third of the STARS begin to GLOW BRIGHTER now.

PATTY (O.S.)

Kids? Where are you? Hello? Is anybody out there? Oh my God…look at all the stars!

We see the VIDEO GLITCH AGAIN.

EXT. OUTER SPACE—CRESCENT MOON

With the SUN PEEKING over its edge. Our VIEW BROADENS to include the Earth. We come alongside a large space station.

We SEE the Latin phrase, ADHUC STAT on the side of it.

Subtitle: "The International Space Station."

Subtitle: "Jewish Passover and Good Friday's Eve, 2004 AD"

INT. SPACE STATION

The SOUND of an electronic warning BEEPS to alert the crew, but they fail to see a small spaceship already headed towards Earth.

HAL, an Asian in his mid-twenties, turns the warning light off as a nearby computer indicates the UFO was an asteroid.

INT. CHAPEL

Other astronauts of different nationalities are preparing to celebrate Easter by decorating this onboard chapel.

As we HEAR the astronauts of different nationalities SPEAK, a small lapel computer-translating device translates their language.

CLOSER VIEW of the device reveals the Macintosh logo, a multicolored rainbow apple with a bite missing.

INT. RECREATION ROOM

Some of the younger astronauts are playing a video game.

INSERT—VIDEO SCREEN

Grotesque demons help the evil Midgard Serpent take on Thor, who wields his golden hammer in a game called "RAGNOROK."

The game is INTERRUPTED by another SIGNAL...a live feed from Rome on the Global One TV Network.

BACK TO SCENE

The players SHOUT AD LIBS to Hal that "the monitors are screwing up!" Hal's CHINESE speech is translated into English.

> HAL (V.O.)
>
> All right, I'm working on it. It's just some inter-ference.

INT. CHAPEL

An astronaut with rosary beads in his hands is WATCHING the Roman Catholic Mass on a MONITOR, which Hal is adjusting.

In the b.g. is a portal through which we can SEE Earth below.

As our VIEW PULLS US through the window, we MOVE towards Italy.

EXT. ROME—NIGHT—THE PANTHEON

The ancient Roman building still stands and is well preserved.

> NARRATOR (V.O.)
>
> Rededicated to the Virgin Mary.

EXT. THE VATICAN/ST. PETER'S SQUARE—NEAR SUNSET

Crowds fill St. Peter's Square, covering the double-cross within a sphere on the piazza. An obelisk in its center rises above them.

INT. SAINT PETER'S BASILICA

A statue of the Virgin Mary holding the baby Jesus is in the f.g. of the Catholic service. The POPE makes his way to the altar. He wears a two-horned mitre and is followed by other similarly dressed Bishops and Cardinals.

A news anchor refers to him as "Pope Peter the Roman."

EXT. SAINT PETER'S CHURCH—OUTER BALCONY

A man wearing a Masonic ring watches from a window above.

> ANNOUNCER (V.O.)
>
> This new Pope has been viewed by many as very liberal. Since the unification of so many Christian churches, he's really been a global leader in restoring the love and fellowship of so many separate denominations. His love and open acceptance have allowed women priests, gay marriages, abortion, and birth control.

The Pope addresses the crowd below in St. Peter's Square.

The device we saw on the space station TRANSLATES LATIN for us.

> POPE (V.O.)
>
> She warns us of future chastisements. They'll be worse than those of New Year's Eve. We'll know more at midnight.

EXT. SAINT LOUIS ARCH—EARLY AFTERNOON

Subtitle: "St. Louis, USA."

The bottom legs of the arch are underwater, the result of the Mississippi River backing up and flooding the banks.

INT. KITCHEN/PATTY'S HOUSE

A digital clock RADIO is broadcasting the Pope's message. Beside the clock is a tabloid newspaper.

INSERT—NEWSPAPER HEADLINE

"The Mississippi Mud…Serving the Daily Dirt. UFO Abductions on the Rise? Explanation for Missing Kids on 1-1-2004?"

BACK TO SCENE

PATTY is listening to the Pope's message on the clock radio, while coloring Easter eggs.

PATTY

I'm tired of all this Latin stuff about the Virgin Mary.

She reaches over and changes the channel, finding a PREACHER giving a sermon.

PREACHER (V.O.)

St. Louis has been plagued by flooding rain, but that won't dampen our spirits this Easter.

Patty looks out her kitchen window, where she SEES the arch.

PATTY

What did J.J. always say? "It's a big steel rainbow, mama. It's God's promise not to send another flood to St. Louis."

Patty gets choked up as a tear rolls down her face. She has to stop coloring the eggs, BAWLING now, as the preacher continues.

> PREACHER (V.O.)
>
> Computers and technology…Mankind builds his house upon sand, which is what silicon is made from. They put computer chips on that. The FOUNDATION of technology is built upon the SAND of the Earth. Friends, build your house upon the ROCK, Jesus!

As we continue to hear the preacher's message, we SEE

EXT. SEVEN CHURCH STEEPLES

On top of SEVEN different churches. Our FOCUS NARROWS on the spires and steeples of each church, which resemble the TOP of an OBELISK as we get to the last church STEEPLE.

> PREACHER (V.O.)
>
> When the thunder, lightning, earthquakes, and 100-pound hailstones come with God's wrath in the end, you'll not be moved!

The last steeple now

> DISSOLVES TO:

EXT. ROME—NIGHT—TOP OF HUGE OBELISK

The preacher's VOICE fades as we HEAR the familiar sounds of a MAN'S VOICE initiating someone into a mystery religion as we

298   Revelations

                              FADE TO: BLACK.

FADE INTO:

INT. JOHN ROCKWELL SR.'S PRIVATE STUDY ROOM

A DARK room, barely lit. A man with black gloves quietly moves around the room. We can't see his face.

He looks at a shelf of various relics, Knights Templar Maltese crosses, antique swords, a coat of arms and a human skull.

INT. ROME—INITIATION ROOM

The walls are covered with Egyptian hieroglyphs. We HEAR more AD LIBS from the initiation. The WORDS overlap as we INTERCUT

INT. ROCKWELL'S STUDY—MALE PROWLER

Has found an entertainment center with video tapes.

He FOLLOWS the list of titles which all say, "PROPAGANDA."

He takes one from the NBZ/SNL file labeled, "PROJECT 2X2L, 2-6-99" subtitled "SATURDAY TV CARNIVAL HOUSE" and places it in the VCR.

                         MAN'S VOICE

            2X2L…double cross to hell!

INSERT—TV SCREEN

An animated image appears on the video screen. It's a cartoon of former President Bill Clinton's impeachment trial.

SPEAKER OF HOUSE

...but Representatives, the Constitution SAYS...

The Constitution, on display nearby in a glass case, somehow comes to life. It develops teeth.

It starts killing people involved in the proceedings.

REPRESENTATIVE

I think this is a job for the Four X-Presidents.

He summons the Four X-Presidents: Ford, Carter, Reagan, and Bush. Their SHIELD resembles the Knights Templar CREST.

The prowler FAST-FORWARDS.

The Four X-Presidents COMBINE FORCES to destroy the Constitution. Together they spin like a BUZZ SAW, cutting up the Constitution.

BACK TO SCENE

The prowler's gloved hand PAUSES the video, REWINDS a few frames, then SLOWLY PLAYS back the buzz saw part several times.

He takes out a picture from his vest, comparing it to the video.

INSERT—PHOTO—A DRAWING

Of a Nazi swastika, rotating. On each of the swastika's four ends is a knife, which cut up people in concentration camps represented by skulls, bones and the Star of David.

BACK TO SCENE

We now SEE the man's face. It's JOHNNY ROCKWELL, now seventy-nine.

> JOHNNY
>
> Ford, Carter, Reagan, and Bush...the four presidents responsible for FEMA, which replaced the Constitution.

His curiosity further piqued, Johnny picks up a "LOST IN SPACE" episode. As he reads aloud, we INTERCUT with the initiation.

> JOHNNY (V.O.)
>
> "My Friend, Mr. Nobody." A disembodied spirit, Mr. Nobody, dwells secretly in a cave. He befriends Penny, who gets trapped in the cave when Dr. Smith blasts open its mouth to gain entry.

An Egyptian-like priest dressed like the Jackal-headed Anubis, acts out the opening of the mouth of a mummy with a hammer. This takes place in front of a hooded initiate.

> JOHNNY (V.O.)
>
> Thinking Penny died, Mr. Nobody seeks to avenge her murderers. Fighting the forces of nature coming against the crew, the robot is torn to pieces.

Several Masons dressed like bandits are tripping up the initiate, now bound and blindfolded, as he is led to the altar.

JOHNNY (V.O.)

But he is put back together and lives again. The opening of the cave's mouth released the spirit, which is reborn as a new galaxy of stars in the heavens. This is observed on an oval monitor, adjusted by reptilian hands.

Johnny's face lights up even more.

JOHNNY

All Masonic rituals and symbolism...zero means nobody. Zero in the Chaldean was a circle, the SEED, another name for the false redeemer...Nimrod! Someone in Hollywood is embedding all this into TV shows?

DISSOLVE TO:

INT. ROME—INITIATION ROOM

Where the initiation is concluding.

INITIATOR

You've fought the forces of nature and survived. You've been resurrected with Hiram Abiff so when you die, you'll be reborn in the heavens with the true light.

The initiate's hood is removed. It's the Pope!

EXT. THE VATICAN—NIGHT

The obelisk we SAW earlier is now REVEALED to be the one in the

302   Revelations

CENTER of St. Peter's Square. This obelisk BECOMES

EXT. WASHINGTON DC—DAY

The National Monument, a 6,660 inch-tall white obelisk.

Our VIEW WIDENS to include the Pentagon in the b.g. The pentagon-shaped Defense Headquarters BECOMES

EXT. DENVER—MASONIC TEMPLE—DAY

The inside pentagon shape within a PENTAGRAM, or upside-down five-pointed star. Our VIEW WIDENS to show the star is located on a sign in front of a Masonic Temple.

On the side of the lodge, a compass and square symbol BECOMES

INT. DENVER AIRPORT—DAY

The SAME Masonic SYMBOL on the floor of the airport there. The Latin phrase ORDO AB CHAO is beside the symbol, which a man is standing beside.

The man is wearing headphones, listening to a VOICE.

> VOICE (V.O.)
>
> ORDO AB CHAO—The old order must be completely and thoroughly destroyed before the New Order, the Third Way can be established.

He SEES a mural on the wall. Children all over the world are bringing a German boy swords wrapped in their country's flags.

The boy is beating their swords on an anvil into plowshares and pruning hooks with his iron fist and hammer.

VOICE
(continuing)

The future.

A uniformed man walks past, heading towards a guarded elevator. A gargoyle statue looms overhead.

The guard makes a secret sign with his hand. We NOTICE a Masonic ring on his middle finger.

The other man returns the sign. As he does, we NOTICE a Masonic ring on his middle finger.

The guard allows the man to pass, who enters the elevator and pushes the DOWN ARROW button.

INT. ELEVATOR—UNDERGROUND FACILITY

Where he exits into a huge room filled with activity.

He drops to his knees, as if in the presence of royalty.

EXT. ATLANTIC OCEAN—DAY

Subtitle: "Bermuda Triangle."

Several huge balls of light come DOWN from the sky alongside a patrolling American fighter jet, which doesn't even detect them.

Suddenly, the balls of light plunge DOWNWARD and disappear under the surface of the ocean. This upsets some eels in the water nearby.

EXT. NORTHERN ISRAEL—EARLY EVENING

Subtitle: "Mt. Hermon"

A small spacecraft descends and lands. It's the object that picked up Elijah at the very beginning of the FIRST movie, "ALPHA."

INT. SPACECRAFT

Inside the craft are LAURIANNA, ELIJAH and ENOCH. The two men are dressed in sackcloth, like prophets of old.

LAURIANNA

Oh yeah, I need to bring you up-to-date on a few more things.

INSERT—OVAL-SHAPED VIDEO MONITOR—VIDEO GLITCH

Like the one we've SEEN between every jump in time. VISUALS from last New Year's Eve appear ONSCREEN.

BACK TO SCENE

We now realize this whole trip through the past has been Laurianna updating Elijah, starting when he was first picked up at the beginning of the first movie.

She hands both Enoch and Elijah some currency.

ELIJAH

What's this?

LAURIANNA

It's the new European monetary unit...the Euro Mark. The wars of New Years Day destroyed the USA's economy. Europe united as the Revised Roman Empire, the New World superpower.

We SEE a map of Europe divided into ten sections. Five eastern and five western nations with a common flag: a black two-headed eagle on a red and white background.

LAURIANNA

Germany, France, Spain, Italy and Greece represent the western nations. Smaller countries like Serbia, Romania, Poland, etc. were absorbed by these five. Their western capital is now Paris. Their religious seat is Rome and most are Orthodox Christian or Roman Catholic. Great Britain was destroyed.

The map shows the western half of the flag is white.

LAURIANNA

Algeria, Libya, Egypt, Turkey and Iraq, with its expanded borders including Syria and Iran, represent the five eastern nations. Their religious seat is Mecca. Their eastern capital is near Baghdad, the restored city of Babylon. Most are Muslims.

The map shows their half of the flag is red.

ENOCH

You said the USA and Britain suffered a great attack?

LAURIANNA

Traitors and terrorists launched Russian and Chinese nuclear missiles at both countries.

On the monitor, we can see the damage in London and New York City.

The entire Wall Street financial area is in ruins.

Many Americans are SEEN working in forced-labor camps.

> LAURIANNA

> Most Americans had invested everything into the stock market. Social Security surpluses had been invested. The largest investment banker, THIRD*UNION*, went bankrupt.

> ENOCH

> But why do so many people work in labor camps? I thought it was the land of the free?

> LAURIANNA

> Anyone in debt has to serve time in a labor camp until his or her debts are paid in full. FEMA, or Martial Law, replaced constitutional law.

> ELIJAH

> What about Russia and China?

> LAURIANNA

> Still communist countries. Russia's leader, Vladimir Zhirinovsky, is the king of the north. China, Pakistan, India, and the united countries of Korea and Japan...are the kings of the east.

Laurianna hands Elijah his blue mantle, which looks worn now.

LAURIANNA

Supposedly the rapture happened last New
Year's Eve. Many religious leaders and children
disappeared.

ENOCH
(surprised)

But we know that's not true.

LAURIANNA

There's more. The world believes two witnesses
for God are upon the Earth. One is the new
Pope, who claims the anointing of Elijah. The
other is Our Lady of Fatima. She's supposedly
the mother of Jesus. Together, they're preparing
the world for the return of Peter and Paul, supposedly the two witness of "REVELATION."

ENOCH

Peter, Paul and Mary? Didn't they break up in
the sixties?

EXT. JEWISH TEMPLE (JERUSALEM)—NIGHT—A FULL MOON RISING

LIGHTS up the Temple Mount as we SEE several Orthodox Jews praying alongside the Temple Walls.

OUR VIEW SHIFTS to a small home near the temple.

INT. KATY'S HOUSE (ISRAEL)—NIGHT

Family members at the dinner table join Katy, now seventy-five. We can SEE David's watch hanging from Katy's neck.

Eva, Katy's daughter, is now in her late fifties. She resembles her father, David. A photo of him hangs on the wall in the b.g.

Sitting next to Eva is her son JOSH, early twenties, a uniformed Israeli Air Force Pilot, and her adopted eleven year-old, DAVIE JR.

Josh sits next to his girlfriend REBEKAH, twenty-two, an Air Force cadet.

                    EVA

    You and Johnny should've gotten together.

                    KATY

    He liked women with short hair.

Everyone LAUGHS.

                    KATY
                (continuing)

    I haven't cut my hair since the Germans did it
    for me in 1945.

Davie sets a glass of wine at an empty place on the table. Josh stands with his own wineglass in hand, preparing for a toast.

                    JOSH
                (to Davie)

    Elijah's successor, Elisha, got a double portion
    of God's anointing. The anointing was still
    strong, even after his death. When a dead man's

body touched Elisha's, the dead man came back to life.

Josh tries to scare Davie with his delivery of that last part.

KATY
(comforting him)

Davie, go to the door, as is custom, to look for Elijah.

The boy OPENS the DOOR to discover Elijah standing there!
The Passover cup ritually left for Elijah now becomes empty.
Elijah looks over a passed-out Davie.

ELIJAH

It's time.

INT. ROCKWELL ESTATE/JOHNNY'S ROOM—LATER THAT NIGHT

We HEAR the SOUND of a wrestling match on TV.

ANNOUNCER (V.O.)

Let's get ready to rumble!

Johnny sits on the bed watching TV with JOHNNY JR, twelve. It's J.J., Patty's boy that disappeared on New Years Eve!

RING ANNOUNCER (V.O.)

The N.W.O. uses wrestlers from other countries as part of a unified Earth.

JOHNNY
(to J.J.)

Mind if I change the channel?

J.J. shrugs his shoulders. Johnny SWITCHES CHANNELS.

NEWS ANCHOR (V.O.)

Iraq denies rumors of unrest between its country and Egypt...

Johnny's wife BUFFY, a former Miss America, enters the room.

BUFFY

Dee Dee and I are going for ice cream, want some?

J.J. gets up and bolts out the door.

JOHNNY

I guess that's his answer. None for me, thanks.

As she leaves, Johnny undresses. Standing in his underwear, we SEE the Masonic compass and square embroidered on them.

HILLARY RODNIM, stands at the door unannounced.

HILLARY

Oh, I'm sorry...I heard your wife and kids so I thought you were dressed.

JOHNNY
(covering up)

I was. It's okay. I was hoping to see you before

you left. So, how are you?

HILLARY

Just fine, thanks. Being a New York Senator keeps me busy. Things better between you and Buffy since adopting the twins?

JOHNNY

Much…her not being able to have kids really had her depressed. But everything is great now. I'm glad Dad found them for us.

HILLARY

Well, got to run. Gotta discuss last minute election strategies with your father.

JOHNNY

You'll be the first woman US President. You'll see.

INT. KATY'S LIVING ROOM—NIGHT

Everyone is watching the late-night news.

ANCHOR

Finally, NASA reports the Cassini mission to Saturn is going well. We should have our first look at the moon Titan in November.

INT. DAVIE'S ROOM

Davie is asleep. His TV is on a music channel now.

> V.J. (V.O.)
>
> The pop singer Madonna has a new video...a remake of Heart's "CRAZY ON YOU" using the crazy man himself, Charlie Manson.

The video SHOWS Madonna sporting dozens of tattoos, one is a tiny swastika on the back of her right hand. Charles Manson has a swastika tattooed on his forehead.

The CHANNEL CHANGES to a movie channel.

It's the movie "CONTACT" where we HEAR the explanation about Hitler's speech being the first television broadcast signal of any real power sent into outer space. Our FOCUS ends on the swastika and Adolph Hitler.

The CHANNEL CHANGES again.

It's a television commercial for a "Psychic Hotline."

INT. COLLEGE DORM ROOM—NIGHT

As this commercial plays in the b.g., we overhear a GIRL talking on the telephone.

> GIRL
>
> But how did you know that? Oh my God...you guys are for real!
>
> (listening)
>
> No, this is the first time I've ever called a psychic before...

INT. PSYCHIC HOTLINE PHONE CENTER—SAME TIME

Dozens of people on phone lines assist people, posing as psychics.

Our SUPERNATURAL EYES are opened momentarily to reveal DEMONS are assisting them with the information.

> DEMON
> (to a psychic)
>
> I've known this girl since she was born...I can tell you anything you need to know.

INT. MASON HEADQUARTERS—MJ12 MEETING—NIGHT

Twelve men are sitting around a table. They're watching news feed from the Vatican via a computer connected to the Internet.

> NEWS ANCHOR (V.O.)
>
> We are about to begin. His Holiness has been briefed.

Sitting at the head of the table is JOHN ROCKWELL, ninety-nine. He's struggling to breathe and is attached to an oxygen tank.

> JOHN
>
> Here today on this panel, the Majesty Twelve, are three FBI agents, three CIA, three Secret Service and three fellow Masons.

> MASON
>
> We have good news on the planned New Year's attacks.

CIA

We have made house to house searches legal.

SECRET SERVICE

People gave up their rights one by one for peace and safety…from us!

FBI

Millions of inferior races were rounded up and later transferred to labor camps after we provoked them into rioting on New Year's Eve. We took care of people opposing tax, prisoners, demonstrators, militia members and die-hard Christians in one night.

JOHN

Our media called it the rapture! We're the new Round Table. Let's begin *our*…Reign of Terror.

EXT. THE VATICAN—NIGHT

Subtitle: "Midnight. Good Friday morning."

Thousands are gathered in St. Peter's Square.

Muslims, Catholics, and Orthodox Christians alike are in attendance with prayer beads, rosaries, and photos of Mary.

POPE (V.O.)

Our Lady of Fatima appeared to three girls in Fatima in 1917. Secrets revealed to them warned of chastisements. Tonight, we await her return.

Suddenly, a beautiful multicolored LIGHT appears in the sky. A female apparition appears. It's SEMIRAMIS, Lililea's twin!

SEMIRAMIS

> My children, I come to you as mediator between God and man. I plead with you, listen to my words of caution.

EXT. JERUSALEM—DEPARTMENT STORE WINDOW TV

Enoch and Elijah are watching the live newscast.

ENOCH

> It's time.

Forgetting to look both ways, they cross the street into the path of a taxi. The driver flips them off, extending his middle finger.

ENOCH & ELIJAH
(together)

> Sun god worshipper!

EXT. THE VATICAN

The crowd listens to every word from the apparition's mouth.

SEMIRAMIS

> Soon, two suns will appear in the sky. One is a ball of fire guided by the Eternal Father to bring mankind to its knees. A sign before this

happens...a red cross in a blue, cloudless sky.

Suddenly, another LIGHT appears. It's a male ANGEL.

> ANGEL
>
> Fear God and give glory to him, for the hour of his judgment is come. Worship Him that made heaven, Earth, and the sea.

EXT. ABOVE ST. PAUL'S CATHEDRAL

SATAN hovers INVISIBLY, watching this with shock. APOLLYON, Satan's sidekick, observes the events CLOSELY on Satan's monitor.

> SATAN
>
> Where's OUR two false witnesses, Peter and Paul?

> APOLLYON
>
> It's the Angel of the Lord.

> SATAN
>
> I can see that! Are the troops ready?

> APOLLYON
>
> Everything is ready, sire.

INT. MASONIC HEADQUARTERS—MJ12 MEETING

Satan magically appears. He turns to John Rockwell.

SATAN

You know what to do.

John nods and bows as Satan turns to leave. Apollyon hands Satan his sword of fire and serpent-shaped helmet.

SATAN

It's Black Friday.

EXT. EGYPT'S NORTHEAST BORDER—DAYBREAK

Subtitle: "A few hours later."
Egyptians begin attacking Syrian forces along Israel's borders.

EXT. EARTH'S ATMOSPHERE—DAY

Michael SHOUTS to the angels of the four winds, SOUNDING like a TRUMPET.
The angels suddenly appear, each riding a different colored horse: white, red, black and gray.

MICHAEL

Do not harm the Earth or sea until the servants
of God have been marked. Hold back the winds
until I've marked the 144,000.

MONTAGE

A)   The wind blowing across the desert suddenly stops blowing.

B)   A hurricane being tracked on radar SUDDENLY dissipates.

C)   People all over Earth react to the lack of a breeze.

END OF MONTAGE

EXT. SYRIA—DAY

UDAI is briefing his troops when suddenly the winds die down.

UDAI

It's the calm before the storm.

EXT. EARTH'S ATMOSPHERE

An ANGEL carrying God's seal descends to Earth from the east. He gives God's seal to the Prince of Israel, Michael.

ANGEL

Of the twelve tribes, mark 12,000 from each...6,000 male and 6,000 female.

MONTAGE

A)   The angels head all over Earth, since the Ten Lost Tribes are still scattered and not all dwelling in Israel.

B)   We SEE Josh and Rebekah getting marked, but Katy does not.

C)   Afterwards, Michael and the other angel head towards Heaven.

D)   The four angels of the wind return whence they came.

END OF MONTAGE

EXT. CAIRO (EGYPT)—DAY

A tour guide, FAROUK EL BAZ, is talking about Egyptian pharaohs to a group of tourists with the Sphinx in the b.g.

> FAROUK

> A secret chamber was discovered under the paw of the Sphinx containing a tablet made of a substance alien to Earth. It would require three of the tablets to make a complete disk. Two of them have been found.

He points to a photo of a wedge-shaped green tablet.

It's the tablet Apollyon buried here in the past.

> FAROUK

> The other was found under a pyramid complex in Mexico on the Yucatan Peninsula. Hieroglyphic writings on both pieces are similar. Found on separate hemispheres, we believe extraterrestrial origin is the only explanation. They have not yet been deciphered.

Egyptian terrorists in the b.g. are mobilizing for war.

EXT. UDAI'S DESERT CAMP—DAY

Several Egyptian spies are tied to stakes in the hot sun. Udai SEES a bow and some arrows and gets an idea.

> UDAI

> Put an apple on each of their heads.

Soldiers obey his order, while Udai takes up the bow and arrows.

Udai takes aim at the first spy. He releases the arrow.

It pierces the Egyptian's head, missing the apple, which falls.

UDAI

Ah, the forbidden fruit...still the downfall of man.

INT. HEAVEN—GOD'S THRONE ROOM

Jesus holds a scroll, sealed with seven rainbow-colored seals.

Seven archangels: Michael, Raphael, Uriel, Raguel, Zerachiel, Haniel, and Gabriel stand before him with seven trumpets.

Seven men in white robes: Seth, Enos, Cainan, Mahalaleel, Jared, Lamech, and Methuselah stand before him with seven vials.

Twenty-four elders: the twelve apostles and the twelve sons of Jacob are sitting on thrones surrounding God's throne.

The four cherubim are at the four corners of God's throne.

Jesus holds up the book with the seven seals. Michael gets his horn into position, as does Seth with his vial.

EXT. UDAI'S DESERT CAMP—DAY

Udai RELEASES the arrow, which misses the last spy, instead hitting the apple upon his head dead center.

Suddenly an ALARM SOUNDS, alerting Udai's troops.

MESSENGER

Egypt is attacking now!

Udai turns to his troops, signaling it's time to move.

GUARD

What about the last spy?

UDAI

They worship the sun...leave him to die in its heat.

EXT. HAWAII—SUNSET (8:00 PM)

A WWW (World Wide Wrestling) match is beginning its live broadcast. We HEAR the announcer's "Let's get ready to rumble!"
The CROWD ROARS. The round BELL RINGS several times.

ANNOUNCER

In this corner, the newest threat to the N.W.O. The adopted giant son of Thor...the God of Thunder. His opponent...just released from his chains below the Earth, the God of fire, the mischievous trickster, Loki!

INT.GOD'S THRONE ROOM

All angels are dressed in armor and battle gear.

ANGEL

Satan is approaching.

EXT. HEAVEN'S GATES

As Satan enters the gateway, he MORPHS into full armor.

Satan's armies, dressed in battle gear, follow him as they make their entrance inside Heaven's gates.

SATAN

It's time!

INT. THRONE ROOM

ANGEL

The war in Heaven begins!

Jesus OPENS the FIRST violet-colored SEAL.

The lion cherub motions for US to LOOK through his monitor.

CHERUB

Come and see!

INSERT—MONITOR

We SEE a cloud of dust forming. A CLOSER VIEW reveals a white camouflaged jeep carrying Udai leading his Islamic troops.

He carries the bow, now supporting a banner displaying a swastika. On the jeep's side are the military ID numbers, 666.

NARRATOR (V.O.)

I saw a white horse, and he that sat on him had
a bow; and a crown was given unto him; and he
went forth conquering, and to conquer.

EXT./INT. GREAT PYRAMID

The FIRST relieving stone over the King's chamber where Adam was buried is supernaturally HIGHLIGHTED.

INT. MASONIC HEADQUARTERS—A COMPUTER MONITOR

Showing Udai is being watched by the MJ12 members.

> JOHN
>
> Udai has retaliated against Egypt's attack with a terrible and sudden force.

John becomes noticeably concerned now.

> CIA
>
> But we're safe, underground in our labyrinth of tunnels.

> MASON
>
> John, what's the matter? You look nervous.

> JOHN
>
> An Oracle predicted my downfall would come through my own seed, and that of a prostitute. I've had all my children killed except one. I've already killed the prostitute.

EXT. HAWAII—NIGHT

WWW title match is about to begin.

> ANNOUNCER
>
> The WWW World Champion...Pluto and sidekick Charon!

The crowd ROARS and BOOS!

INSERT—TV MONITOR

Someone is watching the wrestling match.

The CHANNEL CHANGES to NEWS as we OVERHEAR someone AD LIBBING about what's happening in the Middle East.

GTV News is covering the war and after showing the above atrocities in Egypt, they CUT TO their correspondent in Israel.

Subtitle: "Jerusalem. 8:00 a.m."

> ANCHOR
>
> Thanks Tom. We're outside the steps of the restored Jewish Temple on the Temple Mount. We'll let you hear what's being said for yourself...

EXT. JERUSALEM—TEMPLE MOUNT—MORNING

Enoch and Elijah are addressing Jews inside the restored Temple. Many have GOD'S SEAL, the X-shape within a circle.

Davie is there but he's NOT marked. He's reading ALOUD to himself from a Dr. Seuss book, "GREEN EGGS AND HAM."

> ELIJAH
>
> We are God's two witnesses sent from Heaven.

> ENOCH
>
> God's wrath and judgment are coming upon the Earth.

ELIJAH

If anyone tries to kill us, by the same method shall they themselves die.

EXT. PLATEAU OF TIBET—DAY

Subtitle: "Somewhere near the Gobi Desert."

From an opening in the ground, a huge DOOR OPENS. From this tunnel comes some kind of UFO. It SHOOTS OUT quickly, disappearing.

EXT. EGYPT—DAY

Udai is LOOKING across the desert horizon reflecting a watery mirage. The false water image

DISSOLVES TO:

EXT. NAZCA PLAINS—DAY

A similar VIEW in the desert plains of Nazca. Our VIEW RISES from the ground to an AERIAL VIEW as we are now...

INT. FLYING AIRCRAFT'S POV—NAZCA LINES

...inside the UFO now flying over the Nazca Lines, which resemble an airport landing strip in the sand.

The craft we're in CLIMBS HIGHER and suddenly speeds up as it heads towards Mexico City, as indicated by an ONBOARD DISPLAY.

INT. UFO'S POV—TEOTIHUACAN—SUN AND MOON PYRAMIDS

Come into VIEW. A display shows coordinates of 19.5 degrees S.

Latitude. We bank west towards the Pacific Ocean.

INT. UFO'S POV—EASTER ISLAND—STONE STATUES

Come into VIEW. Pausing, we now head west once again.
Passing over the Pacific, we approach

INT. UFO'S POV—HAWAII—NIGHT

As we pass over the main island heading towards Honolulu, WE SEE it's
at the same coordinates of 19.5 degrees S. Latitude.

EXT. WWW MATCH—LOKI AND MANKIND

Are fighting and seem evenly matched.

Just as it looks like Loki is getting the advantage, a BRIGHT LIGHT
from ABOVE the outdoor arena APPEARS over the ring.

The announcers and crowd seem surprised by this.

A man silhouetted by the light COMES DOWN from the hovering aircraft, which we can't make out.

> COMMENTATOR ONE (O.S.)
>
> The WWW's newest wrestler may be a little
> early tonight.

> COMMENTATOR TWO (O.S.)
>
> Yes. Thor, the God of Thunder, is supposed to
> appear tonight.

Sure enough, the man descending down a rope is dressed like Thor,
complete with winged-helmet, cape and golden hammer.

INT. UFO'S POV—THE ARENA BELOW

As we rejoin our flight, we realize we weren't aboard Thor's helicopter. We leave Hawaii, crossing the Pacific until we arrive...

INT. UFO'S POV—THE GROUND

...along the coast of eastern Asia. We PASS OVER many religious temples along the way until we end up

EXT. GIZA PLATEAU—DAY

Near the pyramids and sphinx, where the UFO seemingly lands.

Udai is still LOOKING across the desert when he SEES a man walking towards him. Guards beside him raise their weapons.

As the man gets CLOSER, we realize he's VERY tall and dressed in camel hair and sandals, with long hair, fingernails, and beard.

The giant-sized man now stands in front of Udai, dwarfing him. Tattooed across his forehead are four letters: S-T-U-R.

Also tattooed there is an ANKH, the Egyptian symbol of life.

He raises his right hand in the form of an open-handed salute, revealing he has SIX fingers and a SWASTIKA tattooed there.

SATURN

Sieg Heil!

Udai and his military leaders scratch their heads with disbelief. They NOTICE he has a mechanical-looking left hand.

An Arab HOLY MAN standing beside Udai advises him.

HOLY MAN

This must be the long-awaited Muhadee, or

twelfth Emon.

Udai and our giant visitor from outer space, SATURN, are standing before television cameras at a huge press conference.

SATURN

I'm Saturn, from the Tribe of Teitan. I'm from your past.

He pauses, looking at the crowd. His eyes begin to water.

SATURN

A reptilian race left their dying home planet long ago. These flying serpents came here and created your race in our image from the elements of your planet.

A group of REPORTERS have made their way to the front.

REPORTER

In the Garden of Eden?

SATURN

Yes...the sacred name of your birthplace. The serpents lived for many years on your fifth planet, Tiamet. We are from your fourth planet, Mars. A nuclear accident on Tiamet destroyed the planet, now an asteroid belt. A fragment of Tiamet hitting Mars forced us to come here. Most reptilians perished except for three. They came here, creating your race.

REPORTER

Your race came from Mars?

SATURN

Yes. We lived in pyramid cities much like this
one. In fact, we built these stone monuments.

He points to the three Giza pyramids in the b.g. Another reporter holds
up a photo taken of the Cydonia region on Mars.

REPORTER

Some people believe there are pyramids located in the Cydonia region of Mars.

SATURN

Yes. That's where we last lived before coming
here. The reptilians gave us advanced technology, which is how we traveled here. Wars
between humans and giants broke out one day
causing many of us to escape and set up a new
home elsewhere. From there, we've been
watching your race and learned of your own
advancements after receiving your first transmission.

He now plays the black and white Hitler speech from the opening cere-
monies at the 1936 Olympics on a 3-D holographic device.

SATURN

We felt it was safe to return to you since you
proudly displayed our most sacred symbol of

330   Revelations

life.

He raises his right palm displaying the SWASTIKA tattooed there.

REPORTER

You expect us to believe your race built these monuments?

SATURN

We left our written record and buried them safely underneath.

Farouk, the Egyptian tour guide we saw earlier, comes forward.

FAROUK

That record has been found.

Egyptian soldiers bring the tablets to Saturn for inspection.
The giant puts them together, a perfect match. It's obvious a THIRD piece is missing.

SATURN

One day, the three flying serpents or the Divine Trinity will return. On that day, they will bring the third piece.

The giant reads the glyphs and translates their meaning.

SATURN
(translating)

Man was created in OUR image, after our likeness. He was created male and female and given dominion over the Earth. He was commanded to multiply.

He SEES a photo from a temple wall in Abydos showing ancient flying vehicles. One of them resembles his craft.

SATURN

This is the ark that carried us safely from Earth.
We found a new home, a moon in this system.
We've been there ever since.

REPORTER

Which moon is that?

SATURN

The moon you call Titan.

The crowd of people begins MURMURING among themselves.

REPORTER

We've sent a probe to the planet we call Saturn.

SATURN

Yes. We've been tracking it along with all your
other probes.

He pulls out a stack of disc-shaped greeting plaques sent with the Voyager and Pioneer space probes.

REPORTER

Why do you travel alone?

SATURN

After receiving your "WAR OF THE WORLDS" transmission, we felt it wise to send only one ambassador.

REPORTER
(shouting his
comment)

Christians and Jews believe a God created them!

A look of rage fills the giant's face.

SATURN

There is no God! Our people who survived here settled in Canaan. Wars with these Jewish people as they TOOK our land, made us flee...and did this.

He raises his left arm, revealing a cybernetic hand.

SATURN

It angers me to know their race survives to this day.

REPORTER

Two of their prophets are in the city of Jerusalem now. One of them, Elijah, claims he can call fire from Heaven.

A smile returns to the titan's face.

                    SATURN

That's easy. A Titan named Prometheus was the
first to bring fire from Heaven. I'll demonstrate
this by calling fire from the sky myself.

INT. GOD'S THRONE ROOM

The battle is in full force. All angels are engaged in warfare. The cherubim protect God's throne with their swords of fire.

EXT. HEAVEN'S GATES

The Archangel Michael fights with Satan. Both are fighting with flaming swords. Michael NOTICES a swastika on Satan's forehead.

                    MICHAEL

You always TWIST the Word of God to further
your LIES, so now I see you've taken God's
Holy Seal and TWISTED it too!

                    SATURN

Your God marks his servants with his CROSS,
so why not mark my followers with my
TWISTED CROSS?

Michael gets a break from fighting Satan by knocking him down. Then,
being the first archangel, he BLOWS the FIRST TRUMPET!

INT. VIENNA (AUSTRIA)—HOFBURG TREASURE HOUSE—DAY

One of Hussein's officers is stealing the Sword of Destiny.

EXT. BANKS OF THE NILE (CAIRO)—DAY

Saturn prepares to call fire down from Heaven.

INT. SPACE STATION

Sensors are going crazy as LIGHTS FLASH and BUZZERS SOUND.

> HAL (V.O.)
>
> Incoming particles…a meteor shower or SOMETHING!

INT. MASONIC HEADQUARTERS

The commanding officer is YELLING into various headsets.

> OFFICER
>
> Get the space station to the other side of the planet! All movable GPS satellites are to move as well…NOW!

EXT. MOON BASE (FAR SIDE)

Everything is going underground, becoming invisible to us from the surface. The moon is directly over Israel, which we can see below in the b.g.

INT. SPACE STATION

All the onboard lights go RED!

> HAL
>
> NORAD, something big is coming from outer

space.

SERIES OF SHOTS

A)   NORAD, under FEMA control, goes to DEFCON FOUR.

B)   Soviet and Chinese forces go on their first level of alert too.

C)   Egyptian battlefields receive HAIL mixed with FIRE and BLOOD.

D)   Israel is not touched as the moon blocks it.

E)   Moon bases on the far side are being pelted.

F)   The hail-fire affects a THIRD of all trees and burns up all the grass, but only in the Revised Roman Empire.

G)   Areas where Christians are sealed by the Holy Spirit, the 144,000 and the entire nation of Israel are spared.

EXT. SUEZ CANAL—DAY

Udai witnesses the alleged firepower of his new giant friend. As Saturn prepares his spacecraft, Udai turns to his generals.

> UDAI
>
> Attack Greece and Turkey now as planned.
> We're headed to Jerusalem to shed the blood of
> two false prophets!

EXT. JERUSALEM—TEMPLE MOUNT—DAY

Enoch and Elijah stand on the steps outside leading into the Jewish Temple. They look up and see Saturn's ship coming down from the sky. As they exit the ship and begin to approach the temple, Udai's armies completely surround them.

A COURIER brings news from the front lines.

> COURIER
>
> The defeat of Egypt, Greece and Turkey has led to the surrender of Germany, Spain, France, Italy, Libya and Ethiopia.

A soldier brings him the Spear of Destiny.

> UDAI
>
> I am invincible! Nobody can stop me! I am the King of the World!

They march boldly to the temple door.

> NARRATOR (V.O.)
>
> Daniel foretold of the day that the great Prince of Israel Michael, who was busy in Heaven, would step aside and allow the greatest time of trouble in the history of all the nations. He had to let the lawless one come and fulfill his destiny.

Udai takes the Sword of Destiny and plunges it towards Elijah.

> UDAI
>
> Die...prophet of death!

But the sword doesn't find its mark.

Instead, as if by magic, it turns upon him and pierces Udai's own forehead, all the way through and coming out the back.

His blood gushes out upon the altar, where he slumps over dead.

SATURN

Stand back! Leave him to me!

Saturn pulls the sword out of Udai's head.

Udai's officers try to retaliate against Elijah but whatever method they use backfires, killing them instead.

Saturn places Udai's body on the Jewish altar. He dips his finger in blood and makes the symbol of a swastika on his forehead.

INT. USA PRISON—CLOSE ON—CHARLES MANSON'S

SWASTIKA as he's watching this with the rest of the world on GTV.

CHARLES MANSON

Far out! I mean...crazy!

EXT. JEWISH TEMPLE (JERUSALEM)—DAY

The Jews SEE this and begin fleeing the city; AD LIBBING they just witnessed the "abomination of desolation."

Josh and Rebekah get a good jump, as does Davie.

But Katy stumbles and falls. She's captured immediately. Eva tries to assist her mother and gets SHOT! She falls to the ground, dead.

Josh tries to turn back, but the crowd pushes him further away. As he's carried along with them, Josh keeps YELLING Eva and Katy's name.

EXT. ISRAELI/JORDANIAN BORDER—DESERT—DAY

Udai's armies chase the Jews fleeing into the desert regions of Jordan. Udai's troops close in.

Enoch leads the Jews. Josh, Rebekah and Davie are among them.

Just as they clear the desert and make it to the mountains, Enoch turns around and smites the ground with his staff.

The ground opens up, swallowing the entire army except one.

He gets on his radio, informing his commander of the events. A lone cameraman carries this from a distance on global TV.

INT. RUSSIAN HEADQUARTERS

Russian and Chinese leaders are watching the events on TV.

INT. UNDERGROUND—NORTH AMERICAN RADAR DEFENSE BASE

NORAD steps up to DEFCON THREE.

EXT. TEMPLE MOUNT—SATURN

Takes Udai's right hand and places it over the crude swastika, making the opposite impression on his hand.

                                SATURN

        I'm taking him with me. I will make him live
        again.

EXT. HAWAII—WWW MATCH—NIGHT

Thor is trying to strike Loki on the head with his hammer.

                                COMMENTATOR

        There must be some bad blood between these
        two.

EXT. HEAVEN'S GATE

We SEE the various fallen angels being tossed out of Heaven now. One by one, they fall through the tunnel back to Earth.

EXT. HAWAII—NIGHT

Finally, Thor's hammer finds its mark and Loki goes down. Mankind, who had stepped in the ring to help Loki, is TERRIFIED, now running out of the ring.

Thor pins the unconscious Loki, winning his debut match.

EXT. HEAVEN'S GATE

Satan and Michael are fighting. Satan gets the upper hand.

Laurianna tries to help. As she does, Satan knocks off her two bracelets with the two keys dangling from her wrists.

Apollyon grabs them as Michael casts Satan from Heaven.

Laurianna trips her brother, causing him to fall right behind Satan. But, he still has both bracelets and the keys.

> MICHAEL
>
> Don't worry. We'll get 'em back.

He takes his golden slingshot and hands it to Laurianna.

> MICHAEL
>
> Give this to David. He'll know how to use it.

EXT. HAWAII—NIGHT

In a moment of compassion for his adopted son, Thor places his hand upon Loki's forehead. He awakes.

EXT. THE VATICAN—DAY

Saturn's ship LANDS inside St. Peter's Square.

Saturn gets out. He LOOKS UP at the cathedral, then all around the square, ending with the obelisk in the center.

> SATURN
>
> So…this used to be the City of Saturn.

INT. ST. PAUL'S CATHEDRAL

Saturn walks up to the Pope, pushing other cardinals and bishops out of his way as they try to protect their leader.

> SATURN
>
> You're coming with me. And bring all of your cute little outfits.

He grabs the Pope's two-horned mitre and puts it on his own head.

> SATURN
>
> I'll be wearing the pants in this religion from now on.

INT. BERGEN-BELSEN CONCENTRATION CAMP—NIGHT

A teary-eyed Katy arrives to the newly constructed camp.

A guard begins cutting off her long, gray hair.

NARRATOR (V.O.)

History…repeated.

EXT. PARIS—SUNRISE

Subtitle: "Three days later. Easter Sunday."

The Eiffel Tower fills the skyline with Paris in the b.g.

NARRATOR (V.O.)

The Eiffel Tower was the first manmade monument to top the height of the Great Pyramid.

THROUGH the Arch de Triumph, we SEE Saturn standing in the Pope Mobile leading the procession ahead of Udai's body.

The Pope is bound and gagged as a prisoner in the last car, which is Udai's jeep with the "666" on its side.

Saturn wears the Pope's mitre and clothing, but they are tight fitting. Our FOCUS ends on the Pope's SYMBOL of the TWO KEYS.

EXT. ST. PETER'S SQUARE—DAY—ANGLE ON—THE SKY

Like a BOLT of LIGHTNING, Satan and Apollyon come to Earth with a great THUD. The ground begins to shake from the TREMORS.

The place where Satan fell was right THROUGH the spike atop the obelisk centered in St. Peter's Square.

Michael witnesses this, as does his fellow archangel Gabriel.

MICHAEL

NOW I understand why the phallic symbol is used with the phrase 'Up yours.'

342   Revelations

Gabriel nods with agreement.

As Apollyon HITS the ground, the keys he took HIT the ground.

Satan MORPHS THROUGH the obelisk, angrily picking up the keys.

                    GABRIEL

> Woe to the inhibitors of the Earth and of the
> sea! For the devil is come down unto you, hav-
> ing great wrath, because he knows that his time
> is short.

EXT. EUPHRATES RIVER—UNDERWATER

Subtitle: "Somewhere in the Euphrates River."

VIBRATIONS from Satan's fall LOOSEN chains from three angels bound here.

GADREL, fallen Prince of the old Grecian Empire, wears the skin of a leopard.

KESABEL, fallen Prince of the Medes and Persian Empire, wears the skin of a bear.

YEKUN, fallen Prince of the ancient Babylonian Empire, wears the skin of a lion.

They rise to the surface, breathing air for the first time in centuries.

                    YEKUN

> We're free at last!

                    KESABEL

> It must be time.

> GADREL

Remember that I'm to be the strongest. Where
are they?

They LOOK all around with their ultra-sensitive vision.

> YEKUN

I've found them!

They become INVISIBLE to our eyes as they head west.

EXT. NOTRE DAME CATHEDRAL—HIGH ANGLE—GROUND BELOW

With a hideous gargoyle in the f.g., we SEE Udai's coffin parked in front.
Saturn heads into the church.

> NARRATOR (V.O.)

Notre Dame, French for Our Lady…the Virgin
Mary.

INT. CATHEDRAL

Saturn walks up to the altar. He motions for the priests there to place
Udai's body on the altar.

Saturn pricks Udai in the side with the Spear of Destiny.

He takes some of the dark blood oozing from the wound on his finger
and retraces the dried swastika on Udai's forehead.

He takes Udai's right hand and places it over the mark, making a fresh
reverse print of it on his right hand.

EXT. NOTRE DAME CATHEDRAL

The three freed Princes FLY PAST the hideous gargoyles on their way DOWN and inside through an open window.

INT. NOTRE DAME CATHEDRAL

Udai begins to move as Yekun, Gadrel and Kesabel now POSSESS him as one UNITED BEAST, bringing him back to life.

> SATURN
> (to Udai)

Happy birthday, boys.

> (to the crowd)

As foretold by our prophets, the Teitans, and stolen by the Jews...after three days, the man to save mankind would be resurrected!

> UDAI/GADREL

After I set up my kingdom, our creators will come and help me establish a 1,000-year reign of peace on Earth.

> UDAI/YEKUN

I change my name to TEITAN, adopted son of the Teitans...like Muslims taking the name Mohammed...like Egyptian kings, the name Pharaoh.

TEITAN/KESABEL

Saturn was hidden but now revealed, thus the name of his people shall be mine.

EXT. NOTRE DAME CATHEDRAL

Gabriel and Michael observe this from the cathedral's top. They're on one tower. Apollyon and Satan are on top of the other.

SATAN
(to Apollyon)

You know what to do.

Apollyon VANISHES. As he does, the Prince of Revised Rome, TAREL, APPEARS beside Satan.

TAREL

It's not fair. My kingdom was the shortest.

GABRIEL

Will you go peacefully?

TAREL

I will. But is it true my brother and I will lead the largest army ever on earth?

MICHAEL

Amazarak and Penemue also.

SATAN

That chain you're holding for me...you won't
need it.

MICHAEL

Don't count on it.

INT. CATHEDRAL

Saturn places a three-horned crown on TEITAN'S head. Then, he wraps
a leopard skin cape around his shoulders.

SATURN

This country's great revolution yielded the
Second Empire. Uniting Eastern and Western
Rome revived its own Second Empire. Today,
we go where Hitler once dared to go. On
Teitan's rebirth, the Third Empire, much like
the Third Reich, is born.

EXT. JERUSALEM'S JEWISH TEMPLE—DAY

Elijah witnesses the events in Paris via a television monitor.

ELIJAH
(to us)

This is how I learned your past.

EXT. PARIS—DAY

Saturn and Teitan make their way through the crowded streets.

Everyone is amazed that Teitan survived his deadly wound.

They come to the Arc De Triumphe, in the Place Charles de Gaulle where the twelve avenues meet, riding in Teitan's jeep.

The Eternal Flame of the Unknown Soldier burns brightly.

SATURN

> This arch celebrates your victory from oppressors. Nameless soldiers honored with a living, breathing, eternal flame. You once worshipped your sun as the light of the world. Now give this honor to another life-giving light…Teitan.

MONTAGE

Masonic secret societies watch this on TV in underground bases in America, Italy, Germany, on the moon and the space station.

END OF MONTAGE

EXT. PLACE CHARLES DE GAULLE (PARIS)

Europe's Ten Kings stand at ten of the twelve avenues. Saturn stands at the end of the eleventh dressed as the Pope. Teitan stands at the twelfth, dressed as a king.

Saturn walks up to a scaffold rig in the circle's center, where something HUGE is covered up.

He LOOKS over at the miniature Statue of Liberty near the river.

SATURN

> You celebrated freedom by erecting this Statue of Liberty. She stands enlightening the world.

Your enlightenment became the new Age of
Reason.

He uncovers the object, revealing a statue made of gold.

It stands sixty feet high and six feet wide and resembles an ancient statue of Nebuchadnezzar but with Teitan's face.

The statue holds a key in its hand, and from our SIDE VIEW, it resembles the ankh. It's the abyss key, stolen from Laurianna.

> SATURN

> The Pope had two keys symbolizing his authority to open and shut heaven. I give this authority to Teitan…and to his image.

Saturn gives Teitan Laurianna's other key. The Pope's ensign displaying two keys is in the b.g.

Saturn takes a golden hammer and chisel. He starts HAMMERING out a swastika on the statue's forehead.

SPARKS fly everywhere, reminding us of when God created angels by hammering on a rock causing fiery sparks.

He also chisels an ankh, and with the final stroke, the STATUE COMES to life. His mouth moves as he begins to speak.

> STATUE

> Happy Birthday!

Everyone GASPS with amazement. One woman faints. Some people start running from the scene.

> NARRATOR (V.O.)

> God's greatest achievement of taking a clay statue and giving it life would finally be imitated by

evil, mocking God.

STATUE

Fear not! I will not harm you. Teitan, in whose image I'm made, will save you. He'll save you from the two false witnesses. He will kill them for all to see and will restore order to the world. Worship Teitan. Take his MARK, the swastika, his NAME, or his NUMBER, 666, and place it on your forehead or right hand to show your allegiance.

The statue holds up his right hand, revealing a swastika.

STATUE

Do it with your own blood.

The statue looks at a live BAND that is waiting to play.

STATUE

When the band begins playing, worship me, made in the image of Teitan. Show your loyalty. If you do not, you will surely die.

MONTAGE

A)   Many are WATCHING large VIDEO SCREENS at the front of their churches. Most churches are filled to near capacity.

B)   One by one, we see priests, preachers, and other various ministers following the statue's instructions.

C)   Entire congregations follow their spiritual leaders.

D)   Teitan's soldiers prick themselves and use their own blood to make the mark in their forehead or right hand.

END OF MONTAGE

BACK TO SCENE

SATURN

Peter founded your church. As the last Pope of his church of lies, I will now be known as Peter...the Terrible. The first and the last!

MONTAGE

Many Jews and Christians AROUND THE WORLD outside of Teitan's Empire witness this, but do NOT take this mark.

END OF MONTAGE

INT. GOD'S THRONE ROOM

The FIRST saint, Seth, pours out the FIRST VIAL.

EXT. EARTH—SERIES OF SHOTS

All people with the mark, suddenly SCREAM with pain.

Great boils come upon their skin where they have the mark.

The mark becomes a permanent scar now.

EXT. NOTRE DAME CATHEDRAL—ROOF

Satan SEES what has happened on his monitor.

> SATAN
>
> My cattle have been branded.

EXT. PLACE CHARLES DE GAULLE

Teitan receives news of his army's demise in the Jordan desert.

> SOLDIER
>
> The ground just opened up and swallowed them.

This angers the antichrist very much. He addresses his armies.

> TEITAN
>
> Kill the Jews! Advance to Jerusalem and wipe them from the face of the earth!

INT. GOD'S THRONE ROOM

Jesus now opens the SECOND indigo-colored SEAL.
The cherub like a CALF motions to US.

> CHERUB
>
> Come and see!

INSERT—CHERUB MONITOR

Where we SEE dust stirring over a desert horizon. The RED army flags of Russia AND China move quickly across the FRAME.

These BECOME the totally RED flag with a two-headed eagle, the new flag of the Third Empire.

Teitan's white jeep has been painted RED!

> NARRATOR (V.O.)
>
> And there went out another HORSE that was RED...

EXT./INT. GREAT PYRAMID

The SECOND relieving stone over the King's chamber is SUPERNAT-URALLY highlighted.

EXT. NEAR ARCH DE TRIUMPH

Just as Teitan is about to lead his armies back to Israel, another MES-SENGER arrives.

> MESSENGER
>
> Russia is attacking from the north...

Before that messenger finishes, MESSENGER TWO breaks in.

> MESSENGER TWO
>
> ...China and its eastern allies are attacking from the east at this very moment.

Teitan signals his troops to halt.

> TEITAN
>
> First, we must protect our kingdom. The Third

Empire declares war on the King of the north and the Kings of the east.

NARRATOR (V.O.)

...and power was given to him to take peace from the Earth and that they should kill one another. And there was given unto him a great sword.

He raises the Sword of Destiny in the air, preparing to lead the charge. He turns to the ten kings, now wearing his mark.

TEITAN

I promise all of you continued reign with me as kings of the Third Empire. Send me all of your troops and weapons. Anyone who is against us...kill them!

He leads his troops back through the Arch de Triumph. As he does, his jeep snuffs out the flame of the Unknown Soldier.

EXT.PLACE CHARLES DE GUALLE

The Ten Kings and Saturn are all admiring the living statue.

FIRST KING

Our kingdoms unite with Teitan's.

SATURN

Do away with any other religions in the Third Empire, including the Catholic Church and Greek Orthodox Church.

All of the kings nod in agreement.

SECOND KING

We know what to do my lord.

The GERMAN KING is dressed as a Templar Knight, complete with a red sash, decorated with a Maltese cross.

GERMAN KING

Let's begin minting new German marks for all of the Third Empire. The swastika will be on the back; much like it was on coins minted in ancient Greece. Only with this new mark can anyone buy and sell.

GRECIAN KING

I like this revising of the old Grecian Empire. Let's bring back all of the past.

FRENCH KING

I want the former Pope, Peter the Roman, placed in the prison where Jacques De Molay was held.

ITALIAN KING

The new Babylonian Captivity? What will you do with Peter?

SATURN

I have special plans for him. Don't Christians claim to be the light of the world?

EXT. NOTRE DAME CATHEDRAL—NIGHT

Subtitle: "The Nativity of Saint John. June 24, 2004"

A huge bonfire burns in front of the church.

> NARRATOR (V.O.)
>
> Midsummer fires lit up the hillsides on St. John's Eve.

Upon CLOSER inspection, we SEE that the bonfire is being used to light the former POPE, PETER the Roman!

> POPE PETER
>
> Oh Lord, my God...is there no help for the widow's son?

> NARRATOR (V.O.)
>
> Just before his own death, Joseph Smith, founder of the Mormons, made this Masonic plea for mercy.

The smoke from his body RISES, turning from WHITE to RED! The smoke travels all the way to

INT. GOD'S THRONE ROOM—ALTAR FIRE AND SMOKE

Mix together with the smoke from Peter's bonfire.

The SECOND archangel, Uriel, SOUNDS his TRUMPET.

SERIES OF SHOTS

A)   Atomic silos open all around the nations of the Third Empire. Rockets lift-off simultaneously.

B)   NORAD in Colorado goes to DEFCON ONE.

C)   On the nose of one of the missiles, we see the words, "Funded by THIRD*UNION*. The mountain will come to you!"

INT. THE VATICAN

Bishops and cardinals are casting ballots for an election.

> FIRST BISHOP
>
> We must not let the Papacy be moved to French soil again.

> SECOND BISHOP
>
> We must elect a new Pope.

EXT. ST. PETER'S SQUARE—DAY

Crowds of unmarked onlookers anxiously WATCH a chimney.

> NARRATOR (V.O.)
>
> They wait to see if the smoke burns black or white. This way they learn if a Pope has been elected or not.

INT. THE VATICAN

A ballot with a black circle FALLS from a pile of ballots. The pile was being held together with a PAPERCLIP.

A gust of wind catches the ballot, taking it out a window.

David Allen Rigsby

EXT. ST. PETER'S SQUARE—THE BALLOT

Lands on a statue of Jupiter, now believed to be that of Peter.
The smoke from the chimney turns from white to red!

INT. THE VATICAN

> BISHOP THREE
>
> This cannot be a good sign.

They immediately clear the room. We see a computer monitor in the
b.g. It's tracking the incoming missiles.

INSERT—COMPUTER MONITOR

WITH A WARNING LIGHT FLASHING BESIDE A FILE NAMED
"WORMWOOD."

MONTAGE

A)   The bombs IMPACT with a great EXPLOSION.

B)   Many bombs land in and around the city of Rome.

C)   The Pantheon is destroyed.

D)   St. Peter's Square and the Vatican are demolished.

E)   Many bombs strike all around the Mediterranean Sea.

END OF MONTAGE

> NARRATOR (V.O.)
>
> The impact and radiation killed a third of the

fish. Stray bombs and tidal waves destroyed a third of all ships in the Great Sea.

EXT. VATICAN REMAINS

Among the burning debris, we see the Latin phrase, ADHUC STAT, on a broken-off piece of brick.

> NARRATOR (V.O.)
>
> ADHUC STAT. It's still standing.

EXT. OFFSHORE

A FISHERMAN is watching the city of Rome burn.

> FISHERMAN
>
> Rome was burned in a day.

EXT. SPACE STATION

We SEE the phrase, ADHUC STAT, on the space station as we PASS.

INT. SPACE STATION

Looking at a GPS monitor, we SEE that a third of the Mediterranean is as red as blood, mostly around Italy. Hal informs crews below.

> HAL
>
> Satellites are relaying images of the damage. The space station is returning from the other side.

EXT. EARTH'S ATMOSPHERE—ABOVE MEDITERRANEAN SEA

Subtitle: "July 4, 2004"

The SECOND saint, Enos, pours out the SECOND VIAL upon the Mediterranean Sea.

EXT. MARSEILLE (FRANCE)—DAY

Saturn has moved from performing miracles in Paris to the banks of the Mediterranean, just off the coast of France.

Since giants are really half angel, he SEES the spirit world. He prepares to CLAIM Enos' water-to-blood miracle.

> SATURN
>
> With the world watching, I'll turn the Mediterranean to blood.

INT. SPACE STATION—OVER EUROPE

Through a portal, we see the ENTIRE Mediterranean turn to blood.

> HAL (V.O.)
>
> How could anything still be alive in that ocean?

EXT. MARSEILLE—DAY

Saturn is standing naked and bathing in the blood of the waters.

> SATURN
>
> This little blood bath is nothing. I'll move to Avignon, so I can be close to the real bloodshed.

EXT./INT. AMPHITHEATER OF NIMES—DAY

Hundreds of people that refused the mark are being slaughtered in gladiator-style fights against soldiers of the Third Empire.

EXT. BATTLEFIELD IN EUROPE—DAY

Teitan's armies are engaged in warfare with the Soviets and the Chinese. There's much bloodshed on all sides.

EXT. CAPITOL BUILDING—WASHINGTON DC—DAY

Crowds fill the White House lawn to capacity. The obelisk-shaped National Monument is in the b.g.

Hillary Rodnim is introduced and makes her way to the podium.

> HILLARY
>
> I'm pleased to announce on this nation's birth-day, that FEMA will finally give way to our her-itage, a constitutional government.

Crowd CHEERS!

> HILLARY
>
> George W. Busch has done his best during this difficult time. But, he's a Republican and will be running against me in November.

The crowd breaks into scattered LAUGHTER and APPLAUSE.

> HILLARY
>
> Now, some bad news. Americans with Christian beliefs must report to the nearest

relocation center today for your own protection. We've received threats from extreme left-wing hate groups. We don't have National Guard troops to protect you, since they're overseas. This will be a temporary solution, I'm sure. We'll reunite you with loved ones as soon as the trouble in the Middle East subsides.

MONTAGE

A)   George Washington's statue at the Smithsonian, where he's seated semi-nude, in the pose of the Greek god Zeus.

B)   An MJ12 party with John Rockwell, Sr. wearing a party hat with a "Happy 100th birthday" sign in the b.g. He smiles.

C)   The Statue of Liberty in NYC.

D)   The statue's replica in Paris.

E)   The LIVING statue of Teitan in Paris. It smiles.

END OF MONTAGE

EXT. JORDAN DESERT—DAY

Elijah is standing before the huge rift separating Israel from Jordan.

Elijah's SPIRITUAL EYES are opened, SEEING yet another plague from God being CLAIMED by the false prophet.

ELIJAH

You want the world to believe you can affect the water? Then by your own deception will you pay...again.

He takes a bottle of water and pours it into the desert sand.

> ELIJAH
>
> You who serve other gods and worship them...the Lord's wrath will be kindled against you. He will shut up the heavens so there will be no rain, and that the land will not yield her fruit.

Elijah stretches his staff towards the heavens.

> ELIJAH
>
> From this day forward, no rain will fall upon the Third Empire.

EXT. BABYLON MARKETPLACE—DAY

Elijah's words are being picked-up and rebroadcast by the space station. Arab shoppers are listening via LOUDSPEAKERS. They wave their hands, dismissing the prophet's words.

One by one, some of them turn around and start grabbing water bottles from a shelf until they're all gone.

EXT. JORDAN DESERT—DAY

Elijah throws his mantle across the rift. The ground magically covers the void for him as he walks across.

After he gets to the other side, the land bridge disappears.

INT. GOD'S THRONE ROOM

Jesus opens the THIRD blue-colored SEAL.

The third cherub resembling a man motions for US to LOOK THROUGH his monitor.

CHERUB

Come and see!

INSERT—MONITOR

A skinny Egyptian BANKER rides through the barren streets of Cairo on a BLACK HORSE. He carries weights and measures.

BANKER

I'll pay a day's wage for some bread and water.

EXT./INT. GREAT PYRAMID

The THIRD relieving stone over the King's chamber is SUPERNATURALLY highlighted.

EXT. JORDAN DESERT—DAY

Enoch is in the wilderness with the third of all Jewish people.
Enoch smites a rock for water. Manna falls from heaven to feed them. The plagues of the Earth do not affect them here.

INT. SPACE STATION

Hal is spying on Elijah with sensitive listening devices.

EXT. JORDAN DESERT—DAY

Elijah looks up, as if he knows the world is eavesdropping.

ELIJAH

Fire from Heaven will be the rain of judgment upon the wicked.

He falls to the ground in prayer. Enoch joins him.

ELIJAH

Lord, it's time for them to receive...their great ball of redemption. Let it come from Heaven and poison their waters.

INT. GOD'S THRONE ROOM

The THIRD archangel, Raguel, blows his trumpet.

EXT. OUTER SPACE—ASTEROID BELT

Suddenly, an asteroid CRASHES into another. The collision now sends one of the asteroids careening from the belt.

NARRATOR (V.O.)

The asteroid 4179 Toutatis was scheduled to come within four times the distance from our moon on September 29, 2004. This little course correction placed it on a direct path with Earth.

The rock is SEEN hurtling straight towards Earth.
Subtitle: "September 27, 2004"

INT. SPACE STATION

Warning lights and BUZZERS go off like crazy.

HAL

Not again!

EXT. JORDAN DESERT—DAY

Enoch and Elijah LOOK UP and see the bright ball of fire in the blue, cloudless sky.

ELIJAH

Not to worry…it won't affect any of us here.

CROWD'S POV—COMET IN SKY

As it suddenly DIVIDES in two! One continues its DESCENT to Earth, while the other curves around and crosses its original path. This creates a bright, fiery cross in the sky.

NARRATOR (V.O.)

Nostradamus wrote that the great star would burn for seven days when the great pontiff changed countries.

SERIES OF SHOTS

A) NORAD'S security goes to DEFCON FOUR as sensors pick up something huge coming towards the Earth from outer space.

B) Americans grumble AD LIBS, "Now they warn us."

C) Underground secret societies are safe and very carefree. Some are even playing games, like chess and "MONOPOLY."

D) People around the world look up and see two suns in the sky.

E)   Bomb and fallout shelters become crowded with people.

F)   Cities are abandoned as air raid SIRENS fill the air.

EXT. CITY ALLEY—A BUM

Urinating, notices an old movie poster for "ARMAGEDDON."

> BUM
>
> Where are those space cowboys when you need them?

In disgust, he urinates on the poster.

EXT. RESORT ISLAND—DAY

Subtitle: "Isle of Lesbos, off the coast of Greece."
Several gay and lesbian couples are lounging in the sun.
TWO WOMEN wearing dark sunglasses are sunbathing and chatting.

> WOMAN ONE
>
> Who can believe what you hear these days? Like an asteroid's gonna hit Earth. As if!

> WOMAN TWO
>
> Same people that say Sodom and Gomorrah were destroyed with fire and brimstone from Heaven. It's all just a scare tactic to push their conservative agenda on us.

> WOMAN ONE
>
> They're jealous 'cause we've come out of the

closet and having our day in the sun.

She compares her sunburn to her pale skin underneath her bikini.

WOMAN ONE

I think I need a stronger sunscreen. I'm burnt already and I just turned over.

NARRATOR (V.O.)

Toutatis was a couple days early and a few thousand miles off its projected course. It also came with a new name...Wormwood.

SERIES OF SHOTS

A) WORMWOOD hits the island dead center!

B) Huge tidal waves wipe out coastal cities near its impact.

C) We SEE someone drinking water in this area, and making a face as if it tastes bitter. He then grabs his stomach.

D) The THIRD saint, Cainan, pours out the THIRD VIAL upon the rivers and springs near Wormwood's impact.

E) The waters become as blood. The man who drank the water earlier is seen lying beside the now bloody water. He's dead.

F) While fighting Russian and Chinese forces, an Empire sergeant takes a drink from his canteen filled with blood.

NARRATOR (V.O.)

They shed the blood of saints and prophets. God has now given them blood to drink.

INT. GOD'S THRONE ROOM

Jesus opens the FOURTH green-colored SEAL.

The flying eagle cherub motions US to LOOK through his monitor.

> CHERUB

Come and see!

INSERT—CHERUB'S MONITOR

Supernaturally, we see a green horse whose rider is the angel of DEATH. He's dressed like the GRIM REAPER.

Another horse follows carrying the angel of HELL. She has flaming red hair. It's LILILEA—Lilith's mother!

> NARRATOR (V.O.)

I saw a pale horse: and his name that sat on him was Death and Hell with him. Power was given unto them over the fourth part of the Earth, to kill with sword, with hunger, and with the beasts of the Earth.

EXT./INT. GREAT PYRAMID

We see the FOURTH relieving stone over the King's chamber SUPER-NATURALLY highlighted.

MONTAGE

A)   People are being killed by sword. This mirrors Denver's murals showing women and babies killed by a large sword.

B)   Skinny people are dying from starvation. This includes the many relocation centers, labor and concentration camps.

C)   Wild animals are killing people, as they have grown bold due to gnawing hunger and thirst. A snake strikes and kills one man.

D)   Amphitheater of Nimes is where Christians are being fed to lions for the amusement of Third Empire audiences.

END OF MONTAGE

EXT. JORDAN DESERT—DAY

Elijah now prepares for his final miracle.

> ELIJAH
>
> Since your hearts are still hardened and you will not hearken to the Lord, I will bring yet another plague upon you. You, who worship the sun as god, will see that the sun is vulnerable.

EXT. DEEP SPACE

A HUGE asteroid is heading directly towards the sun.

EXT. THE SUN

The FOURTH TRUMPET archangel, Zerachiel, and the saint with the FOURTH VIAL, Mahalaleel, circle the sun.

As Zerachiel SOUNDS his TRUMPET, Mahalaleel pours his vial upon the sun.

The huge asteroid on a collision course with the sun approaches.

INT. SPACE STATION

NASA computers DISPLAY impact at 19.5 degrees S. Latitude.

As the asteroid IMPACTS, there's a huge EXPLOSION!

Heat sensors quickly SOUND. Warning lights and ALARMS go crazy.

Astronauts AD LIB warnings to their respective countries.

EXT. OUTER SPACE

GPS satellites and the space station scramble to the other side of Earth, trying to escape the maddening heat.

One satellite doesn't make it and gets FRIED!

SERIES OF SHOTS

A)   People across the globe SEE the sun getting brighter.

B)   Thermometers get so hot that some break.

C)   Everywhere, the intense heat is scorching people.

D)   Some lakes and streams dry up quickly. Steam is everywhere.

E)   On the Earth's dark side, where the moon is full and its reflection is so bright, it almost looks like daylight.

F)   Many are dying from the intense heat.

G)   As the intense heat flare ceases, the world gets colder everywhere as people start reaching for blankets.

H)   One-THIRD of the sun is now MISSING.

I)   The full moon's glow is very dim now.

J)   A ship captain looking up notes a THIRD of the constellations and Milky Way stars have stopped shining.

NARRATOR (V.O.)

A third of all stars, which stopped shining when a third of all angels fell, finally withhold their light from Earth.

EXT. JORDAN DESERT

Enoch strikes a rock and water gushes out. Elijah fills a jar.

EXT. EARTH'S ATMOSPHERE

The WOE ANGEL flies over SHOUTING to the inhabitants below.

WOE ANGEL

Woe to the inhabitants of Earth...when the three remaining trumpet angels begin to sound...

FADE TO:

EXT. PARADISE

We HEAR ELVIS PRESLEY SINGING as we SEE a mansion on a hill in the b.g. On the front gate is the word, "Graceland."

Elvis, dressed in white, is serenading a young Princess Diana.

ELVIS
(singing)

In my Father's house are many mansions, full of love and grace, in a place called Graceland.

EXT. SOMEWHERE ELSE IN PARADISE

John F. Kennedy, Joe Dimmagio, and Marilyn Monroe are all sitting in a field of flowers.

David Smith is SEEN riding a white horse, a mustang.

> NARRATOR (V.O.)
>
> Everyone's paradise is different. It's their own place of rest.

INT. HELL

We HEAR SCREAMS as we enter the fiery depths of the underworld. As we go DEEPER into the depths of Hell, we SEE a man in great pain as he is completely engulfed in flames. It's Adolph Hitler!

EXT. EARTH

Subtitle: "Wodensday, Thanksgiving Eve, later that year."

> GLOBAL NEWS TV
>
> The numbers are in now. One-fourth of the world's population has died since the terrible plagues began last spring. A trade agreement has been reached with the Third Empire by the United States to exchange water supplies for oil.

EXT. MIDDLE EAST—DAY

Children dying of thirst sweat by the flames of an oil heater.

EXT. ATLANTA AIRPORT—DAY

Oil from the Middle East arrives.

The new oil shipments go underground. A UN guard observes.

GLOBAL TELEVISION

A promotional spot for the upcoming event: "WWW's Babylon 3!"

> ANNOUNCER (V.O.)
>
> It's the return of World Wide Wrestling with a
> grudge match Between Thor and Loki.

The Midgard Serpent, a new character wearing a snake mask and body suit, AD LIBS he's gonna "squeeze Thor to death."

The PROMO introduces HELA, Goddess of the Underworld. She has flaming red hair, bright green eyes, and is very shapely.

> ANNOUNCER (V.O.)
>
> This Thanksgiving night, live from Babylon!

EXT. NEW YORK CITY—DAY

Subtitle: "Thursday, Thanksgiving Holiday, 2004 AD"

The Macy's Thanksgiving Day Parade is finishing up. We SEE Santa Claus with one of his elves riding in a sleigh float.

Satan and Apollyon are WATCHING this atop Rockwell Center. Satan is wearing a Santa suit. Apollyon is dressed like an elf.

He NOTICES some rooftop graffiti spelling out: "S-A-N-T-A."

374 Revelations

APOLLYON
(imitating
Dana Carvey)

Oh, who could that be...Satan?

He magically moves the 'N' to the end, after the second 'A' so it now reads, 'S-A-T-A-N.'

Satan, who is studying a lump of coal in his hand, looks up to see Apollyon's graffiti.

SATAN

The writing has been on the wall for a long time.

APOLLYON

Thanks for letting me be part of the myth by using dwarfs as Santa's magical elves.

SATAN

Kids believe in many things when they're young...the Tooth Fairy and the Easter Bunny. They learn about Jesus and the virgin birth in Sunday school. As they get older, they stop believing in all those...fairy tales.

He studies the piece of coal again.

SATAN

Free presents overnight replaced the free gift to mankind through the overnight miracle birth. Coal...kids are taught this came from the

Carboniferous Age, almost 220 million years ago.

> APOLLYON
> (admiring himself)

I look good for my age.

He takes the coal from Satan.

> APOLLYON

This is what happened to bad boys and girls from the Old World.

> (imitating Carvey)

'Isn't that CONVENIENT?' They receive a rock made by the flood when they've been naughty?

INT. DENVER AIRPORT—UNDERGROUND CITY

A secret society is enjoying their bountiful feast.
They are standing comfortably around HOT heaters.
Some men are sitting around playing "MONOPOLY."
Many men are watching the Thanksgiving Bowl via television.

INSERT—TV SCREEN

The Tennessee Titan's are hosting the New York Giants.
We HEAR a COMMENTATOR talking to Tennessee's Governor, JERRY LAWLESS, former wrestler and past commentator for the WWW.

COMMENTATOR (O.S.)

You're from Memphis and they call you the King?

LAWLESS (O.S.)

That's right. I even wear my crown when officiating.

We SEE a Greek building in Nashville, home of the NFL Titans.

Going back to the game, a SPECIAL EFFECT WIPE resembles a mechanized flying machine with an oval-shaped monitor, dropping down a wheel within a wheel where the network's logo is inserted. A CLOSE VIEW of a player's colorful jersey reveals a puma embroidered on his sleeve. OUR VIEW WIDENS, revealing it's from a red Saturn blimp above the stadium.

BACK TO SCENE

Johnny and John Sr. are watching the game. A man WALKS PAST them, going to the elevator, where he presses the UP button.

INT. AIRPORT—UPPER LEVEL

Getting out of the elevator, the man walks up to an odd-looking keypad. He enters some kind of command. In the b.g., we see Christian slaves being transported in over-sized baggage bins.

INT. SPACE STATION

Hal is also watching the game on TV, while keeping an eye on other screens monitoring deep space.

The Titans' tie the game again with the Giants as the Cassini probe's weak signal comes in.

HAL

Hey guys...I'm getting some really strange readings on Saturn. I don't know what it is, but I've got a fix on it at 19.5 degrees S. Latitude.

The atmospheric probe is arriving on Titan.

INSERT—PROBE FEED

Something unusual is beneath the clouds of Titan's atmosphere.

As we get below them, entire cities appear! Pyramids, skyscrapers, obelisks and other HUGE monuments!

Titans look human but are almost twenty feet tall.

We see the swastika everywhere.

BACK TO SCENE

ALARMS SOUND. There's something HUGE on Hal's radar screen.

HAL

Uh...guys. I don't mean to worry you or any-thing...but I think we got company.

EXT. SPACE STATION—ORBITING EARTH

A HUGE space ship passes OVER the space station.

A smaller escort ship comes from the belly of the mother ship. It descends to Earth, heading towards the Middle East.

EXT. JERUSALEM—DAY—LIGHTNING FLASHES

Fill the skies. A large UFO flies over the Dome on the Rock.

EXT. MECCA, SAUDI ARABIA—DAY (STORMY)

A Muslim Imam runs from the mosque to the Kaaba's south wall.

He grabs the sacred Black Stone, preparing to defend it with his life as the largest UFO lands beside the Kaaba.

> NARRATOR (V.O.)
>
> This Kaaba contains the Muslim's most sacred relic—the Black Stone. They believe God sent it down from Heaven.

Teitan makes his way through the crowds, followed by Saturn.

A ramp from the bottom of the UFO opens. A TITAN walks down the ramp. He's carrying a black box in his hand.

He walks up to Teitan and offers him the black box.

The Titan gestures for him to open it. He does.

Inside the box is a black stone—EXACTLY like the one enshrined in the Kaaba, being guarded by the Imam.

> TITAN
>
> The Black Sun.

Teitan and Saturn salute him, displaying the swastika in their palms.

The Titan returns the salute revealing a swastika in his palm.

As the Titan presses his palm into Teitan's palm, a camera FLASHES, freezing the mirror image of the swastikas.

INSERT—NEWSPAPER

Headline: "THE BROTHERHOOD," is above the photo just taken. The photo's caption reads, "The new symbol of unity?"

EXT. SAUDI ARABIA—MARKET SQUARE—LATER THAT AFTERNOON

An Arab boy peddling the papers SHOUTS the headlines.

> PEDDLER
>
> Scientists confirm Muslim and Titan Stones are identical!

INT. BABYLON—WRESTLING ARENA—LATER THAT NIGHT

The Titans are sitting ringside with Teitan and Saturn as the much-anticipated WWW rematch begins.

A commentator interviews the WWW's newest heroes, Thor and Loki.

> THOR
>
> I'm firstborn of Odin, father of the Gods. Loki, a member of the giants, was adopted into my family and is now my brother.

> LOKI
>
> But today, brother shall fight against brother. And the giant race shall win!

The BELL RINGS, beginning the match. Thor quickly gets the upper hand. He's about to use his golden hammer on Loki when the Midgard Serpent jumps into the ring.

He drop kicks Thor, takes his hammer, then hits him in the head.

TITAN

(to Saturn)

I like this Midgard.

With Thor out cold, the referee announces Loki as the winner.

LOKI

Midgard will be my new tag team partner. We challenge Thor and the partner of his choice in a rematch.

Facing Teitan, Loki and Midgard take their own blood and make a swastika on their foreheads.

LOKI

When in Rome, do as Romans do.

Hela has made it to Thor's side and revives him with a kiss.

HELA

I'll stand by Thor's side in this rematch.

The Titans are enjoying this soap opera.

TITAN

We will join the arena in this next event. But, we'll only fight other Titans.

Teitan LAUGHS and stands up to make an announcement as well.

TEITAN

This day, the day the Titans came to us, will no longer be known as Thursday. It will be

Thorsday, to honor these new gods of force.

NARRATOR (V.O.)

And so calendars were changed and the gods of Greek and Roman mythology were given new temples and shrines.

EXT. ATHENS, GREECE—DAY

The Oracle at Delphi debuts alongside Apollo's restored temple. The ORACLE, a young girl, talks indecipherably to world leaders. SUPERNATURALLY, we SEE demons are channeling through her.

ORACLE

Titans will give man a substance lighter and stronger than Titanium, called Titanium Three. It comes directly from Titan.

The leaders are all nodding in agreement, impressed.

ORACLE

The Titans will help the Third Empire, but won't intervene in our wars. They'll set up bases in Berlin and Babylon.

EXT. BABYLON—DAY

The Titan is talking to a group of Masons.

TITAN

If you build a tower at least a mile high and

place a beacon on top of the tower, after three days, the serpent race that created man will return.

INT. JEWISH TEMPLE

Teitan is roasting a pig on the altar. After picking one rib clean in his mouth, he holds it up and studies it.

> TEITAN
>
> I could make myself a wife from this rib. But I have no need for the love of a woman.

He throws the bone to a little white dog, his companion.

In the Holy of Holies, he's set up a statue of Zeus but with his own face.

INT. MASONIC UNDERGROUND CITY

A FEMA GUARD discovers water stockpiles have turned to blood.

> GUARD
>
> Uncontaminated supplies must be reserved for Masons only.

A Mason tests the blood. The blood type comes up UNKNOWN.

> JOHNNY
>
> Here, use my own blood to see if the machine works at all.

He notices a Christian slave girl nearby.

JOHNNY

You there…what's your name and where are you from?

PATTY

I come from a relocation center. My name is Patty.

JOHNNY

Let him sample your blood. Just double-checking this machine.

The tester pricks her finger and administers the test.

A DNA warning goes off.

JOHNNY

What does that mean?

TESTER

It must be malfunctioning. It shows her DNA close enough to be your own daughter.

Johnny looks at the tester, then the results, and finally the girl. They're interrupted by an announcement over the speakers.

SPEAKER (V.O.)

Everyone will temporarily have to stop bathing until water supplies are restored.

MONTAGE

A)   Dried-up lakes and rivers across the USA.

B)   The Mississippi shore along St. Louis. There's no water.

C)   Patty's house in the b.g. is in ruins.

END OF MONTAGE

EXT. WASHINGTON DC—DAY

Hillary Rodnim is making a speech before the PRESS.

> HILLARY
>
> I vow to make a deal with the devil himself if necessary, to get more oil and water.

EXT. BEER FACTORIES—GERMANY—DAY

Premium German beer factories are all boarded up and closed.

INSERT—TV SET

A home shopping channel shows a six-pack of beer going for $1,000. CHANNEL CHANGES.

A news program has a special bulletin.

> NEWS ANCHOR
>
> The Titans announced a plan to help mankind with his water problem. They're going to build HUGE ships, the largest ever, and go to Antarctica to get ICE. They'll melt it for all

Third Empire kingdoms.

EXT. CASABLANCA, MOROCCO—DAY

"TITANIC TWO" is complete. It's three times larger than our old Titanic, which sank on April 15, 1912.

Teitan, wearing his leopard-skin cape, christens the new ship. The ship's CAPTAIN, a Titan, steps up to the microphone.

> CAPTAIN
>
> If there even was a God, He Himself couldn't sink this ship!

EXT./INT. BERLIN—DAY—BEER FACTORIES

Beer production starts back up. Germany is prosperous again.

INSERT—TV MONITOR

Titans have become regulars on World Wide Wrestling.

> TITAN WRESTLER
>
> When the restraining talisman of the Christian cross is broken in Germany, then the fury of ancient warriors will surge up again!

Another Titan WRESTLER smashes a large crucifix.

> WRESTLER
>
> The old stone gods will rise from forgotten ruins and rub the dust of a thousand years from their eyes.

EXT. ATHENS, GREECE—DAY

Many of the old temples to the Greek gods are being restored.

> ANNOUNCER (V.O.)
>
> And Thor with his giant hammer will leap up and smash the gothic cathedrals. When that crash comes, it will be like nothing before.

GLOBAL TV

A wrestling commercial SHOWS Thor smashing his hammer down on a Jewish Star of David and a Christian cross.

INT. PARIS—NOTRE DAME CATHEDRAL

A group of TITANS are addressing the crowd of beast worshippers.

> TITAN ONE
>
> The Jewish plagues have become self-fulfilling prophecies. You must prevent the remaining ones.

> TITAN TWO
>
> You must eliminate all Christians and Jews. Also, Native Americans and blacks since Israel's lost tribes could've joined with them.

INT. DENVER AIRPORT

We SEE the murals painted on the walls again. CLOSER VIEW of three caskets, which contain a Jew, a black, and an Indian.

TITAN (O.S.)

Their seed must be cut off or we'll be cut off.

EXT./INT. THIRD EMPIRE—CONCENTRATION CAMPS—DAY

Christians that refused to accept the mark are in captivity.

A PRISONER quotes from the Bible.

PRISONER (O.S.)

He that leadeth into captivity shall go into captivity. He that killeth with the sword must be
killed with the sword. Here is the patience of
the saints. For you will be hated and persecuted for His sake.

He starts singing the chorus to "AMERICAN PIE." The other prisoners
join in. "This will be the day that I die" hauntingly ECHOES.

INT. BERLIN—WWW MATCH—RINGSIDE—NIGHT

Subtitle: "Summer Solstice, June 2006"

John and Johnny are ringside.

The first match is between a black prisoner and a Titan.

While watching the black man die, John whispers to Johnny.

JOHN

We never let blacks join our Masonic lodge.

As John looks away, Johnny is noticeably disturbed by his father's
words.

A Titan and Christian male prisoner are next up.

The guest Titan is the new Pope himself, Saturn.

During the match, Saturn's opponent cuts him.

Johnny rushes to get a dab of the blood as a souvenir.

Realizing he still has the DNA analyzer, he takes it out.

INSERT—DNA ANALYZER

Patty's DNA reading is still being displayed.

He places the newly collected sample in the portable machine.

BACK TO SCENE

The next match involves the female giant, HELA.

Hela tortures her victim to the delight of the crowd.

The DNA analyzer in Johnny's coat SOUNDS a familiar ALARM. Johnny takes it out to look at it.

INSERT—DNA ANALYZER

Patty and Saturn's blood are a perfect match…mother and son.

However, his blood-type reading shows half of it as UNKNOWN!

BACK TO SCENE

Johnny's puzzled look changes to shock as he looks up and SEES Patty is the next slave to fight Hela.

Right behind Patty, is an old lady…it's Katy!

Song "THIS IS YOUR TIME" by Michael W. Smith, begins.

The CROWD is cruelly hysterical.

Johnny makes eye contact with Katy as she YELLS for him.

KATY

Johnny! Help me!

PATTY

Father! Help us!

JOHNNY'S FACE as he realizes this *is* his daughter!

Hela prepares for the kill on Katy.

Another giantess prepares to kill Johnny's daughter.

Johnny can't bear to watch and suddenly LEAPS UP into the ring.

Hela THROWS Johnny back.

Hela breaks Katy's neck instantly. David's watch falls from her broken neck, HITTING the floor.

Johnny reaches across the mat, grabbing the watch.

In the commotion, Patty lives. They are led off together.

INT. BEER FACTORY—GERMANY

Saints killed in matches are being burned in great ovens.

This visual BECOMES a beer commercial.

ANNOUNCER (V.O.)

Our beer is brewed with an international fire-brewing method so unique...we patented it.

Katy's body is put into the oven brewing the beer.

The SMOKE from the chimneys once again RISES to Heaven.

EXT./INT. PARADISE

David catches the scent of smoke as it passes his nose. As he turns around, a single tear falls from his eye. SONG ends.

EXT. JORDAN DESERT—DAY

Subtitle: "Jewish Passover, 2007."
The Jews are celebrating Passover with Enoch and Elijah.

> ELIJAH
>
> Soon, we'll return to Jerusalem and the Temple.

INT. RUSSIA—DAY

Teitan is shaking hands with VLADIMIR, the Russian Federation's leader, as they make peace between the north and the Third Empire.

> TEITAN
>
> I've signed a treaty with my brother and companion, Vladimir Zhirinovsky. Together, we face anyone who defies us. United, we'll rule the Middle East.

The crowd APPLAUDS and repeatedly CHANTS, "Peace!"

> VLADIMIR
>
> China agrees to remain within its borders, as will all kings from the east. I embrace my brother…and peace.

The two men embrace to the CHEERS of the CROWD.

NARRATOR (V.O.)

"Then shall the lords be two in number, in the north, victorious against Eastern ones. They shall quake for fear of two brothers who are not brothers of the north." June 27, 1555. Nostradamus.

EXT. PAKISTAN/SYRIAN BORDERS—DAY

Titans stationed along Empire borders wear UN peacekeeping uniforms. Their armbands and helmets display the swastika.

EXT. SYRIAN DESERT—DAY

Empire and Russian troops begin mobilizing towards Jerusalem.

VLADIMIR

We will annihilate the Jews!

TEITAN

I'll hang their two false prophets from my Hanging Gardens!

INSERT—TV MONITOR

The big WWW revenge match is about to begin.

ANNOUNCER

The event you've all been waiting for…tag team partners Thor and Hela take on the Midgard Serpent and his partner, Loki!

The BELL RINGS as the match begins.

INT. GOD'S THRONE ROOM

Jesus opens the FIFTH yellow-colored SEAL.
The FIFTH angel, Raphael, SOUNDS his TRUMPET.

EXT./ INT. GREAT PYRAMID

The FIFTH relieving stone over the King's Chamber is SUPERNATU-RALLY highlighted.

EXT. ISLAND OF ABYDON (OFF COAST OF IRAN/IRAQ)—DAY

An angel walks across the water TOWARDS US. It's Apollyon.

He holds the keys to the abyss, stolen from Laurianna.

A huge whirlpool FORMS under him, clearing the water from around the ocean floor and creating a circular wall of water.

Underwater pipelines BURST, causing oil to mix with the wall.

The angel of DEATH leaves the area on his green horse.

HELL stays, standing at the edge of the abyss.

Apollyon opens the abyss with his key.

The FIFTH saint, Jared, pours his VIAL into the opening.

HUGE amounts of smoke come billowing out. The fire from the abyss ignites the wall of oil, adding to the smoke.

Hundreds of demons, souls of slain giants, exit the abyss.

LILITH comes out last. She SEES Lililea dressed as HELL.

> LILITH
>
> Hello mother, excuse me while I kick some

human ass!

EXT. PLATEAU OF TIBET—DARK

Subtitle: "Somewhere near the Gobi Desert."

From an opening in the ground, a huge DOOR OPENS. From this tunnel come wave after wave of Apache helicopters.

INT. HELICOPTERS

Piloted by men with long, black hair. They look as if cloned from the same person with dark eyes on an expressionless face.

SERIES OF SHOTS

A)   The Apaches head towards the smoke-covered Third Empire.

B)   We SUPERNATURALLY SEE Lilith guiding a pilot's hands.

C)   All other pilots are being guided by various demons too.

D)   Apollyon leads the Apache brigade through the smoke cover.

INSERT—TV SCREEN

The WWW match is heating up. Hela has Thor's golden hammer and wields it, trying to knock out Loki.

A News Bulletin interrupts the match as an ANCHOR breaks in.

> ANCHOR
>
> We interrupt to bring this late-breaking story. A huge fire has erupted in the Middle East. It's feared Israel is now preparing to send bio-chemical weapons into the Third Empire. With

the latest, here's Teitan.

TEITAN

We are sending a massive helicopter evacuation force through my entire Empire. Everyone must be evacuated to a sheltered area capable of surviving germ warfare.

EXT. JORDAN DESERT

There are no clouds over the Jews celebrating Passover here.

Enoch is still teaching Davie Jr. to play the shofar.

EXT./INT. WORLDWIDE—VARIOUS PEOPLE

The 144,000 with God's SEAL on their foreheads are safe.

Christians SEALED by the Holy Spirit are not affected either. A Christian LEADER reads from the Bible.

LEADER

Ye were SEALED with that Holy Spirit of promise, which is the earnest of our inheritance until our redemption. Ephesians 1:13-14.

EXT. THIRD EMPIRE—DARK AND CLOUDY

Crowds line the streets. Titans wearing gas masks are herding them.

INT. APOLLYON'S HELICOPTER

APOLLYON

All demons hosting a clone...hearken to my voice again. Fire at will!

NARRATOR (V.O.)

They were commanded to hurt only those not sealed by God.

EXT. APACHES—WIDER VIEW—MISSILES FIRING

Into the crowds of people, armed with chemical warheads.

FIRE from the missiles EXTENDS back to the helicopter's tail section, completing the illusion of the missiles coming FROM the TAIL of these iron, scorpion-like machines.

NARRATOR (V.O.)

And to them it was given that they should not kill them, but that they should be tormented five months: and their torment was as the torment of a scorpion, when he strikes a man.

EXT. CROWED STREET—PEOPLE

Grab at their throats, trying to breathe. Huge boils appear on their skin alongside the mark on their foreheads and hands.

INT. HOUSE—A COUPLE

Hiding here tries to avoid contamination. Children's VOICES outside the door beg for them to "Please, let us in."

Upon opening their door, they discover they've been tricked by DEMON VOICES.

They grab their throats as the airborne chemicals take effect.

> NARRATOR (V.O.)
>
> And in those days, shall men seek death, and shall not find it; and shall desire to die, and death shall flee.

DEATH leaves on his horse. He heads toward the United States.

> DEATH
>
> After six millenniums on the job, I'm going to Disney World.

EXT. ATLANTIS—DARKNESS

Covers the ocean. A ball of LIGHT shoots out of the water.

Two smaller balls of light join the first, heading into space.

EXT. THE ABYSS OPENING—DAY

Subtitle: "Three days later."

Holy angels stand beside HELL. Michael taps his foot.

> HELL
>
> Don't look at me. I knew it was only for three days.

Finally, Apollyon arrives with a horde of transparent demons.

While demons enter the abyss, Apollyon tosses the keys to Michael.

> APOLLYON
>
> Here's the key to Hell, pops.

EXT. THIRD EMPIRE—AERIAL VIEW—CLOUDLESS DAY

People everywhere writhe in extreme pain, including Russian and Empire soldiers. This obviously halts their advance to Israel.

Construction work on the mile-high obelisk has also been halted.

EXT./INT. JERUSALEM TEMPLE

Jews are returning to the Temple to cleanse it.

INT. GOD'S THRONE ROOM—NEAR ALTAR

Naked souls of Saints killed gladiator style are here, including Katy. She studies events on Earth through a cherub's monitor.

> KATY
>
> When will we be avenged? When will our mur-
> derers die?

> GOD
>
> Be patient. Your fellow servants and brothers
> must be killed first as you were.

God hands Katy and the other Saints killed a white robe.

EXT. MGM THEME PARK, DISNEY WORLD—DAY

DEATH is standing in line with others waiting for a ride. A sign indicates "the wait from here is ninety minutes."

DEATH

I'm in no hurry. I've got five months to kill.

EXT. PARIS—PLACE CHARLES DE GUALLE

Is in the f.g. as the Eiffel Tower looms in the distance.
Our VIEW SHIFTS to a nearby jail window covered with bars.

INT. PARIS JAIL

Patty and Johnny are chained to a wall in the same cell.

PATTY

Sorry I got you in this mess.

JOHNNY

Don't be silly. I would've helped you sooner if
I'd known you were my daughter. At least now
we can get better acquainted.

PATTY

I don't know anything about you...or my
grandparents...

JOHNNY

Forget your grandfather. But your grandmother
was special. When pregnant with me, she said I
kicked nonstop on a flight to Paris from St.
Louis. "The Spirit of St. Louis was in me," she
said. A movie made the same year of

Lindbergh's 1927 flight; "WINGS," had "Shooting Star" written on the nose of the hero's plane. That's what I named my plane during WWII.

PATTY

I wish we had your plane right now and could fly all the way back to St. Louis.

Johnny looks down at his chest where David's watch now hangs.

JOHNNY

Our time to fly is coming soon.

EXT. EUROPEAN BATTLEFIELDS—DAY

Subtitle: "Five months later"
Badly wounded soldiers begin dying again.

NEWS ANCHOR (V.O.)

After what's been dubbed the five months death took a holiday, people are again dying.

EXT. PARIS—NOTRE DAME CATHEDRAL—DAY

Teitan conducts a press conference. The ten kings, Saturn, and Vladimir are all attending this State of the Empire address.

TEITAN

The Jews caused us all to suffer these past five months. We also believe they're responsible for the disappearance of my statue.

We can SEE that the golden statue of Teitan is not on its pedestal.

TEITAN

We must now continue our charge to Jerusalem
and wipe out their entire race...forever!

SATURN

All remaining Christians must be
killed...NOW!

President of the WWW, a Titan, stands beside Midgard and Saturn.

TEITAN

During the upcoming match, Christian prisoners in Germany, now the capital of World Wide
Wrestling, will be slaughtered. Then, the long
awaited rematch between Thor and Hela and
the Midgard Serpent and Loki.

The crowd CHEERS wildly as Teitan steps back to the microphone.

TEITAN

The Sun Tower must now be completed before
the Armageddon timetable set in motion by the
Jews can complete itself.

SATURN

The beacon must be placed upon the mile-high
obelisk. We must work nonstop to complete it.

EXT. SPACE STATION—AN EIGHTY-THREE FOOT MIRROR

OPENS, beaming sunlight to Babylon on the dark side of Earth.

EXT. BABYLON—NIGHT—SATAN AND APOLLYON

Are atop the nearly complete obelisk, soaking up the sun's rays.

Slaves work on a scaffolding rig just below them. Satan creates a gust of wind, causing a slave to lose his balance.

Together they watch as he

FALLS

All the way to the bottom, where his body SPLATS next to a Masonic compass and square symbol engraved on the cornerstone.

> SATAN (O.S.)
> (laughing evilly)

Only I'm the Prince of the Air.

EXT./INT. JERUSALEM—TEMPLE MOUNT—NIGHT

Enoch, Elijah, and the entire Jewish third are here now from Jordan's desert. They are in prayer, rededicating the temple.

> ENOCH

The Temple is clean and ready to receive our Lord.

> ELIJAH

Prepare the shofars for the final blast. The Jewish New Year is about to begin.

Subtitle: "Rosh Hashanah"

Davie Jr. takes his own HORN and tries a NOTE. It's SQUEAKY.

EXT. TEMPLE MOUNT—HANGING GARDENS—NEXT MORNING

Enoch and Elijah are deep in prayer.

> ENOCH
>
> Our hour of darkness is upon us.

> ELIJAH
>
> Let your will be done.

A drop of blood drips as sweat from his forehead.

EXT. BOTTOM OF TEMPLE WALL

Titan guards and Empire troops quietly surround the Jewish Temple. A titan marksman scouts the Temple Mount THROUGH binoculars. He HEARS a car pull up behind him and swings around.

TITAN'S POV—THROUGH BINOCULARS—A RED SATURN CAR

Pulls up and stops. Teitan steps out. He sets his car alarm.

> CAR (V.O.)
>
> Protected by Viper! Stand back!

Our BINOCULAR VIEW SHIFTS back around to the top of the wall, where Davie Jr. is looking right at US.

BACK TO SCENE

Davie BLOWS his HORN, barely making an audible SQUEAKY SOUND.

The Titan levels his rifle, aiming it at the boy.

EXT. TOP OF TEMPLE WALL—JOSH

As he HEARS the GUNSHOT.

                    JOSH

        Oh my God…Davie!

He runs to Davie's post but SEES only his shofar lying there.

He SEES him on the ground, with Empire troops in the b.g.

He picks up the shofar, and BLOWS the horn LOUDLY.

EXT. CITY'S WATCHTOWERS—VARIOUS ANGLES

Israeli watchmen SEE the enemy surrounding Jerusalem and BLOW their TRUMPETS.

EXT./INT. JERUSALEM RESIDENCES—VARIOUS HOUSES

Jews HEARING the warning, are SEEN scrambling for cover.

                NARRATOR (V.O.)

        The watchman, seeing the sword come upon
        the land, blows the trumpet, warning the peo-
        ple. He who hears the warning but does not
        take heed, his blood is upon his own head. But
        he, who takes heed, delivers his soul.

EXT. WATCHTOWER—ONE WATCHMAN

Fearing for his own life, drops his horn and runs for cover.

> NARRATOR (V.O.)
>
> But if the watchman see the sword come and blow not the trumpet, and the people be not warned, any persons taken away in their sins, his blood will be required at the watchman's hand…by God.

EXT. JERUSALEM ALLEY

The fleeing watchman runs right past a deaf and blind beggar, who is unaware of the impending danger.

EXT. TOP OF TEMPLE WALL

Enoch and Elijah join Josh, who's still BLOWING his HORN.

TITAN SNIPER'S POV—THROUGH RIFLE SCOPE—JOSH'S FOREHEAD

With God's seal, line up with the cross hairs of the scope. It makes the sign of the double-cross.

> TITAN (O.S.)
>
> Joshua blows his mighty horn.

BACK TO SCENE

He FIRES!

The bullet magically diverts, hitting Josh's horn.

Josh loses his balance, taking Enoch and Elijah with him.

EXT. BOTTOM OF TEMPLE WALL

All three land on the ground beside Davie's body.

TITAN

And from the walls, they came tumbling down.

Rebekah opens the temple door and runs toward them, but is captured.

GLOBAL TELEVISION

Enoch and Elijah have nooses around their necks.

Teitan kicks the chairs out from under them.

TEITAN

Your plagues will be upon us no more!

INSERT—VARIOUS TV SCREENS

News reports from around the world SHOW people hugging, leaping for joy, feasting, celebrating and exchanging gifts.

One report shows Enoch and Elijah lying in the streets of Jerusalem.

EXT. JERUSALEM STREET—DAY

A titan soldier takes Elijah's blue mantle and tries it on. Not fitting, he throws it over Davie's dead body lying nearby.

A CLOSER VIEW of Davie as he comes back to life!

DEATH is INVISIBLY looking over him. He winks at Davie.

Davie gets up and sneaks past Empire soldiers being addressed by Teitan.

TEITAN

Round up ALL Jews. Prepare them for public execution. Send the next train to Berlin. We'll let the Titan's kill this batch.

Josh and Rebekah, handcuffed together, are being led to an awaiting railroad cattle car.

INT. DENVER AIRPORT

A noted Mason leader activates the beacon with the keypad.

EXT./INT. TOWER OF BABYLON—TOP

We SEE the beacon atop the mile-high tower being activated. A torch is lit and placed on the obelisk's highest point.

INT. ATLANTIS—SS HEADQUARTERS

Subtitle: "Three days later."
Johnny and Patty are in chains standing before MJ12 leaders, Buffy and John Sr. Buffy walks up to Johnny.

BUFFY

Traitor! You had it all.

She spits in Johnny's face. John LAUGHS.

JOHN

You were right about Roswell, son. Aliens

didn't land there. We made people think they did though...on the day your Jewish friend visited us in '47.

HEAD MASON

Hitler found an ancient flying machine buried below the Gobi Desert. His pulse jet engine came from it. The Nazis found something else...giants, frozen in ice. They were all dead, of course. That's where we found the real Saturn. And an angel called Azazyel.

JOHN

Azazyel gave us the computer chip, which we began using in '47. It was time for mankind to have technology again. Which leads us to UFO's.

He looks at Patty, who looks horrified now.

JOHN

Oh yes. Those abductions were real. Angels were punished for mating with mankind and creating giants. This time it had to be more...impersonal.

Patty is getting very nervous now.

FBI AGENT

We allowed these fallen angels to abduct people for creating giants from our human seed. They also needed blood and tissue, thus the cattle mutilations in the 70's and missing children. These sacrificial lambs helped cure diseases for us elderly. All of our genetic advancements came from this titan nursery including cloning and test tube babies.

JOHN
(to Johnny)

You got a prostitute pregnant in St. Louis, Patty's mother. She tried to blackmail me. She died, of course. I kept track of her daughter for years, but lost her. Thanks to you, we found her.

Johnny and his daughter exchange looks.

JOHN
(to Patty)

It wasn't a dream dear. You really were abducted. You should be honored though. From your seed we created Saturn, the false prophet from the Earth, inspired by the dead Saturn found in Gobi.

Patty breaks down in tears.

Johnny's anger turns to rage. He tries to rush at his father but his chains keep him back.

JOHN

Obviously, giants never came from Titan…an illusion the Cassini probe helped create. The world bought it along with other lies.

JOHNNY

I saw your propaganda tape file. Shows promoting anti-family values. You even used your propaganda machine to influence kids, you bastard!

John's breathing becomes strained again and is forced to temporarily put on his oxygen mask.

JOHN

Yes, we even funded the Halloween broadcast and radio experiment known as "WAR OF THE WORLDS."

CIA DIRECTOR

That taught us how to set up FEMA. Wall Street was an obvious target in order to cripple our own economy. We had to set up Europe as the new super power.

A five-star GENERAL from the US enters the room, joining in.

GENERAL

Our Cold War machine kept funding alive from taxes to fight an enemy WE created and controlled. As the "Four X-Presidents" would say, "Aliens and communism are one and the same." CREATED foes.

HEAD MASON

Hitler was right...people just don't think

anymore. They're more focused on pleasure.

MJ12 MEMBER

We became your kid's babysitters with year-round schooling. We kept them…well conditioned.

Johnny's anger has reached its peak!

JOHNNY

You've set yourself up as gods! Remember March 2, 1999? On that day, I read "GREEN EGGS AND HAM," to little kids on national TV. That story has a "SAM, I AM" character. Could that be…Uncle Sam? Getting the world ready to eat your story about aliens creating our very life…the egg? And through the seed of Ham…Nimrod? You've been conditioning the world to accept little green men for years now, father. Well, where are they?

Video monitors all throughout the secret underground city simultaneously lose their signal, leaving only VIDEO NOISE or snow.

JOHN

…They're h-e-r-e.

EXT. SPACE STATION—OUTER SPACE

A large UFO and two smaller ones appear above the space station.

MONTAGE

A)   The three UFO's land in Babylon, greeted by Teitan and Saturn. The Grey aliens look like the serpent from the Garden of Eden.

B)   Children greet the ET's. They're not afraid of them.

C)   Dozens of little Greys exit the ship, mixing with children.

D)   Parents just smile, as their kids become ambassadors to these similar-sized aliens.

E)   Babylonian merchants are selling alien dolls.

F)   Another vendor is frying green eggs and ham.

END OF MONTAGE

EXT. BABYLON TOWER—PRESS CONFERENCE

The larger GREY approaches the microphone. A computer-translating device interprets into various languages, including English.

> GREY (V.O.)
>
> The Titans have told you the truth. We created your species in their image. Ever since our home planet in the Pegasus system got too close to our sun, we've been looking for a new home and sewing seeds of life.

One of the smaller Greys comes forward with a triangular-shaped piece of metal with strange markings engraved up its center.

Saturn brings the other two similar pieces found on earth.

The Grey places his piece at the bottom of the disk shape formed by the three pieces. MARKINGS up the center, human chromosome strands, combine with the EDGES of each piece resembling a PEACE SIGN!

412

Revelations

GREY

We come in Peace!

The crowd breaks into a thunderous APPLAUSE.

TEITAN

The Jews are liars and a danger to mankind.
They must be destroyed so we can endure!

The crowd CHEERS! Many can be SEEN in the b.g. burning Bibles.

SATURN

The seven-year treaty has expired and their
Messiah has NOT come. More proof of their
lies! Only by destroying them will we be rid of
their plagues…forever!

A little girl and boy have made their way up to the platform.

She holds a stuffed ET doll resembling a Teletubbie, a rainbow-colored alien doll with a monitor in its belly in one hand and a dead, potted flower in the other.

The little boy is holding a plate of green eggs and ham.

SATURN

We've not had rain in three and one-half years.

The Grey stretches out his longest finger, touching the flower. As he does, his finger and monitor-like belly begin to glow.

GREY

This is how we created life…

The flower comes back to life, blossoming before our very eyes!

Suddenly, a small dinosaur-type dragon exits the larger UFO. It stands next to the Grey and appears to be smiling.

The little boy offers the dragon the plate of green eggs and ham, which he swallows hungrily.

A fly lands on top of the little girl's head, getting the attention of a smaller Grey.

Suddenly, the Grey uses his tongue like a frog, catching the fly.

The little girl blushes as the Grey smiles, licking his chops.

NARRATOR (V.O.)

> And mankind believed the lie from the serpent beings, that they created all living things. They had swallowed the story…about green eggs and ham.

The crowd begins chanting "Armageddon!"

INT. DENVER, UNDERGROUND TRAIN STATION

Hundreds of Secret Service agents are everywhere. England's Queen Elizabeth and Prince William are being escorted.

Several guards carry the coronation stone and chair in a procession.

EXT. SARGASSO SEA—DAY—THREE UFO'S

Hover above the ocean, then dive beneath the surface.

INT. ATLANTIS—UNDERGROUND CITY—THRONE ROOM

Members of the secret society are here, preparing for some kind of ceremony. Priests and guards line the aisles.

Johnny and Patty are chained to a wall in the b.g.

Queen Elizabeth and Prince William enter.

The three Greys follow them.

John Sr. kneels before Elizabeth, who curtsies.

He then kisses Prince William's hand, bowing his head.

Walking up to the Grey, John kisses him on the cheek, causing him to MORPH into SATAN!

> JOHN
>
> Kiss a frog and he turns into a Prince...of Darkness.

The other two Greys MORPH into Apollyon and Azazyel.

> JOHNNY
>
> The three frog-like spirits of *Revelation*...

Satan takes a golden canteen from his belt, offering it to John.

> SATAN
> (to Johnny)
>
> Water...from the original River of Life that flowed from your Garden of Eden. It has kept your father alive all these years, waiting for this day. It's how we struck our little deal.

John takes a sip and magically becomes twenty years younger.

> JOHN
>
> Yes. Our plan is almost complete. God promised David he'd always have an heir on his throne. His throne was the stone known as Jacob's Pillow. Believe it or not, Jeremiah

brought this stone to Ireland. He also brought the king's daughters and continued the royal line. The Stone of Scone went from Ireland to Scotland to England. But, it still roars like a lion when true nobility is crowned. Today, after Jesus is defeated, we'll be crowning young William as the New World Order's first king.

JOHNNY

So, you killed Princess Diana to keep an Egyptian from taking your coveted throne?

JOHN

Yes. We had her killed where legends say your soul goes straight to Heaven. Why do you think we chose Paris to set up the image of the beast? At least Christians that died for their cause went straight to Heaven.

SATAN

God only saved eight people during the flood in order to preserve only His good seed...and His promised Redeemer. I failed to prevent His birth, but I won't fail to wipe out His chosen ones.

AZAZYEL

We'll use Earth's nuclear weapons to purify the Earth by fire.

SATAN

This time the only survivors will be onboard the space station...our ark of safety.

JOHN

Lucifer gave us the design for the Saturn rockets, which took man to the moon. Five rockets, like the original five cherubim. Like the five computers now needed to fly the space shuttle. Even the names of the shuttles were handpicked. "A Colombian Enterprise to Endeavor for the Discovery of Atlantis...and all Challengers shall be destroyed!"

SATAN

After we destroy the rest of mankind, only MY chosen disciples will repopulate the Earth. Like the Phoenix, I'll rise from the ashes.

JOHN

Here's the best part. After we've helped defeat Jesus, Satan will ascend to Heaven and take the Tree of Life. We'll have eternal life in our sinful state—something God prevented Adam and Eve from doing.

PATTY

What have you done with my kids?

JOHN

You mean the ones we abducted and allowed your father to adopt? They're safe onboard the space station. We're making a special sacrifice when this is all over. The flesh of children is most tasty. Ever had any? But you don't eat meat offered to pagan gods, do you?

Patty manages to slip out of her restraints and charges John.

PATTY

You BASTARD!

MI6 secret service agents SHOOT her dead over John's LAUGHTER!

EXT. CHINA—KARAKORAM HIGHWAY—DAY

Subtitle: "October 13, 2007."
Subtitle: "700 years EXACTLY after Jacque De Molay's arrest."
Subtitle: "The Day of the Templars' Revenge."
Subtitle: "becomes…the Day of the Lord."
200,000,000 Chinese tanks are using all lanes of the highway as they are headed west, towards the Euphrates.

NARRATOR (V.O.)

There shall be in a month of October a great revolution. Everyone shall think the Earth has gone down into perpetual darkness. After this shall be extraordinary changes, reversals of kingdoms and a great earthquake. Nostradamus.

GLOBAL TV

Wrestling matches are being broadcast from Berlin and Babylon.

JOSH AND REBEKAH

Are ringside in Berlin, waiting their turn to die.

Christians slaughtered in these death matches are being burned.

The SMOKE from their bodies burning in the crematories RISES

EXT./INT. HEAVEN—TO GOD'S NOSE

Smoke mixes with incense from a golden censer.

The angel of the altar and fire is holding the censer.

> GOD
>
> It's time for wicked man to taste and feel my wrath.

He signals Jesus to open the last TWO SEALS, the orange and the red.

Jesus opens the sixth AND seventh seal, together.

The sixth and seventh archangels, Remiel AND Gabriel, BLOW their TRUMPETS.

The sixth AND seventh saints, Lamech and Methuselah, pour out their vials.

EXT./INT. EGYPT—GREAT PYRAMID

We supernaturally SEE the two stone slabs, forming the roof of the King's chamber, being HIGHLIGHTED.

INT. HEAVEN—GOD'S THRONE ROOM

The angel with the golden censer fills it with fire from the altar and casts it DOWNWARD INTO the Earth.

> GOD

It is done.

> HEAVENLY VOICES
> (shouting)

The kingdoms of this world are now the kingdoms of our Lord and he shall reign forever and ever.

The twenty-four ELDERS come off of their thrones.

> ELDERS
> (in unison)

Your wrath is come, and the time of the dead, that they should be judged, and that you should give reward to your servants, the prophets, and to the saints, and them that fear your name, small and great; and should destroy them which destroy the Earth.

GLOBAL TV

Wrestling matches in Berlin and Babylon are heating up now as Josh and Rebekah are next to be killed.

EXT. DAY—EUPHRATES RIVER

RECEIVES the sixth vial upon it, causing it to dry up.

Four angels bound there: AMAZARAK, PENEMUE, TURYAL, and TAREL are released as the SOUND of the sixth TRUMPET reaches them.

EXT. SYRIA—KARAKORAM HIGHWAY—DAY

Chinese tanks are lined up and waiting to cross the lower Euphrates.

A Chinese FLAG waves over a Chinese tank. The flag's four smaller stars DISSOLVE INTO the four angels just released.

They lead the tanks across the dried-up river, heading west.

EXT. OUTER SPACE—THE SUN

Now burns completely out. Its COLOR goes from the bright YELLOW to a dark RED. The moon reflects the sun's changing colors.

NARRATOR (V.O.)

> Just ten thousand years after its creation, the sun became black and the moon as blood.

The sun becomes completely dark now.

EXT. VALLEY OF MEGIDDO—NIGHT

Roads leading here are filled with Russian and Empire troops carrying banners with the SWASTIKA.

More troops arrive carrying bright red Muslim flags, which also display the swastika.

Darkness is upon all the Earth. Only a few stars fill the sky.

EMPIRE CAPTAIN

Bring me a thousand Christian prisoners. Burn
them as torches. A thousand points of light on
the road to Jerusalem!

EXT. ROAD TO JERUSALEM

Is now lined with human torches, as we HEAR them SCREAMING.

EXT. SATURN'S ORBIT—CASSINI PROBE

Suddenly EXPLODES!

This explosion causes ANOTHER ring to form around Saturn from the
impact. The double ring looks like an "X" or a cross.

The explosion literally obliterates the moon Titan.

INT. SPACE STATION—A TITAN ONBOARD

Witnesses this on Hal's monitor. He's OUTRAGED!

TITAN

I knew Cassini's plutonium would jeopardize
Titan's safety.

He addresses Hal, who is backing up with every word.

HAL

Don't blame me! I didn't put the stupid probe
up there.

TITAN

Maybe not, but your race did. An eye for an eye, huh?

EXT. EARTH'S MOON—FAR SIDE

A huge Titan ship positions itself over our moon. A HUGE BEAM of LIGHT comes from the Titan ship, HITTING moon bases HARD!

EXT. JERUSALEM—NIGHT—CROWDS OF JEWS

Are staring up at the heavens with amazement.

CROWD'S POV—THE NIGHT SKY

The huge explosion on the moon's far side PUSHES the moon TOWARDS Earth. Earth's gravity starts pulling it in on a collision course.

As the moon approaches Earth's atmosphere, its surface becomes blood red, BURNING on entry.

Suddenly, we HEAR the SOUND of THUNDER. LIGHTNING fills the night sky as bolts begin arcing between the Earth and moon.

EARTH—OVERHEAD VIEW

The moon's gravity is pulling on the seas, causing the high tide to go crazy. Waves become tidal waves.

NARRATOR (V.O.)

And there were signs in the sun, and in the moon, and in the stars and upon the Earth, distress of nations, with perplexity, the sea and the waves roaring.

EXT. TEMPLE MOUNT—NIGHT

A soldier is guarding the bodies of Enoch and Elijah. He receives an urgent message on his remote laptop computer.

INSERT—COMPUTER SCREEN

Where Teitan's face appears.

> TEITAN
>
> Burn the bodies of the two dead witnesses, NOW!

EXT. NEARBY JERUSALEM STREETS

Jewish bystanders are looking up at the sky.

CROWD'S POV—THE MOON

EXPLODES into shooting stars, heading towards Earth.
A comment can be HEARD from a BYSTANDER.

> BYSTANDER (V.O.)
>
> My God, look at all the stars!

BACK TO SCENE

Another man, looking up, grabs his chest. He falls to the ground, suffering from a heart attack.

NARRATOR (V.O.)

And the stars FELL from heaven. And men's hearts failed them for fear, looking at those things, which are coming upon the Earth.

SERIES OF SHOTS

A) Drops of rain mix with the THUNDER and lightning followed by a monsoon as the first rain in over three years begins to fall.

B) As the soldier begins to set Enoch and Elijah's bodies on fire, the rain puts out his torch.

C) Rain extinguishes the burning bodies of all dead Christians.

EXT. JERUSALEM—NIGHT—RAINING

People are dancing in the rain. Many are looking up as

THE SKY

Opens like a scroll. We can see the light of God's Temple.

Christ is in the air now, holding a key. He has obviously used it to open Heaven. The SOUND of the last TRUMPET reaches Earth, causing a GREAT EARTHQUAKE to begin.

An ANGEL comes from the Temple in Heaven.

TEMPLE ANGEL
(shouting to Jesus)

It's time!

Jesus holds a sickle in his hand.

TEMPLE ANGEL

Thrust in your sickle and reap for the harvest is ripe.

With the trumpet still ECHOING, Jesus reaps.

JESUS

Come up hither.

EXT. JERUSALEM STREETS—ENOCH AND ELIJAH

HEAR the ECHOING WORDS of Jesus and the SOUND of the archangel's last TRUMP, and RISE as they ascend UPWARDS towards Heaven.

EXT. GRAVEYARD—GRAVES

Opened by the earthquake allow the resurrection of dead saints.

NARRATOR (V.O.)

At the last trump, the dead shall be raised, and they shall be changed. The sound of a trumpet could raise heavy stones. Now, it removed the tombstones of saints.

EXT. BABYLON—HANGING GARDENS

We SEE all the hanged men resurrected.

INT. ATLANTIS—UNDERGROUND CITY—THRONE ROOM

Patty awakes from the dead. Her body has changed to an immortal one now. She looks at Johnny.

SATAN

The gateway has been opened! We must send all our firepower to Heaven now!

As a guard OPENS FIRE on Johnny, he VANISHES!

David's watch drops to the floor with a CLANG!

INSERT—DAVID'S WATCH

As the second hand stops.

NARRATOR (V.O.)

The time of the Gentiles…ends. Those still alive are changed instantly, and ALL the saints meet Jesus in the air. For behold, I show you a mystery; not all will sleep but shall be changed, in a moment, in the twinkling of an eye. For God has not appointed His Saints to wrath, but to salvation.

EXT. EARTH'S ATMOSPHERE—HIGH ANGLE

We NOTICE that the 144,000 marked Jews do NOT get raptured.

NARRATOR (V.O.)

144,000 were taken with Jesus as the first fruits of the resurrection. That same number was now left behind, marked from the Four Corners of the Earth.

David is reunited with his body, appearing in his early twenties.

Katy is reunited with her body as a young sixteen-year-old.

As SAINTS go UP, God's WRATH comes DOWN, SNATCHED AWAY at the LAST SECOND!

The Woe Angel comes again.

> WOE ANGEL
>
> The second woe is past. Behold, the third woe comes quickly.

EXT. HEAVEN

It's very quiet here. An ANGEL looks at his watch.

> ANGEL
>
> This is the quietest half-hour ever in Heaven.

Suddenly, a little girl appears before the angel. It's HEATHER O'ROURKE, the star of the "POLTERGEIST" movies.

> HEATHER
>
> They're h-e-r-e!

A great multitude that cannot be numbered APPEARS.

> NARRATOR (V.O.)
>
> These were they, which came out of the great tribulation. They shall hunger or thirst no more, neither shall the sun light on them, nor its heat.

EXT. BERLIN—RAINING—JOSH AND REBEKAH

Are running from the arena, escaping during all the chaos.

REBEKAH

Now what?

A squadron of German fighters flies overhead.

JOSH

I have a plan.

EXT. PARADISE

The SOUND of THUNDER mixes with the JETS as it ECHOES beneath. Saints are receiving white robes.

David and Katy tearfully embrace as they're reunited.

Eva and Levi meet again. They hug.

Saints are mounting thousands of white horses.

David, who's still glued to Katy's side, goes to Jesus.

Saints surround Jesus with happy tears in their eyes, which He wipes away with His hand. We can SEE a nail print in His hand.

DAVID

Can I ride my own personal mustang when we return to Earth?

JESUS

You'll ride it well.

EXT. JERUSALEM

Troops advancing towards Jerusalem are killing Jews as they enter the outskirts of the city. Women are being raped.

EXT. MEGIDDO

Chinese tanks have crossed the Euphrates River and are now lined up FACING the antichrist's armies.

Their four angelic leaders give the COMMAND. China begins BLAST-ING away at Teitan's troops.

Some of their nuclear missiles are FIRED at Teitan's ten kingdoms.

EXT. BETHEL (ISRAEL)—HEAVEN'S GATE—JESUS

Arrives with His army of saints and angels through the tunnel.

Darkness is lifted as a new light comes with Jesus. It's seven times brighter than our sun used to be. There is no more night.

JESUS

Let the truth be known!

Chorus from the song "RIGHT HERE, RIGHT NOW" by Jesus Jones begins.

MONTAGE

A)   The twenty-seven global positioning satellites orbiting Earth begin sending a signal to the Earth below.

B)   This causes every video screen worldwide to display the final speeches made by John, Satan, etc. to Johnny in Atlantis.

C)   The world now knows the real truth. This causes fighting to

430

Revelations

break out as men realize they've been double-crossed.

END OF MONTAGE

SERIES OF SHOTS

A) Suddenly, nations turn on each other.

B) Satan, demons, giants, and all his angel forces hidden underground now come against the holy angels and saints.

C) Jesus stands on top of the Mount of Olives, watching.

D) Suddenly, from the same place in the sky where Jesus and the Saints appeared, a white airplane appears.

E) It's David, flying an all white P-51 Mustang! He's dressed in an all white WWII style military uniform.

F) Hell's Angels, aided by modern JETS from countries around the world, appear now FLYING towards Israel.

G) A Titan fighter engages David in a dogfight.

H) David reverses and closes in quickly. He uses his MACHINE GUNS to splash the Titan ship.

I) Before he can even catch his breath, a UFO comes in from behind, as LASER FIRE spits out green bursts at David's plane.

J) To make matters worse, two Syrian jets join in the fight.

K) Despite the Mustang's older technology, its supernatural abilities give it some advantages.

L) After much maneuvering, one of the jets gets a radar lock on David's plane. The WARNING in David's cockpit SOUNDS LOUDLY.

M) Just as the jet's pilot is about to squeeze off a missile, his own jet EXPLODES in a huge ball of flame!

INT. DAVID'S PLANE

David HEARS a familiar voice in his headset.

> JOHNNY (O.S.)
>
> Just like old times…still making the air a safe place for angels to fly.

He comes flying alongside David in his own white P-51 Mustang. The nose of his plane reads, "Spirit of St. Louis."

> DAVID
>
> Thanks buddy. We'll catch up on old times later. Right now, how would you like to be my wingman on one more mission over Germany?

> JOHNNY (O.S.)
>
> Berlin?

> DAVID
>
> Yes…I lost my wife there. Also, we're headed to Bergen Belsen. She lost a friend there…a girl named Anne.

> JOHNNY (O.S.)
>
> I lost a friend there myself. Best wingman I ever had…

EXT. BERLIN—OVERHEAD VIEW—WWW ARENA

Johnny and David arrive on the outskirts of the city. German surface-to-air missiles EXPLODE all around them.

In a Blitzkrieg-style maneuver, both dive-bomb these forces.

Hela and other giants fleeing the arena are BLOWN to pieces.

INT. DAVID'S PLANE

David's RADAR indicates two fast-moving jets approaching.

> DAVID
>
> We've got company!

> JOHNNY (O.S.)
>
> Roger. Two German F-22's.

A VOICE comes over their RADIO from the German jet.

> JOSH (O.S.)
>
> Hello gentlemen. Need some help?

EXT. TWO SHOT—P-51 MUSTANGS—VIEW WIDENS AS

Josh and Rebekah come alongside the older Mustangs.

> REBEKAH (O.S.)
>
> We needed a ride back to Israel. Wanna join us?

> DAVID (O.S.)
>
> First, we're going to right a wrong for all the Jews who died here. Wanna join us?

JOSH (O.S.)

Grandfather, we'd be honored to accompany
you as your wing.

EXT. BERGEN-BELSEN—OVERHEAD VIEW

We can SEE the concentration camp below. Anti-aircraft tracers are
coming from the ground, exploding all around.

DAVID'S PLANE

Where two bombs are attached under each wing. One says, "BERGEN"
on it, the other says, "BELSEN."

DAVID (O.S.)

Bombs away!

All four planes drop bombs on the concentration camp below.

JOHNNY (O.S.)

Now it's my turn to ask a favor. Would all of
you accompany me to a place in the Atlantic?

EXT. MOUNT OF OLIVES—DAY—JESUS

STOMPS his foot three times. The Earth starts to SHAKE.
The GROUND SPLITS under Jesus' feet and WATER starts GUSHING
out.

JESUS

Mountains and islands hear and obey my
voice…be removed and cast yourself into the sea.

EXT. EARTH—OVERHEAD VIEW—VARIOUS ANGLES

Mountains are removed from their place and every island sinks into the ocean. This causes even bigger tidal waves.

EXT. SOUTH ATLANTIC OCEAN—DAY—TITANIC TWO

Is SLAMMED into an iceberg, breaking in half and sinking.

> NARRATOR (V.O.)
>
> Did I mention…history has a way of repeating itself?

A male and female Titan are on the bow of the ship. They're holding hands as they await their impending doom.

The female Titan displays a flower tattoo with the name, "Rose."

MONTAGE

A)   During the EARTHQUAKE, we SEE major cities destroyed.

B)   Babylon gets a double portion of wrath as the mile-high Sun Tower falls over, smashing Teitan's Palace.

C)   The torch on the tower's top ignites oil seeping from below the ground.

D)   The entire city becomes a huge fireball as we SEE Babylon was built upon a huge bitumen pit.

E)   We HEAR AD LIBS from people in ships from far off wailing their cries for the fallen city.

END OF MONTAGE

EXT. TEMPLE GATE—JERUSALEM—DAY

Satan comes before Jesus now.

> SATAN
>
> You should've accepted my offer a long time ago because now you *will* bow before me.

Satan notices the nail-prints on Jesus' feet.

> SATAN
>
> Looks like someone has bruised your heel.

Satan charges, but Jesus quickly sidesteps the advance.

> JESUS
>
> Go ahead. Make my Millennium.

Teitan pulls up in his red Saturn car.

Jesus has a rock attached to a chain. He's swinging it.

> JESUS
>
> What was the one thing that could bring down Superman? Kryptonite...a piece of the rock from his home planet. Remember Tiamait? The rock from which you were made?

He swings it, STRIKING Satan squarely in the head.

Satan is HIT hard. He falls to the ground too weary to get up.

                          JESUS

Looks like someone has bruised your head.

Teitan gets out of his car, sets his alarm with a DOUBLE BEEP then
walks towards Jesus with the Sword of Destiny in hand.

Suddenly, a huge hailstone, the first meteorite fragment from the moon,
HITS his arm. He DROPS the Sword of Destiny.

                    NARRATOR (V.O.)

     When separated from the sword, his downfall
     was soon to follow.

The IMPACT from the meteorite causes the car's ALARM to SOUND.

                      ALARM (V.O.)

     Protected by Viper! Stand Back!

Another hailstone completely OBLITERATES the car!

Teitan, now LOOKING UP, SEES the next one HIT him squarely upon
his helmeted head. He's KNOCKED out instantly.

EXT. RUSSIA—RUSSIAN SOLDIERS

Are dissolved by fire from the incoming Chinese missiles.

                    NARRATOR (V.O.)

     Their flesh shall consume away while they
     stand upon their feet, and their eyes shall con-
     sume away in their holes, and their tongue shall
     consume away in their mouth.

EXT. RUSSIA—OVERHEAD VIEW

Five-sixths of the Russian troops are destroyed. Their heavy tanks are stuck in the mud, caused by heavy rain.

One hundred-pound hailstone's pelt them, further crippling their attempt to flee Chinese missiles being fired upon them as well.

JESUS (V.O.)

When Gog comes against Israel, I will rain upon him and upon his bands and upon the many people that are with him, an overflowing rain, great hailstones and fire and brimstone.

EXT. VALLEY OF MEGIDDO—DAY

An eagle swoops down over the dead bodies. Vultures follow.

NARRATOR (V.O.)

For wherever the carcass is, there will the eagles be gathered together. One third of mankind was killed in one hour. Here, for over two hundred miles, the valley was filled with blood reaching a standing horses bridle.

The eagle dives and retrieves a snake trying to slither away.

EXT. JERUSALEM—MOUNT OF OLIVES—JESUS

Looks at a dazed and confused Satan, who's nursing his head wound.

NARRATOR (V.O.)

Man's redeemer full-filled his destiny, bruising the head of the serpent.

The archangel Michael arrives as another eagle swoops DOWN, picking up the Sword of Destiny.

Teitan is nearby lying unconscious on the ground.

The three fallen archangels possessing him COME OUT.

The fallen archangels Amazarak, Penemue, Turyal and Tarel arrive.

All seven fallen archangels surround Michael.

The other six holy archangels: Gabriel, Raphael, Uriel, Raguel Seraqael, and Haniel appear suddenly, joining Michael.

JESUS

It's time!

The angels fight each other using their own strengths.

Amazarak, dressed like an Egyptian sorcerer, throws his staff.

The staff BECOMES a huge serpent wrapping around Michael.

Penemue, holding an ink pen, throws it like a dart at Gabriel's hand as he goes for his fire sword.

PENEMUE

The pen *is* mightier than the sword.

This pins Gabriel's hand, denying him his sword.

Yekun and Raguel are locked in various wrestling maneuvers, as are Kesabel and Seraqael.

YEKEN

For we wrestle not with the flesh…

KESABEL

…but with principalities, thrones and

dominions.

Gadrel, proficient in martial arts, engages Raphael in mortal combat.

Twins battle twins as Turyal and Tarel take on Haniel and Uriel.

All seven fallen chiefs currently have the advantage.

INT. ATLANTIS—THRONE ROOM

Prince William is about to sit on the throne when something HITS him squarely in the head, KNOCKING him out cold.

Everyone turns around to discover it's Israel's KING DAVID. He has used Michael's golden slingshot.

> KING DAVID
>
> I believe that's my throne.

Every guard with a GUN FIRES at him.

But the bullets seem to MAGICALLY bounce off his resurrected body and back at the person who fired it, killing them.

John SEES this and disappears down a secret passageway.

Saturn picks up Prince William's crown, placing it on his head.

> SATURN
>
> I've tasted water from the River of Life, shorty.
> I don't think you can stop me.

Saturn sits on the coronation chair, which remains silent.

King David puts another stone in the slingshot.

> KING DAVID
>
> Maybe so, but man doesn't live by water alone.

He releases the stone, hitting Saturn in the forehead.

He falls out of the chair, stone cold!

> KING DAVID
>
> This is how I became king to begin with, isn't it?

Laurianna now APPEARS in the secret room.

> LAURIANNA
>
> I'll take him to his new kingdom.

As Laurianna takes Saturn, King David notices David's watch.

> LAURIANNA
>
> Sir, we must leave quickly. We're running out of time.

King David nods as he picks up the watch.

EXT. JERUSALEM—MOUNT OF OLIVES

SERIES OF SHOTS

A)   The seven fallen chiefs still dominate the seven holy ones.

B)   The seven saints, who poured out the vials, show up.

C)   The saints assist the seven holy ones, helping them gain the upper hand. They hold the seven fallen princes while the holy angels bind them.

D)   Michael, Raphael, and Uriel grab Yekun, Kesabel, and Gadrel.

E)   The archangels take these fallen ones to the abyss' entrance.

F)   Laurianna arrives with Saturn, handing him to Gabriel.

G)   She takes one of the keys from her wrist and opens the pit.

H)   Gabriel, Raguel, Seraqael and Haniel cast Amazarak, Penemue, Turyal and Tarel into the pit.

I)   Gabriel casts Saturn alive into the lake of fire as Michael and company throw in their captives.

J)   Teitan regains consciousness. He leaps up to run away.

K)   Michael and Gabriel grab him and toss him into the lake of fire.

MICHAEL AND GABRIEL
(together)

Go to Hell!

EXT. MEGIDDO BATTLEFIELDS—DAY

HAIL comes down as the last moon fragments reach Earth.

The hail utterly destroys any of the Third Empire army left standing, along with ALL of the Chinese tanks.

JESUS (V.O.)

I will tread down the people in mine anger, and
make them drunk in my fury.

One-sixth of Russia's army retreats. Vladimir stands alone.

A meteorite hits his left hand. Another hits his right hand.

Then, a huge chunk of burning debris hits him squarely in the head, killing him instantly.

JESUS

Behold, I am against thee, oh Gog, chief prince

of the land of Magog. I will smite thy bow out of thy left hand, and will cause thine arrows to fall out of thy right hand. Thou shalt fall upon the mountains of Israel, thou, and all thy bands, and the people that is with thee: I will give thee unto the ravenous birds of every sort, and to the beasts of the field to be devoured.

Two holy angels are standing over Vladimir's body. An evil angel APPEARS beside them, coming FROM the dead Russian leader.

A CLOSER VIEW of the dark-clad angel reveals the name "GOG" written in his forehead.

An eagle nearby is tearing a snake's head off and eating it.

EXT. ATLANTIS—LAUNCH PAD—DAY

John has been watching this on TV. He gives a launch command.

JOHN

Begin Operation Samson.

EXT. AMERICAN MILITARY BASES—MISSILE SILOS

Open all across America. Missiles LAUNCH towards the Middle East.

INT. SPACE SHUTTLE ATLANTIS

John and other MJ12 members are onboard.

INT. SPACE SHUTTLE ENDEAVOR

We HEAR the COUNTDOWN. Pilots onboard monitor the five

David Allen Rigsby 443

onboard computers and their various readouts.

EXT./INT. MISSILES—DAY—OVER ATLANTIC OCEAN

Targeting computers guiding the missiles show they are on course. Some are targeting the Middle East and some the open gateway in the sky.

INT. SPACE SHUTTLE ATLANTIS

John watches the shuttle pull away from Earth on his own personal monitor. Suddenly on his screen, he sees an old lady.

> KATY
>
> I don't think you should've trusted the ones who gave you your computer chip. After all, it's built on sand.

She's transforming into her sixteen year-old self.

> KATY
>
> Let's see how the secret government of the United States and Germany likes wearing the color red.

She clicks away on a computer keyboard.

All missiles change course. One turns back 180 degrees.

INSERT—MISSILE TIP

Which displays the swastika symbol beside the Masonic compass and square symbol.

BACK TO SCENE

Its onboard computer shows its new heading—Atlantis!

JOHNNY'S POV—MISSILE

Going to Atlantis underneath the ocean.

> JOHNNY
>
> It had their name on it.

INT. UNDERWATER ATLANTIS—BOMB EXPLODES

Destroying Satan's throne and the Masons' hideout.
The BLAST goes through tunnels connected to the underwater city, killing all giants inside.

INT. SPACE SHUTTLE ATLANTIS

Shuttle pilots can't take controls off autopilot.

EXT. ATLANTIC OCEAN

Another missile is now heading towards the shuttle Atlantis.
The missile IMPACTS the shuttle causing it to EXPLODE.

> JOHNNY (O.S.)
>
> As Challengers to their Colombian Enterprise, we Endeavor for the Discovery and destruction of…Atlantis.

EXT. SKIES OVER ATLANTIC—FOUR SHOT

The two planes roll-off, followed by the two jets.

> JOSH (O.S.)
>
> Where next, gentlemen?

> JOHNNY (O.S.)
>
> You two can't follow us on this next mission. Your flesh must preserve the Jewish seed now. We're immortal and must tread where only angels dare fly.

INT. UNDERGROUND CITIES—DENVER

Men continue to blaspheme God throughout the EARTHQUAKE.

Others throw idols of silver and gold to the fleeing moles.

Masons and secret society people are "begging for the rocks of the caves to fall on them to hide them from God."

The WALLS do CAVE IN on them, killing them all.

EXT. WASHINGTON DC

The EARTHQUAKE topples the National Monument.

Its pointed top section lands upside down in the…

INT. SMITHSONIAN

…where it smashes George Washington's statue as Zeus. The "Spirit of St. Louis" survives.

EXT. JERUSALEM—FROM THE SKY

Michael comes down from Heaven with a GREAT chain in his hands.
He grabs the dazed and confused Satan and binds him.

EXT. THE ABYSS

Laurianna opens the bottomless pit with her key as Michael casts Satan
in.
She locks the abyss and places a "CLOSED" sign over the door.

INSERT—SIGN

With "For a Thousand Years" handwritten under "Closed."

BACK TO SCENE

Thousands of buzzards and vultures are airborne.

EXT. JERUSALEM—AN EAGLE

Flies DOWN towards Jesus. In one claw, he has the Sword of Destiny. In
the other claw, he holds an olive branch.
Jesus takes the sword. He smiles as the eagle takes off.

EXT. OUTER SPACE—SPACE STATION

Two P-51 Mustangs arrive alongside the space station.

                    DAVID (O.S.)

        Hal…open the shuttle bay doors…NOW!

INT. SPACE STATION

Hal frantically tries to reach anyone on his radio but with no success.

HAL

I'm sorry Dave…but I can't do that.

J.J. and D.D. are watching in the b.g. They spot two space-walking suits.

EXT. OUTER SPACE—TWO SHOT—DAVID AND JOHNNY'S PLANES

Johnny SEES something near the back of the space station.

JOHNNY (O.S.)

I've got a fix on something.

David joins him. They both spot J.J. and D.D. coming out an emergency door dressed in the space suits.

DAVID (O.S.)

I'll get the girl.

JOHNNY (O.S.)
(laughing)

You always do. I'll meet you in St. Louis.

EXT. NEW YORK CITY (IN RUINS)—VARIOUS ANGLES

Our FOCUS NARROWS on the United Nations statue of a man beating swords into plowshares with his hammer. The statue is melted.

INT. STATUE OF LIBERTY

Hillary Rodnim is inside the statue's torch. Miraculously, she has survived. A lone cameraman accompanies her.

HILLARY

I want you to get a shot of me taking a bite out
of an apple…the Big Apple, get it? It's meant to
be that I alone lead this nation as it rises out of
the ashes. Get ready to start taping. Wait until I
take the first bite. This proves that it's okay to
eat the forbidden fruit. Nothing bad will happen. You can do whatever you want! You won't
DIE!

EXT. STATUE OF LIBERTY—TORCH

As the LAST moon meteorite hits the torch, obliterating it!

EXT. ST. LOUIS—A HUGE RAINBOW

Has replaced the metal arch, now destroyed. A FATHER and DAUGH-
TER stand along the overflowing Mississippi again.

DAUGHTER

A rainbow! It's over now!

The father SEES something shiny near the base of the rainbow.

FATHER

Come here. I see something.

As they head towards the rainbow, Johnny's plane, the "Spirit of St.

Louis" APPEARS in the sky.

It flies right through the rainbow.

David's plane now APPEARS, following the same path.

INT. DAVID'S PLANE

D.D. is sitting behind David.

> DAVID
>
> Are you all right?

> D.D.
>
> I am now.

We can see that D.D. is *the* very little girl that was dressed like an angel in all of David's flashbacks while he was alive.

> D.D.
>
> I always dreamed I'd be rescued by a guardian
> angel. They always watch over and protect you.

EXT. BOTTOM OF RAINBOW

The father and daughter have reached the rainbow's end. He SEES something shiny and bends over to pick it up.

It's a gold bar with the words, "Federal Reserve" written on it. There are lots of them, apparently exposed by the earthquake.

> DAUGHTER
>
> Wow! There really is gold at the end of a
> rainbow!

INT. DENVER AIRPORT—MURAL—CLOSE ON

German boy beating swords into plowshares. It's ruined.

A CLOSER VIEW shows a handwritten letter from a Jewish boy who died during the holocaust of World War II.

BOY'S VOICE (O.S.)

"I was once a little child who longed for other worlds. But I am no more a child for I have known fear, I have learned to hate. How tragic, then, is youth, which lives with enemies, with gallows ropes. Yet, I still believe I only sleep today, that I'll wake up. A child again, and start to laugh and play."

DISSOLVE TO:

EXT. ISRAEL—GREEN MEADOW—DAY

Kids of all colors are playing together.

Katy's little brother is SEEN playing with Anne Frank. Katy's mother and father are watching the kids play in the b.g.

Davie Jr. is seen playing with two other kids, fraternal twins.

Subtitle: "The Millennial Reign of Peace. In the year 2525."

A lion and a lamb play together in the f.g.

Other children are beating swords into plowshares. We NOTICE they each have the Name of God written upon their foreheads.

NARRATOR (V.O.)

Instruments of death are a distant memory. No one learns war anymore.

EXT./INT. JERUSALEM—THE TEMPLE

It has been completely rebuilt. Pagan shrines are gone.

King Jesus holds the Sword of Destiny as his rod-of-iron scepter. He stands next to King David, as both are rulers in Jerusalem.

The throne chair is the coronation chair, formerly of England and the stone under it is Jacob's pillow.

JACOB LOOKS at the stone under the chair.

> JACOB
>
> It never was a great pillow.

The SOUND of a lion ROARS as Jesus sits down.

Water flows from the Mount of Olives into the Dead Sea, healing it.

ADAM and EVE, who look as young as they did when they were created, drink from the water there.

> ADAM
>
> The Fountain of Youth, like I remember it tasting.

> EVE
> (tasting)
>
> It's a perfect world...again.

David and Katy, standing in the b.g., HEAR this and smile at each other. Katy's hair drags along the ground.

As Katy lifts her glass to her lips, we NOTICE she's wearing David's restored watch.

KATY

I'll drink to that...

DAVID

I have the girl, the watch, and everything.

Eva and Levi are in the b.g. and are smiling at each other.

EXT. ISRAEL MEADOW—HIGH ANGLE—A BUTTERFLY

FLIES slowly to the ground, above the kids we saw earlier.

It LANDS between Josh and Rebekah. They are watching Davie Jr. play with their own fraternal twins, JOSH JR. and BECKY.

Johnny and Patty stand next to them, watching J.J. and D.D.

All the kids are playing softball. Their uniforms say "Saints."

THE BUTTERFLY

MORPHS into Laurianna. She then MORPHS into a twelve year-old version of herself. She wears an "Angels" softball uniform.

LAURIANNA

Everyone should get in touch with his or her kid inside.

JOSH

Since none of us age much now, that's easier to do.

LAURIANNA

I have something I want to give your boy and
girl.

REBEKAH

I'll call 'em. Josh! Becky!

The twins come running.

JOSH JR.

You need us?

Laurianna takes out two gold bracelets with matching symbols, the
same ones she made for herself and Apollyon.

She gives them to Josh Jr. and Becky.

They each give her a kiss on the cheek.

JOSH AND BECKY
(together)

Thanks!

UMPIRE
(interrupting)

Game time! The Saints are in the field first.

The angels all MORPH into children as the Saints take the field.

CRACK! The SOUND of the first HIT ECHOES LOUDLY.

As Becky goes deep for the well-hit ball, she stumbles into a crack in the
ground.

Josh Jr., backing her up, comes to her rescue.

Upon removing her foot, Becky discovers something buried in the crack caused by the great earthquake over 500 years earlier.

It's THE golden box that used to belong to Laurianna.

Becky opens it, discovering its contents: seeds. They're from the fruit Adam and Eve ate from—the tree of Good and Evil.

The bracelets Laurianna gave the twins shine brightly around their wrists as they hold the golden box.

Laurianna runs up and SEES them holding something.

LAURIANNA
(laughing)

What did you find?

She NOTICES the golden box, then realizes it used to belong to her. Her expression turns more serious.

BECKY

It's a gold box with some kind of seeds in it. Would it be okay to plant them?

Laurianna holds out her hand to receive the seeds.

JOSH JR.

Yeah, maybe it would be something good to eat.

As the seeds are poured into her hand, we SEE her mark on the back of her hand.

DISSOLVE TO:

INT. THE ABYSS—CLOSE ON—MALE HAND

In chains with the SAME mark. As our VIEW WIDENS, we are expecting to see Apollyon. As we get to the man's face, we see it's SATAN! It's the first time we've seen the glove off of his left hand since his fall.

Satan begins laughing a long, sinister LAUGH.

> MALE VOICE (O.S.)
>
> When God created the first angel, there was enough fire to create a sister angel. Enough was even left over to create a third, but smaller angel…the only angel triplets. The smaller was named Apollyon. The first was Lucifer, now Satan. Laurianna was the sister of the two.

EXT. EARTH—HIGH ANGLE—MINUTES LATER

We HEAR Satan's LAUGH over OUR VIEW of the children in the field as OUR VIEW PULLS BACK, taking us farther away.

> MALE VOICE (O.S.)
>
> As in the millennial day of rest from creation, the same circumstances have presented themselves during the final day of rest for mankind. History repeats itself…until the end.

The Earth is literally covered with hundreds of rainbows.

Song "I CAN SEE CLEARLY NOW" begins.

EXT. EGYPT

An altar has been set up in the middle of Egypt.

The Great Pyramid has new white outer casing stones. An inscription on one says, "It's still standing."

FADE TO: BLACK

VIDEO GLITCH

A computer readout displays words typed ONSCREEN over BLACK:

> When the thousand years have expired, Satan shall be loosed out of his prison. He'll deceive the nations once more but they'll be defeated as God purifies the Earth by fire. After which, the Holy City, the New Jerusalem will come down from Heaven, as will God, to dwell with men forever.

Our VIEW WIDENS, revealing the MONITOR to be oval-shaped.

Further WIDENING reveals it's the MAN CHERUB'S monitor we've been reading. As the cherub SPEAKS, we realize the MALE VOICE is his.

MAN CHERUB

> Around 10,500 BC when darkness was upon the face of the deep, God became three-dimensional. Like separating the three isotopes of hydrogen, the Trinity separated from Itself. God chose symmetry or mirror images in all created flesh. It's His unique signature. Understand the three isotopes of hydrogen and

the foundation of three-dimensional space reveals itself. God was a Spirit, like protium, the lightest isotope of hydrogen and our simplest atom. From this, come the isotopes of tritium, which is likened to God; and deuterium, which compares to Jesus. The three stars in Orion's belt represent these three, the first three stars created in the Heavens...on the fourth day. The three Giza Pyramids, built by the Righteous Seed of Seth, represent this. The pyramid shape is the basis of three-dimensional geometry. Two inverted tetrahedrons create the male and female Star of David. The pyramid bases are at 19.5 degrees north or south latitude within the sphere. These are the foundation stones. Understand this and you'll understand how God created all things by establishing the laying down of foundations. Like the Trinity, you are a body, soul and spirit. God's very Soul became His only begotten Son. He's your foundation and rock of Salvation. His perfect sacrifice allows you eternal life by simply believing in Him. That's why Peter was the foundation or the rock of the church...he was the first to believe. Church *means* body of believers. Worship the Creator, not the created. God loves you. No matter what you've done, He'll forgive you and take you back. Just ask. But you must repent. What more could I possibly reveal to you?

ROLL CREDITS

As Song, "BE THE ONE" by Al Denson begins.

FADE OUT.

THE END

Conclusions

I respect the Bible and would never have written this story based on the Bible if I felt I was going to deviate from God's Word or blaspheme it in any way. Unlike many today, I do fear God. We're supposed to. *Revelations Alpha and Omega* is a *logical* interpretation that came from my persistent belief that I could, with the help of God's Holy Spirit, finally do what respectable theologians and respected scholars have been unable to do…make *all* the prophecy scriptures agree 100 percent. Have I done that? Yes! And I've gone the proverbial extra mile to further prove my point. I showed how many of the world's mysteries *and* recorded history agree with the Bible as well. Only God's Spirit can truly enlighten and give true interpretation to His Word. Some members in the Body of Christ are *interpreters.* That's my gift in the body.

"*The sun goes black, the moon turns to blood, stars fall, there's a great earthquake and one hundred-pound hailstones.*" That's the key that unlocked the book of Revelation! When Jesus mentioned those things in Matthew 24 and it was one of the first things ever prophesied on the day of Pentecost (Acts 2:17-21) *AND* it kept happening all throughout the book of *Revelation* (other prophecy books as well), then I saw the patterns. The same things kept coming before and after these things. Now, lay it out like a jigsaw puzzle and put the similar pieces together until the entire picture (timeline) emerges. If it doesn't contradict anything else in God's word, you're done! Not convinced?

Nearly all Bible experts and prophecy preachers are teaching that the *seven seals* happen first, then the *seven trumpets* in order followed by the *seven vials.* They do *not* understand the book of *Revelation*! I prove in my story that they go in this order: the first seal is opened, followed by the first trumpet and then the first vial. This continues until the first four *judgments* (seals, trumpets *and* vials) are completed. Then, there's a break before and after the fifth seal, trumpet and vial. Finally, the sixth AND seventh seals, trumpets, and vials are all done *simultaneously*!

Archangels sound the trumpets but the vials are poured out by the seven firstborn righteous sons of Seth's line! They had already been resurrected and dwelled in Heaven *before* John was taken up to write the book of *Revelation*. And I figured all this out using the Bible! John didn't have a word processor in Heaven. Each cherub (zoa *or* living creature) showed him only what they each had to show (vials, trumpets, or seals, etc.) That's the only reason he wrote them as separate events. But if you put the things together, you'll notice that they are in fact describing the same events!

Prophecy preachers like Jack Van Impe (among others) teach the pre-trib rapture. They claim Ezekiel 38 and 39 describe a war with Russia that happens at the *beginning* of the tribulation. Ezekiel 38 and 39 could NOT be fulfilled at the beginning or even the middle of the seven-year tribulation. How do I know? Ezekiel 38:22 says, "...and I will rain upon him, and upon his bands, and upon the many people that are with him, an *overflowing rain, and great hailstones, fire, and brimstone.*" There's only ONE time that all those things could be happening at once...*the Day of the Lord*! And that's at the END of the tribulation! The "him" Ezekiel refers to is Gog of Magog, *not* the antichrist. Gog is NOT the name of the Russian or Northern king either but the name of the angelic Prince that rules that land. It's like the law of double reference used when the Bible talks to the Prince of Tyre *and* the cherub Lucifer at the same time. (Ezekiel 28) That's in the Bible too and proved in my story.

The KEY to understanding this is to know that Deuteronomy 32:8 says, "When the most High divided to the nations their inheritance, when he separated the sons of Adam, he set the bounds of the people according to the number of the...*Angels of God*." I've done my homework. That's what the Bible used to say before 300 BC when "angels of God" was changed to read "children of Israel." Evil men have separated us from our *understanding* of our past. But they left a trail for a guy like me to follow. You can find it too. Just LOOK for it. Seek and ye shall find! If you are not looking, you won't find the TRUTH because only the LIE is being spoon-fed to the public.

So, does this literally mean the sun is going to go out forever? *Yes!* When Jesus comes, He's bringing an entirely new lighting system. The Bible says the day will be seven times brighter than now (Isaiah 30:26). I like to compare it to new and improved automobile headlights over the older, more yellow colored lamps.

Moon turns to blood? That's what it *looked* like to John. An eclipse? Nope. Imagine a huge explosion on the other side of the moon. I can think of many scenarios that could make it happen. That would send the moon TOWARDS us. Gravity locks in and PULLS it until it reaches Earth's atmosphere. Imagine the arcing going on between the Earth and moon creating violent storms where it hasn't rained in three and one-half years where it begins to BURN bright red until exploding into...hundred pound hailstones or meteorites! Will that look like falling stars? Would that cause men's hearts to fail them for the fearful sights in the heavens? *(The real meaning behind Luke 21:25-26).* Would this cause the seas to roar violently? Would this cause a great earthquake? Think about it...

Rain, great hailstones weighing over one hundred pounds each (I'll explain the *fire and brimstone* with the 200 million-man army later) fit 38:22 of Ezekiel's description perfectly when you use the Bible to interpret the Bible...NOT today's popular church doctrine flavor of-the-month. They're mostly teaching about prosperity, wealth, abundant life ("God wants you to be RICH and have lots of money") and the *gifts* of the Spirit. The Son of God had *no wealth* and was hated by the scholars and religious leaders of his day. Is anybody listening?

What is the *seven-year peace treaty* signed by the antichrist and Israel and other nations? Let's see. The Jews believe that their Messiah will come seven years *after* they are allowed to rebuild their Temple. (Daniel's 490 weeks. There's only one week or seven years left to fulfill that prophecy.) Okay, *if you build it...He will come!* Since Palestinians and Jews are fighting over the same capital, let's settle this fairly. Islam doesn't agree with this Jewish claim so why not test it? Let them build their Temple and if their Messiah doesn't come, make those liars leave the land...forever! Sounds logical...and solves everything!

The *three frog-like spirits* of Revelation are *three Grey aliens* that lead everyone to believe they were our creators. Ever see a *normal* frog perform miracles? Remember that John just *described* what he saw. He didn't have our modern vocabulary. Want to know what kind of miracles they'll perform? Watch *E.T.: The Extra-Terrestrial* again. They aren't *real* aliens, of course. And they aren't our creators either. But a lot of people will be fooled and will answer the rallying cry to "crush the evil thing"...the Jews. That's what Armageddon is all about...the world coming together to wipe out the Jews *and* to evict them from Jerusalem after the seven-year peace treaty expires. If they *could* succeed, then the *Second Coming* of the Messiah or promised Redeemer would be impossible. How can He save them if they're all dead? That's Satan's last hope to avert the prophecies concerning his future as foretold in the Garden of Eden. He *must* now prevent Jesus' *Second* Coming. Satan and a third of all angels that are with him will be cast into eternal Hell if they fail to stop God's prophetic words from coming true. What if you were a fallen angel and knew the only way to prevent your fiery fate was to destroy mankind? Would you try to destroy mankind? Of course you would.

Titans *will* return to Earth, as in the past. They'll claim to be from Saturn's moon Titan. It's the only planet or moon in our system with a substantial atmosphere. It's covered by a thick cloud that conveniently blocks our view of the surface. And the timing of all this fits with the Cassini probe mission to Saturn/Titan in 2004, which also fits the time-line of when the first four judgments of Revelation will have already happened. Having a hard time believing NASA would have anything to do with Masonic symbolism? Go to enterprisemission.com on the World Wide Web and look at the facts outlined there. I'll let you decide for yourself as I did.

Why did I portray Jesus returning in the *fall* of *2007*? Because I showed the peace treaty being signed in the fall of 2000 and seven years later would be the fall of 2007. Obviously that date didn't happen. What? No man can know the day or the hour? You're right! Remember that *Revelations Alpha and Omega* is just a story and the future dates are *not* prophecy. But what about the *season* and when it's near, even at the door? Do you understand *why* we can't know the "*day* or the *hour*?" Cause if Satan could know that, then he'd send a full-scale nuclear assault heaven-bound like he wanted to do with the Tower of Babel. On that day and in one hour, Heaven opens like a scroll and all men will see God's throne. It's an open door even wider than the TV show *Stargate* depicts. That's the *gateway* (that's what Babylon means…Gateway City, thus, the Tower of Babel's location) where the New Jerusalem will descend from *after* the millennium of peace.

The false prophet with two horns that's like a lamb but speaks like a dragon also comes from the ground. Check your history. The *two-horned* mitre worn by the Pope (fits the lamb…God's children are sheep, all others are goats) can be traced back to the mitre worn by priests of Dagon, the fish god. Did I mention *Paganism and Christianity* became intertwined in 378 AD? I'm not saying THE pope will be the false prophet but the last pope of the Catholic Church will hold that office *by force*. St. Malachi in his Pope Prophecies foretold this. His accuracy has been one hundred percent. Peter, the Terrible, remember? He comes from the ground (means giant) not the sea (means man). *The next batch of giants comes from the Earth.*

Why? Because fallen angels today are trying to avoid the fate of the first batch of angelic fathers who took human wives, resulting in off-spring of giants. Those angels are now bound in the lowest depths of Hell. The newest angelic *fathers* of giants *took* only the *seed* of men and women and have created their giant children and they're living *under-ground*…out of sight. That *explains* UFO abductions and cattle mutila-tions of the 70's. They've got our seed (without the one-on-one sex) and lots of blood for a giant underground baby farm. They'll be adults by 2004. My guess is they already are. Sound crazy? Of course it does but if you think about it, have you ever had reason to believe there were ever giants on the Earth in the past? Now have you ever noticed that these most recent events coincide with the timing of all our genetic advances like test-tube babies, cloning, A.I.D.S., etc. Is this just a coincidence? Remember, the real purpose of giants before and even after the flood was to prevent the birth of the prophesied Redeemer through the seed of the woman. Satan failed at that, but evil mustn't quit yet. They're still trying to avert their fiery destiny. Mankind must be destroyed and giants only know destruction for they are evil.

The demon locust of Revelation doesn't fit the description of insects but instead…Apache helicopters. "From its tail it did hurt men." Ever seen a chemical-head missile fired from an Apache? The *illusion* of fire goes to the tail. John just described as he saw. They're flown by lifeless clones temporarily inhabited by the *souls* of dead giants from the past or DEMONS, as they're more commonly known. They're released from the abyss for three days only. A tenth of *all* demons are *not bound*. This we know from the Book of Enoch. Let me repeat that for Benny Hinn and all other *Pre-Adamite theorists*: Demons are the SOULS of dead giants from the past. They'll never be bodily resurrected. They are NOT the souls of a race of humans before Adam! That's how I explain psychic hotlines and ghosts…these bodiless souls can never see a resurrection so they seek bodies to inhabit. Isaiah 26:14 explains this but remember that in the translation *deceased* was used in place of *Rephaim* or giants.

(If you need help in truly understanding how words in the Bible have been inaccurately translated, I suggest you study using a Dake's Bible. It's the best King James research Bible on the planet...period!) And these dead giants inhabit our bodies through our minds. If you think that's so far-fetched, remember that Jesus and His disciples regularly had to cast out these demons. This is also how demons can know so much about your past...because they've been around that long and longer. But the Bible is clear that they cannot know the future unless foretold by God. That's how you know a false prophet by whether he's Holy Ghost guided or demon guided...whether the prophecies come true or not. Forget the deception of knowing your past. Demons have that one down pat already.

200 million man army? Chinese tanks! *Fire and brimstone* from *the mouth* (ever seen a tank fire its artillery?) *and tails like serpents* (ever looked at the muzzle of a machine gun mounted on the back of a tank?) *who did hurt men?* John couldn't SEE the bullets. We can't see them either with our naked eyes. He just knew these "serpent-like" tails *hurt* men. Just try and watch a war movie and describe the action without using our modern vocabulary. Let's see what words *you* use.

Lucifer is a serpent cherub, one of the highest of God's creation, as were the ox, lion, eagle and man. The serpent was the wisest of all creatures. The pre-fall serpent and Lucifer look alike...a Grey alien complete with legs, arms and the ability to speak. Lucifer is the Red Dragon and the Serpent of old. Cherubim carry God's throne, are made of gold and covered with precious stones *and* are the only class of angels with wings. (Living GOLD? You are living DUST!) Read Ezekiel's description (chapter one) and tell me otherwise.

In fact, the four living creatures of Revelation are the *remaining* cherubim a.k.a. seraphim. Study the words and break them down. Seraph means fiery ones. Zoa means living ones. All have in common the fact they constantly surround the throne of God. They never rest (they're living machines and immortal) and have in common the appearance of the lion, calf or ox, flying eagle, and a man. Lucifer is a *serpent* cherub and *completed the pattern...*the five-pointed star. They are the same! Read Ezekiel 28:11-19 for more on this. Verse 12 refers to *sealing the sum* or completing the pattern.

What about their heads/faces and wing count of six? *When JOINED for flight by the dreadful rim* (Ever study the five-pointed star with a circle around it? That was the original flight configuration of the FIVE cherubim) *they SHARED each other's characteristics* (*five* faces, then *four* after the fall) *and had only four wings each.* When separated they had their own features...*one* face and *six* wings each. Ever notice United Airlines slogan is "Fly United" and "United is Rising?" It's like Horus on the Horizon from Egyptian mythology. The truly rich of the Earth know things that only the *initiated* could know. Just follow the money and their motives and a trail emerges.

Four angel wings joined together? ("Their wings were joined one to another; they turned not when they went; they went every one straight forward." Ezekiel 1:9.) Seen a helicopter lately? Remember that these men didn't have our modern vocabulary. Need I remind you, these are the only angels ever described as having wings and NOWHERE does it say they are feathered. Having a hard time visualizing this? Look at a ceiling fan with three or four light bulbs hanging below. Turn it right side up in your mind and you have a pretty good idea of what a cherub's head (the bulbs) looks like above their wings (the fan blades).

How did John SEE what he SAW in Heaven? Ever hear of the Teletubbies? No, I'm not delirious or pulling your leg. Five *basic* colors make up a rainbow. Lucifer was the Red Dragon or serpent. That's the color he represented in that rainbow over God's throne he helped carry in the 3-D world. Your eye is oval-shaped. So is the monitor in the mid-section of the mechanical cherubim. The Masonic all-seeing eye, get it? So, *literally* when one of the four living creatures said, "Come and SEE" and John came and SAW, that's HOW he saw the future...while looking into each of their monitors...through the four *eyes* of God. There used to be five, like your five senses that allow you to experience things around you. Is God watching you right now? You bet! Lucifer? At least now you know HOW! Even the Hollywood concept of the *Power Rangers* can be compared to the cherubim, proving someone at the top really understands the Bible better than most Christians. These five differ-ent colored *animals* UNITE to form a big and powerful flying *machine*. And you thought the creator of the *Power Rangers* just had a vivid imagination...

Yes, the cherubim are flying machines! South American legends called the Moche god Aiapaec the winged decapitator A.K.A. the *smoking mir-ror* from which he could view the activities of both men and God(s) from afar. A modern-day computer and monitor have a lot to do with Lucifer, covered with EYES, a.k.a. *spirits* and *flames* or...are you ready? Bulbs! Bright shining star! His legendary name back in Mayan days was Tezcatilpoca, which means, "smoking mirror." That's why divination and magicians use crystal balls complete with "smoke and mirrors" using its cloudy appearance. Having a hard time believing the physical part of God needs these bright and shiny machines to fly around in? God's Spirit is omniscient but his physical body is not. It's as three-dimensional as you and me. Go to an amusement park or the county fair next time it comes to town and look at all the rides at night. Even carnival rides mimic God's own flying machine complete with flashing bright lights, smoke and machines that simulate G-force. We are made in God's image. Why wouldn't we enjoy the same things God likes? That's also why there are so many other galaxies. Not to harbor alien life like modern thinkers believe. God created all those other planets to give you and I something different to do throughout all eternity. Do you like going to the same vacation spot year after year? Of course not. You'll want to do new things throughout eternity too, and God isn't going to create anything else. He's done with all that. If God can fly to other worlds, you better believe He'll let us too.

Light sabers? Swords of fire! Remember the cherubim with their swords of revolving fire that they used to guard the Garden of Eden after Adam and Eve were kicked out? Did you know there's a stele of a Mayan ruler in Palenque (Central America) holding one of these Xiuhcoatl or fire serpents in his hand? It's carved in stone! Flying serpents? There's also carved in stone a man *inside* a flying serpent with what appears to be a monitor in front of him. What did I say Lucifer was? Right! An original serpent that could fly! (To view pictures of these, check out "Fingerprints of the Gods" by Graham Hancock.) *Serpent* also meant *rod* back then. It's interesting to note the Historian Sanchuniation in 1250 BC (over 3,000 years ago) had this to say about a flying serpent: "*The snake has a speed that nothing can exceed because of its breath...Its energy is exceptional...it has illuminated everything with its gleam.*" What? I didn't know snakes could do all that. Perhaps he wasn't talking about a "snake." What does this have in common with a modern rocket? Think about it...

So what was that Tower of Babel, anyway? "*Whose top may reach unto heaven?*" (Genesis 11:4) There are no Hebrew words for *may reach*. But that's what the King James Bible says. If angels don't fly (only cherubim do) but instead travel to Heaven up and down some kind of ramp or "Jacob's ladder," then what if those post-flood rebels intended to send the top of a tower to Heaven this way? Through some kind of wormhole? To make a name for themselves by destroying God's access to Earth and keeping them from being scattered by God? (His command to spread out wasn't being obeyed). Why else would the Bible say "*now nothing will be restrained from them, which they have imagined to do.*" God was that impressed with oven-baked bricks over sun-dried bricks? I don't think so.

You mean we had technology back then? Horus the HAWK god could fly. South American gods wielded CONDOR scepters. Fire worship? People only worshipped that which they feared. Could we have learned how to make a hydrogen bomb from fallen angels? The Book of Enoch teaches that fallen angels did just that. You separate hydrogen isotopes from…water. ALL ancient ziggurats used water for some "unknown" reason. One pyramid in Teotihuacan (near Mexico City) is appropriately named after the "Sun." It even contained mica in its floor…*well below the surface.* Study the use of mica. It is opaque to fast neutrons and can act as a moderator in nuclear reactions. This mica came from very far away (2000 miles away in Brazil) and could not even be *seen* in the pyramid. Central and South American gods were called "hummingbirds" and "condors." Helicopters and planes or jets? Where are they now? Only ONE PERCENT of the cities in the Nazca region has been uncovered due to "religious reasons." Sounds like a good cover.

A German woman, Maria Reiche, has kept anyone from getting close to the famous Nazca lines for years. When asked what she thought about the idea of ancient airplanes ever landing there in the past, she responded that it would've been impossible because they would've gotten stuck in the mud. Hmmm…one of the driest places in the world. Less than half an hour of miserly drizzle every *decade* falls there. Where's the MUD? Where's the TRUTH? Why do we believe these LIES? Why do you think those cities got buried to begin with? Radiation sickness? I have outlined the truth in my story. You should understand my message before Titans (children of angels and mankind) and aliens (the original serpent looked like a Grey) show up and claim they made us…not God. Kind of poetic justice for the serpent cherubim…lying to mankind *again* and most believe him and again…DIE! Half of the entire world will die during the great tribulation. Your Creator doesn't want you to believe their lie. That's why He's trying to get you to *think* for yourself. Stop just taking the word of others who *claim* to have your best interest at heart.

By the way, want to know who the Native American Indians are? Genesis 10:18 mentions only one tribe of people being spread ABROAD after the flood...the Canaanites! Did they cross from China to America through Alaska? Did they have dark hair and almost almond-shaped, dark eyes like their forefathers? You bet they did! Also, I studied the totem pole and discovered its true origin. The Hebrew word Asherah means a pillar of wood. This wooden upright pole used to be worshipped in the center of the Canaanite nations and spread from there. The pole displayed the image of the goddess Astarte, or the queen of heaven. It always was displayed next to the image of Baal. This mother Earth worship came with the Canaanites and many of their dances and religious rites can be traced back to Canaan. Even look at the curse Noah put on the seed of Canaan. (Genesis 9:25-27) Look at the modern implications, i.e. Indian Reservations, etc.

Proof all other angels don't have feathered wings? That's why John confused the seven righteous sons of Seth (Enosh, Kenan, Mahalelel, Jared, Lamech and Methuselah round out the seven vial angels) with the seven archangels (trumpets)...*because none of them have feathered wings.* Remember in Revelation 22:8-9, John fell at the feet of the angel who had just shown him some things and the angel commanded him not to bow to him. *"For I am thy fellow servant, and of thy brethren the prophets, and of them which keep the sayings of this book."* In other words, he was a redeemed MAN...*not* an angel. In fact, they (the seven firstborn righteous sons) were buried in the smaller pyramid at Giza. They were buried in three separate chambers representing the body, soul and spirit of man. The number seven (bodies) to represent the seven spirits of the Holy Spirit. They are among the first fruits of the resurrection. Remember the Law of first fruits and the law of gleanings? (Leviticus 23:22.) Also, when Jesus tells us that sometimes when we entertain strangers we actually entertain angels, do you think they have to keep their wings tucked in? I don't think so either 'cause they don't have feathered wings. (Note: Even though *The First Kiss* angel painting inspired this story, that still doesn't mean Apollyon or Laurianna had wings because they do not. If I ever make this into film, only the cherubim will be depicted as having wings.)

Adam, Eve, and the firstborn sons of Seth's line (from which the Redeemer came) *buried in the Giza pyramids*? Resurrected and now dwelling among the stars (angels)? If evil men had not removed the book of Enoch from the Bible in the fourth century (when paganism and Christianity became mixed, remember?), then you'd know Jared commanded his sons to do this very thing…bury our forefathers in the CENTER of the Earth…where the Giza plateau is located. Giza is the exact geographical center of all the continents. That's why its foundation is solid and still stands today. Jude, Jesus' half-brother, quotes an *entire chapter* from the book we removed from our Bible, the Book of Enoch. *Jude* 14 and 15 is quoting *Enoch* chapter two…*word for word*! Look it up and compare them. Enoch's book has survived and is in print. Also, I strongly urge you to get a copy of Alexander Hislop's *The Two Babylons* (ISBN: 0-937958-57-3) for complete understanding of how paganism became intertwined with the Christian church.

Bible scholars of the fourth century (and even scholars of our own day) refused to accept that angels could have mated with our seed to produce giants. Refusal to accept that will lead you to believe that giants of the future really do come from Saturn's moon Titan. Sounds like a "big lie" to me…

How did a handful of men build these huge monuments of *stone* (sphinx is solid *stone* and was originally a lion, representing the lion from the tribe of Judah) and *brick* (the pyramids)? How did they cut the stone and move them to their final position? Jesus taught if you have enough faith, you can command a mountain to cast itself into the sea. Did our forefathers from the righteous seed of Seth have that kind of faith? I think it would be logical to conclude…YES!

Now, let's talk about Masonic symbolism and their real agenda for a moment. Freemasonry is a mystery religion that started back with the rebellion of Nimrod and the tower of Babel. I've outlined the progression of this in the story. Masons worship the brightest star in the heavens, Lucifer. That's the LIGHT that Masons seek all their life. He caused a THIRD of all angels to fall. That's 33.3 percent of all angels. That's why the 33rd degree is their highest. Washington was a Mason and our National Monument honoring him is an obelisk that stands 555 feet tall. That's 6,660 inches. The Great Pyramid uses inches to tell a story and reveal facts. Why would Washington's monument measure 6,660 inches? Is it symbolic of their defiance against the 66.6 percent that still serve God? Does "up yours" really come from this? Remember that *conspiracy theorist* is a TITLE or label *they* want you to give people who are uncovering the TRUTH...about *them*. And they love titles. They call themselves Worshipful Master, etc. I know much of Freemasonry is supposed to be secret but my own father is a 32nd degree Mason and a Shriner. You can't be one without being the other. I guess things he told me when I was a boy he assumed I'd never remember or be able to add up. But nothing he's ever told me can't be found in books about Masonry available everywhere. Joseph Smith, founder of the Mormons, was a Mason too and his own death resulted in a nationwide scandal against Freemasonry. That historical backlash didn't remain, however. But the records of it do, and I encourage you to study it as I did. The Shriners and their burn centers and children's hospitals are the only real *visible* part of Freemasonry now. I invite you to look *below* the surface. Just remember, you can walk into any Christian church service but you can only become a Mason by invitation *and* initiation into their brotherhood. And only members can attend. And members are sworn to secrecy about the organization through horrible blood oaths. Masons always relished the building of the Tower of Babel but just 200 years ago, they thought it should be changed to Solomon's Temple. This is a documented fact! Just in case people with a conscience had a problem with associating themselves with Nimrod's rebellion. And when I say people with a conscience, I mean white men only. Blacks and women aren't allowed to become Masons. Black Masons are called Prince Hall masons but are NOT accepted by *real Masons*! You mean Masons are racist? What do you think? A good book to read about modern Masons and their history is *"Please Tell Me..."* by Tom C. McKenney.

Anyway, back to the Giza plateau. EVE was buried in the middle pyramid at Giza (its foundation is older than the others cause Jesus is the foundation and the rock) because it represented the redeemer or Jesus since he would come from the seed of the woman. For more FACTS about the pyramids, again read *"Fingerprints of the Gods"* by Graham Hancock. Although I don't agree with his conclusions, his detailed accounts on them are invaluable.

The first man ADAM was buried in the Great Pyramid. That's why Adam's burial crypt (the Great Pyramid) was covered with 144,000 white outer casing stones representing the righteous or virgin-like saints to be resurrected with Jesus. Remember the dead saints that appeared in Jerusalem on that day? (Matthew 27:52-53) That's why they surround him always. (Revelation 13:4 *"...These were redeemed from among men, being the first fruits unto God and to the Lamb."*) They came to South America with Jesus where he became known as Viracocha, which means, "foam of the sea." Natives had just witnessed the first hurricane ever as Jesus showed up...walking on foamy seawater. Ever notice that white, frothy foam on the shore after a hurricane hits? Look at the *one* region where hurricanes hit the *most*...the very area where Eden used to be. Satan still tries to control the place where we, his mortal enemy, were created.

That's also why God *leaves* 144,000 to survive the tribulation...to preserve the Jewish seed through the millennium. The same number he has already taken will be "left behind."

God uses mirror imaging a lot. 6,000 years to create, thus the same time allowing the mystery of iniquity. Look in a mirror and at all animals. Their physical shape is perfectly symmetrical. Draw a line down the center and the right side MIRRORS the left. Mirror images. Sound wave files? Top and bottom match. How could random chance...the backbone of evolutionary thinking...do that? WHY and HOW are all the different species *adapting* so...perfectly? What purpose does symmetry serve? Appears instead to be the DESIGN of a God who established the use of mirror images.

The hydrogen atom and its isotopes are the fingerprint of God, His Son, and the Holy Spirit. Tritium (God), Deuterium (Jesus), and Protium (Holy Spirit). Before the Trinity separated from Itself when three-dimensional space began roughly 13,000 years ago (that's right, before that, the Spirit of God moved across the face of the deep or space), God was not yet the perfectly symmetrical body that Adam was patterned after. STUDY how the isotopes of hydrogen work and separate and you'll understand HOW God became three-dimensional! (God separated FROM Himself. The *wo*man was taken FROM the man.) When the Son was seated back at the right hand of the Father, the Holy Spirit came like a fire. Combining or fusing heavy hydrogen and heavy heavy hydrogen produces FIRE! In fact, stars and angels are synonymous in the Bible. How do you think stars produce light? Through fusion of these hydrogen atoms. Amazing how God's universal laws are everywhere just challenging us to understand them.

Water is two-thirds hydrogen and one-third oxygen. Also, the only substance on Earth occurring naturally in three forms: liquid, solid, and gas (God, Jesus, and Holy Spirit). Every living thing needs water to live. Two-thirds of man and the Earth's surface is water. Think about that.

Check Flavius Josephus' history of Jews claiming they built a pillar of brick (the pyramids are made from cut stones or bricks) and a pillar of stone (first a solid stone lion, later re-carved into sphinx) to preserve their knowledge of mankind's redeemer. That's something great scholars like Sir Isaac Newton even confirmed.

Yes, there was an Atlantis. That's what the devil renamed Eden after God took the sacred trees with him before the flood. Did you know I finally figured out where the original four heads of the one river from

Eden flowed? I can even put the continents back together and tell you when they separated, how and why. I got this from the Bible. Study Genesis 2:10-14 with a Dake Bible and a good map. You'll see what I saw. In case you don't, I describe it in detail in my story. I've also included illustrations at thetruthishere.com.

Dinosaurs? That's easy! Study the Bible's length of man's days before the flood when a water canopy protected us from the sun's harmful radiation. God divided the waters and called the upper firmament heaven. The upper waters were *above* the firmament. A water canopy. Look at Genesis 1:6 again. After its collapse, man's life span shortened. This also explains why flesh will live a LONG time during the upcoming 1,000 years of peace…the sun no longer exists! It won't harm natural flesh anymore. Reptiles grow until they die, not genetically programmed to stop growing like us. Let one live 900 years as pre-flood man did and you've got a dinosaur, behemoth or leviathan. Archeologists recently found huge alligator fossils in Africa. Buried fossils of all reptiles will fit this profile. I laugh at the premise for the *Jurassic Park* movies. Genetics are NOT responsible for the size of dinosaurs. Instead *length of life* is how those ancient reptiles reached great heights. Science and FACTS prove this!

Why have we found so many fossils? Because a global flood would bury them quickly and replace the nutrients in their bones quickly (before decomposing) thus, fossilization. Coal is not 220 million years old. It is the compressed vegetation of a globally warm planet before the floodwater and sedimentary rock (new ocean floor now covering all the Earth) compressed it into coal. That much water would have been very heavy and since it covered all the Earth, it would easily have had the PRESSURE needed to create the coal layer. Not to mention the sedimentary rock all around and right under your feet! And regarding the flood, did you know that there are 270 flood myths globally? In every culture! What are the odds?

The Carboniferous Age was only 4500 years ago! C-14 dating doesn't even account for this little known fact regarding a water canopy. Instead, it makes the assumption we reached carbon saturation tens of thousands of years ago. Even the guy who wrote the book on C-14 dating said a water canopy would make this form of dating invalid. But whoever tells you that? I have a book (Bible) to prove my theories…do they? Furthermore, a water canopy would keep levels of radiation down (like a shield) in carbon-based living matter and that's why it can't be measured in coal. It's like setting your watch. You have to have a reliable source to set yours by. What if scientists have been setting the "age of the Earth" clock by the wrong source? Think about that.

And you better wake up and realize that any real evidence discovered which *disproves evolution* is never revealed on the news. I know. I personally tracked down some *finds* and the men who found them. God bless you, Ed Conrad! And you thought only communist countries lied to their people…This is a global thing. This is spiritual warfare. *They* now want you to swallow the lie that reptiles and birds are related. Why? So you'll never figure out for yourself that reptiles grow until they die and ARE the dinosaurs of the past. It's that simple.

Why? Think about it. If everyone believed in God or a creator, then that means all that bad stuff in the Bible about being good, "*man shall not lie with mankind as with womankind,*" (Leviticus 18:22) and "*no tattoos upon your flesh*" (Leviticus 19:28) etc., would also be true. Why follow the one true God when you can follow many false gods and do whatever you want? It's just the same old lie the serpent told Adam and Eve…"*Surely you won't die if you disobey God.*" Mankind still thinks he's not ever going to be accountable to God. But you and I know better, right?

The antichrist has a great sword and with it takes peace from the Earth. Want to know what that is? It's the Sword of Destiny. Hitler once held it, as did many great world leaders. What does it have in common with Excalibur, King Arthur's sword? Both are supposedly the spear tip that pierced Jesus' side on the cross. Jesus was the rock or the stone formed without hands. The sword taken from the stone would make the man who wielded it King of the World. That's just one of many myths and legends I've taken the time to explain in my "story." Their *origins* and how some of them will *end*.

Writing on the walls? Seen the Denver Murals? There's a picture of a tall man in green army gear and gas mask (do you really understand the fifth *judgment* in Revelation?) and he holds a large sword with a dove sticking to its tip. What scripture does that remind you of? (Revelation 6:4) Now who would put this on those walls and why on Earth would they show a German boy beating swords into plowshares? I thought that was Jesus' job? I smell a Masonic plot and symbolism. Didn't Project Paperclip bring a lot of high-ranking Nazis and their top scientific minds to America after WWII? You reckon they're still here?

The rapture? Yes, it's for real but who can agree as to WHEN it happens? Do you realize that the prophecy books give you the answer? It's just that nobody has been able to see the obvious. I have. I outline exactly how those alive are "snatched away" at the last second as God's wrath is coming down upon the Earth. Yes, some saints will still be here. The one who steps aside or is removed to allow the lawless one is NOT the church…it's the Prince of Israel, the archangel Michael. He's Israel's angelic protector and will be busy with the war in Heaven casting Satan out as the antichrist makes his way to the Temple when he breaks his seven-year peace treaty. Just double-check the book of Daniel's definition of "he who lets." (Daniel 12:1).

Would you believe that this is carved in stone by the righteous seed of Seth, who knew God's timeline firsthand? The seven relieving stones over the King's chamber in the Great pyramid even illustrate how the sixth and seventh "judgments" of Revelation come TOGETHER! The book of *Revelation* makes this clear…if you know how to unlock it.

Remember that an angel stopped Abraham at the *last second* before killing his own son Isaac. That's why the Bible says to hold fast until the very end, lest you lose your reward. And you too (if you're lucky to still be alive) will be "snatched away" at the last second! As God's wrath is coming down…you are going up!

Has it occurred to you that the reason "church theology" (the *understanding* of carnal-minded men) teaches the pre-trib rapture is to *lull* you into a false sense of security? Remember that if evil men have indeed succeeded in dethroning the kings of the world and made their system built upon the wealth of the world the ruling body, then they darn sure don't want you to realize any real truth found in God's word. They want you to stop caring about your own government and the world around you! Why should you care? You're gonna be raptured at the beginning of the tribulation! Just focus on getting to the 100th level of that video game…now THAT'S important! Adolph Hitler said it best: *It's a fortunate thing for governments that men don't think!*

But comfort yourself with this: "He that leadeth into captivity shall go into captivity. He that killeth with the sword must be killed with the sword. Here is the patience of the saints. For you will be hated and persecuted for His name's sake." During the fifth judgment of *Revelation* when the martyrs slain for their testimony receive their white robes, they're told that others must be slain as they were. "…until the number of their fellow servants and brothers who were to be killed as they had been, was completed." If you are still living during the great tribulation…watch your head! You mean, you might have to die for your beliefs? Didn't God do that for you? Didn't the early *church* also do that? Be suspicious of false prophets who claim only peace and prosperity. Israel didn't listen either and they also went into captivity. You'll escape God's Wrath but NOT persecution. You'd better repent.

"I looked and there before me was a great multitude that no one could count, from every nation, tribe, people and language, standing before the throne and in front of the Lamb. They were wearing white robes and were holding palm branches in their hands…

Then one of the elders asked me, "These in white robes—who are they and where did they come from?"

I answered, "Sir, you know."

And he said, "These are they who have come out of the great tribulation..."
Revelation 7:9-14

Van Impe and others claim we'll all be up in Heaven during those seven years (tribulation...that's why they call it the pre-trib rapture) enjoying the marriage supper of the lamb. How can that be when the new Jerusalem (the CITY in which the Saints dwell) or Christ's bride, isn't due to arrive on Earth until AFTER the thousand-year reign of peace? AFTER the Earth is purified by fire and Judgment Day? The Bible's book of Revelation makes it clear as to the timing of this great event. Just get your ducks in a row and keep the facts straight.

It should be obvious by now how I feel about top Bible scholars who believe in the pre-trib rapture. They believe these things because they've failed to understand *Revelation* and its timeline concerning what happens on the Day of the Lord. I've done what they've been unable to, therefore my lack of total respect for them. Don't get me wrong, without their foundation study done on the Bible, I doubt I could've gotten as far as I did. But the truth remains that nobody ever put it ALL together. That's where I came in. God used me for the purpose of interpretation. What does it profit a church service if someone speaks in tongues in which no one interprets? Paul says there is no value to tongues spoken and not interpreted in public. Which, by the way, are actually other languages spoken by men somewhere on this planet. If the tongue is spoken in public and can't be interpreted, perhaps it's a made-up tongue, not the Holy Spirit? And I'm not talking about your PRIVATE prayers in tongues, as that's entirely different.

I'm aware of Pre-tribbers who feel Rev. 4:1 somehow magically explains the rapture. John had to be taken up to Heaven where he would be SHOWN the future. Until I came along, *nobody* (and I do mean NOBODY) could've told you HOW John saw the things he saw. This can be compared to Ezekiel being taken up via the cherubim as well. This is a physical thing. John and Ezekiel were taken bodily. So were Enoch and Elijah. Only those two didn't come back. Not yet, anyway. Just because John was taken to Heaven *after* his letters to the seven churches so he could SEE the future *does not prove* that the church is removed *before* these events take place. Where is the scriptural precedent for this? God's Word always testifies unto itself, as two or three witnesses. So, that should mean this happens in God's Word somewhere else too?

Some argue that on the day of the Lord when the righteous dead and living are *snatched away,* (what the word *rapture* means) a great voice also says, "Come up hither." Now, are these two related? No. On our day of redemption when WE hear these words, they are NOT the same exact time as when John heard them. Two different times. Two different outcomes. Two millenniums apart too, I might add. But when we are resurrected or raptured, we WILL hear that same PHRASE. Just check the timing. When the two witnesses hear these words, they are raised with the DEAD. They are resurrected during that last trump with the other resurrected dead. When does this happen? On the Day of the Lord. You do know the two witnesses come during the last three and one-half years, don't you? So how can that be BEFORE the tribulation? Sounds like it's at the conclusion of the great tribulation, as God's wrath is poured out. But His servants are snatched away, just in the nick of time...GET IT?

If the body of believers, that's what *church* means, isn't mentioned anymore in Revelation like pre-tribbers claim, then they have to explain a lot of things like:

If Christians are raptured at the beginning of the tribulation, then that means the righteous dead must also be resurrected at that time. How many resurrections of the righteous dead are there if the two witnesses are then resurrected with the righteous dead with the seventh and final trumpet blast on the Day of the Lord at the END of the great tribulation? When THEY hear the words, "Come up hither."

"Blessed are the dead which die in the Lord from henceforth: Yea, saith the Spirit, that they may rest from their labors; and their works do follow them." (Rev. 14:13) We're in the great tribulation here, folks!

Not to mention the *great multitude* that appears in Heaven: "These are they which came out of the GREAT TRIBULATION." (Rev. 7:14) This happens in the last three and one-half years.

And to the souls under the altar during the FIFTH seal. This happens during the GREAT TRIBULATION or last three and one-half years. This is when God says, "Rest yet for a little season, until their fellow servants also and their brethren, that should be killed as they were…"

And please don't take the well-known pre-trib *theory* that claims that the 144,000 *Jewish Evangelists* and all those empty cars and planes will convert the rest of the world. Sounds nice in theory and makes for good Christian fiction but doesn't hold water. JEWS don't believe Jesus was their Messiah so how are they going to convince the lost to accept Him?

During the great tribulation, the Dragon makes war with those who have the testimony of JESUS CHRIST. (Rev. 12:17) PROVING that CHRISTIANS (those who *believe* in Jesus) are here at that time.

And the 144,000 Jews that are marked are NOT the 144,000 redeemed first fruits already in Heaven, affectionately referred to as the 144,000 virgins, which when Paul uses that term, he means that they are *righteous*. Bible scholars have been mistakenly classifying these two groups as one. Now you see why I don't always respect modern theology, scholars and mainstream church doctrine.

The real reason those 144,000 are marked to survive the tribulation is to preserve the Jewish SEED…for the millennial day of rest. Also, since the OTHER 144,000 have already been bodily resurrected WITH Jesus, then our God of mirror images MUST leave behind that same amount. That's why the mystery of iniquity lasts for 6,000 years. Cause that's how long it took to create all this for us.

A day is a thousand years...it's mentioned more than ONCE in the Bible. Six days of creation...YES, creation DID take 6,000 literal years. That's why Seth's line roughly showed the date of 10,500 BC when they built the lion in relation to the Nile. The lion from the tribe of Judah, JESUS, is the foundation or the solid rock formed without hands. That's HOW the stone lion was formed. FAITH that MOVES mountains. That's why the lion, later its head was re-carved, thus our modern-day sphinx, would've looked east at the constellation Leo almost 13,000 years ago...because that's WHEN three-dimensional space as we know it BEGAN. That's the message Seth's line wanted us to understand. (Yes! That is the ANSWER to the RIDDLE of the sphinx!)

Remember when Jesus said he could tear down the Jewish Temple but then He'd rebuild it in three days? The millennial reign of peace is in the third millennium after Jesus' first coming. That's when the Bible says the Temple will be rebuilt in Jerusalem and all the nations shall come and pay homage to the King of Kings. More proof a day *is* as a thousand years?

AFTER the millennial reign of peace, 14,000 years will have been completed. Six thousand for creation, plus six thousand for mankind under the curse and the mystery of iniquity to be completed, PLUS the two millenniums for periods of peace and rest EQUALS two periods of SEVEN thousand years...God is the God of mirror images! That is HIS signature. That is why ALL flesh and blood is perfectly symmetrical. One-half MIRRORS the other half. God bears witness unto Himself. That's why His Word says that if men won't praise Him, the ROCKS (pyramids and "sphinx") will testify and cry out.

Don't believe me? The sun was created on the FOURTH day. *Ye are the LIGHT of the world*...that's why Jesus came during the FOURTH millennium of mankind's history. "I am the way, the truth, and the LIGHT." The sun's diameter when created was one million miles, or 1,000 miles times 1,000 miles. How do I know? God is a God of perfection. Here comes the proof. Sun, stars and angels are synonymous with one another in God's word. That's WHY Seth named constellations...because they tell the story of our Redemption. One-third of all the STARS or ANGELS, Lucifer included, caused the Fall. That's the reason for the STARS telling us a story...our story. This is also the reason I use an ANGEL as my NARRATOR in my story. Now, using science and astronomy, the study of stars and the heavens, I reversed the math on our sun's shrinking rate and I found our Sun is only 10,000 years old. *That's when its diameter would have been a perfect one million miles.* THAT fits the Bible's story like a glove. PERFECTLY!

Even astronomy PROVES the stars in the Orion system have been moving apart. They reversed their math to discover a period of only 10,000 years when they were created! Math is the universal language, something Seth's line knew and Hollywood tries to attribute to OTHER life forms in outer space (*Contact*). Using math and science, I figured out where Heaven is located! An atom is the smallest particle with its electron orbiting its nucleus at a *distance* roughly 10,000 times the diameter of its nucleus. IF our sun is the nucleus (we orbit it) with a diameter of one million miles (when created), THEN Heaven would orbit our sun at a *distance* of ten billion miles. Thus, the real reason a day is to the Lord a thousand years! Ah, the elusive *Planet X*.

God's own mark *is* the "X" or cross, surrounded by a circle. How many TV shows and movies use that? The four points of the zodiac make a cross in the sky, like the four cardinal points on a compass (north, east, west, and south...our term "news" comes from this). Because there are only four cherubim in Heaven surrounding God's throne now. Aquarius the *man*, Taurus the *bull*, Leo the *lion*, and *Opheocus* the *serpent* holder or *eagle*, make a cross in the heavens. In the same place where the stars tell our story. From the four corners of Heaven comes the news of our Redeemer. God is in the middle of them (the cherubim), as we (made in God's own image) are in the middle of the zodiac's circle.

God's design and signature is even upon the tiniest of things known to exist. Atom even sounds like Adam. When you die, your *spirit* goes to Heaven, if you're righteous. A spirit has little or no mass. So does an atom's electron. Coincidence? Think about it…Simple logic and simple algebra. IF $A = B = C$, then $A = C$! It's all really that simple. Who can dispute all this? That is the reason Seth's line chose the pyramid shape to tell their story. Because the pyramid is the *basis* for three-dimensional geometry. The three pyramids mirror Orion's belt because they were the first three stars ever created. And because they represent God, Jesus, and the Holy Spirit. That's *part* of the story they tell.

The Bible's measuring system uses cubits, of which inches, feet and miles also use. Think about that. Jews *invented* inches. That's why evil men have come up with the metric system…to distance YOU from the truth about your past AND the message that INCHES reveal in the Great Pyramid, which was built by the righteous seed of Seth—NOT the Egyptians. Something my story also PROVES! Like the lie the serpent told Eve in Eden, mix the truth with the lie. It's the oldest trick in the book. That's why the metric system uses God's number of ten. So you'll not think anything about *digesting* the need for a new system. God also uses the number 27. In grams, the mass of a single electron is written with a decimal point followed by twenty-seven zeroes and a nine. The smaller belt star representing the Holy Spirit in the Orion system is exactly twenty-seven degrees off the plane created by drawing a line through the other two stars. That's also why the book of *Revelation* is the 27th book of the New Testament. The book of *Revelation* is prophecy. The testimony of Jesus is the spirit of prophecy. (Revelation 19:10) It is the Light. Jesus is the light. That's also why the sun is 27,000,000 degrees Fahrenheit. (*I don't even care what it is in Celsius!*)

Remember that my story not only predicted the fall of the World Trade Towers *and* the attack on Washington DC which immediately followed, but my story also predicted that George W. Bush would be our next President. And that was one year *before* the elections. I'm pretty sure that Hillary Clinton will be our next President or Vice President, then President. And since I was so *sure* that the fall of 2000 was *when* the seven-year peace treaty was to be signed, it's interesting to note that the current escalation of violence and unrest in the Middle East between Palestinians and Jews did *begin* in the fall of 2000. (It's the fall of 2001 at time of this writing). I've done my homework. I know more about the true agenda of the world than you may realize. Our real enemy is as old as time itself. But we do have hope. I hope and pray you didn't read this section before you read the story. If you did, you have cheated yourself. Go back and read the story. In it, I've placed everything you need to know. I only included this section to give you a taste of how I arrived at some of my conclusions presented in the story. After you read the story, read it again and again. I can promise you that you'll learn something new every time you do. Then, pick up a copy of God's word. That book has the rest of the answers you seek. It has taken me a lifetime of researching God's word to know what I know. I've given you a head start but nothing will ever replace the learning and understanding that reading God's Holy Bible will give you. Amen.

0-595-21293-X

Lightning Source UK Ltd.
Milton Keynes UK
30 April 2010

153614UK00001B/78/A